Talking about welfare

readings in philosophy and social policy

The International Library of Welfare and Philosophy

General Editors

Professor Noel Timms
Professor of Social Work,
University of Newcastle upon Tyne

David Watson
Department of Moral Philosophy,
University of Glasgow

Talking about welfare

readings in philosophy
and social policy

Edited by

Noel Timms
*Professor of Social Work
University of Newcastle upon Tyne*

and

David Watson
*Department of Moral Philosophy
University of Glasgow*

Routledge & Kegan Paul
London, Henley and Boston

First published in 1976
by Routledge & Kegan Paul Ltd
39 Store Street,
London WC1E 7DD,
Broadway House,
Newtown Road,
Henley-on-Thames,
Oxon RG9 1EN and
9 Park Street,
Boston, Mass. 02108, USA
Manuscript typed by Jacqueline Bayes
Printed in Great Britain by
Redwood Burn Limited
Trowbridge & Esher
© Noel Timms and David Watson, 1976
No part of this book may be reproduced in
any form without permission from the
publisher, except for the quotation of brief
passages in criticism

ISBN 0 7100 8382 3 (c)
ISBN 0 7100 8383 1 (p)

As is the case with social policy in any State . . . the student must eventually make up his own mind and act on his own convictions. Even if the term 'Welfare State' were to pass out of common usage he would still find himself discussing 'The Good Society', for the debate is in fact about the meaning and conditions of the good life, always to be sought, never finally to be attained.
Kathleen M. Slack, 'Social Administration and The Citizen', p.74.

A name is worthless without a backing of descriptions which can be produced on demand to explain its application. P. F. Strawson, 'Individuals', p.20.

Contents

Notes on the contributors		xi
Acknowledgments		xiii
Introduction Noel Timms and David Watson		1
1	**The right to welfare** T. H. Marshall	51
2	**The concept of welfare** Richard B. Brandt	64
3	**The good of man** G. H. Von Wright	88
4	**Alienation and self-realization** Kai Nielsen	117
5	**Human rights, real and supposed** Maurice Cranston	133
6	**Welfare state and welfare society** R. M. Titmuss	145
7	**Respect for persons and public morality** R. S. Downie and Elizabeth Telfer	161
8	**Liberty, equality and fraternity** David Donnison	189
9	**Who is my stranger?** R. M. Titmuss	207
10	**The concept of community** John Benson	237

11 **The function of social work in society** 252
    Peter Leonard

12 **The art and science of helping** 267
    Alan Keith-Lucas

13 **Knowing by living through** 281
    Dorothy Walsh

14 **On not being judgmental** 290
    Ian T. Ramsey

    Bibliography 304

Talking about welfare
readings in philosophy and social policy

Notes on the contributors

T.H. MARSHALL is Professor Emeritus of Sociology at the University of London. Among his many publications are 'Sociology at the Crossroads and other Essays', 1963 and 'Social Policy', 1965.

RICHARD B. BRANDT is Professor of Philosophy at Yale University. His publications include 'Ethical Theory', 1959 and, as editor, 'Social Justice', 1962.

G.H. VON WRIGHT is Research Professor in the Academy of Finland and Andrew D. White Professor-at-Large, Cornell Univeristy. His publications include 'Norm and Action', 1963 and 'Explanation and Understanding', 1971.

KAI NIELSEN is Professor of Philosophy at the University of Calgary. His publications include 'Scepticism', 1973.

MAURICE CRANSTON is Professor of Political Science at the University of London. Among his many publications are a biography of John Locke and 'What are Human Rights?', 1973.

R.M. TITMUSS was Professor of Social Administration at the London School of Economics until his death in 1973. His publications include 'Essays on the Welfare State', 2nd edn, 1963, and 'Commitment to Welfare', 1968.

R.S. DOWNIE is Professor of Moral Philosophy at the University of Glasgow. His publications include 'Roles and Values', 1971. He was chairman of the Working Party on The Teaching of Values in Social Work, set up by the Central Council for Education and Training in Social Work, whose Report was published in 1976.

Notes on the Contributors

ELIZABETH TELFER is Senior Lecturer in Moral Philosophy at the University of Glasgow. Among her publications are 'Education and Personal Relationships', 1974, with R.S. Downie and Eileen M. Loudfoot.

DAVID DONNISON is Director of the Centre for Envrionmental Studies at the University of London. His publications include 'Social Policy and Administration', 1965 and 'The Government of Housing', 1967.

JOHN BENSON is Professor of Philosophy at the University of Lancaster.

PETER LEONARD is Professor of Applied Social Studies, University of Warwick. Among his publications are 'Sociology in Social Work', 1966.

ALAN KEITH-LUCAS, educator and social worker, is Professor at the University of North Carolina. His publications include 'Some Casework Concepts for the Public Welfare Worker', 1957 and 'Giving and Taking Help', 1972.

DOROTHY WALSH is Professor of Philosophy at Smith College.

IAN T. RAMSEY was Nolloth Professor of the Philosophy of the Christian Religion at Oxford until 1966. He was Bishop of Durham from 1966 until his death in 1972. His publications include 'Christian Ethics and Contemporary Philosophy', 1966.

Acknowledgments

We gladly acknowledge the assistance of Professor P.F. Strawson, Professor R.S. Downie, Vernon Pratt, Rita Timms and Rosemary Watson by way of comment on earlier drafts of the Introduction, and of Beverley Symes, Anne Valentine and Wilma White by way of typing.

All the essays printed here, except that by Professor Leonard, have been published before and details of previous publication are given below. We thank the authors, editors and publishers concerned for permission. We reprint T.H. Marshall, The Right to Welfare from 'Sociological Review', 1965, pp. 261-72; Richard B. Brandt, The Concept of Welfare, from Sherman Roy Krupp, ed., 'The Structure of Economic Science: Essays on Methodology', (c) 1966, reprinted by permission of Prentice-Hall, Inc., Englewood Cliffs, New Jersey, pp. 257-76; G.H. Von Wright, The Good of Man, ch. 5 of 'The Varieties of Goodness', London, Routledge & Kegan Paul and New York, Humanities Press, Inc., 1963; Kai Nielsen, Alienation and Self-Realisation, from 'Philosophy', vol. 48, 1973; Maurice Cranston, Human Rights, Real and Supposed, ch. 4 in D.D. Raphael, ed., 'Political Theory and the Rights of Man', London, Macmillan, 1967; R.M. Titmuss, Welfare State and Welfare Society, ch. 11, of 'Commitment to Welfare', London, George Allen & Unwin and New York, Random House, Inc., 1968; R.S. Downie and Elizabeth Telfer, Respect for Persons and Public Morality, ch. 2 of 'Respect for Persons', London, George Allen & Unwin, and New York, reprinted by permission of Schocken Books, Inc., 1969; David Donnison, Liberty, Equality and Fraternity, reprinted from 'The Three Banks Review', no. 88, December 1970, published by the National and Commercial Banking Group Ltd, pp. 3-23; R.M. Titmuss, Who is my Stranger?, ch. 13 of 'The Gift Relationship',

London, George Allen & Unwin, and New York, Random House, Inc., 1970; John Benson, The Concept of Community, from L. Bright and S. Clements, eds, 'The Committed Church', London, Darton, Longman & Todd, 1966; Alan Keith-Lucas, The Art and Science of Helping, from 'Case Conference', vol. 13, 1966; Dorothy Walsh, Knowing by Living Through, from 'Philosophy and Phenomenological Research', vol. 31, no. 2, 1970-71; Ian T. Ramsey, On not being Judgmental, from 'Contact', no. 30, 1970, pp. 2-16.

Introduction

Noel Timms and David Watson

This introduction does not consist of abbreviated versions of the essays and extracts which follow. Our main purpose is to bring a particular philosophical perspective to bear on 'welfare talk', and in our view, such a purpose can best be realised through a substantive introduction concentrating on a major theme - in this case, identification. In using this book it is important to keep in mind that all the readings, and our introductory essay, should be examined carefully and critically.

Our introductory essay falls into two sections, A and B. Section A is divided as follows:
1 Conceptual clarification
2 Talk and welfare talk
3 Identification
4 Explanation
5 Identification and explanation in welfare

The first part of Section A explains our conception of the role of conceptual analysis and the contribution it might make to discussion of welfare, where technical, would-be technical, and everyday terms are somewhat haphazardly used and insufficient attention is given, for example, to the distinction and connections between evaluative and descriptive meaning. In the second part we introduce the main general argument of this section that (i) every subject of welfare discussion must be capable of a certain sort of description, and that (ii) every welfare activity must be capable of a certain sort of explanation. Questions of identity and explanation are first considered in terms of everyday examples. A philosophical theory of identification is then introduced, in part three, largely through the work of Professor P.F. Strawson. This particular part may seem too abstract at a first reading, but it has an important role in our argument for it provides detailed justification of point (i) above and declares our conception of adequate identification. We see conceptual analysis as an important means to the adequate identification of subjects of welfare discourse.

The value of conceptual analysis for welfare discourse may be questioned on the grounds that there are countless cases in which we understand a word perfectly well *without* being able to give a philosophical account of it. However, some of these words, and in particular those which are key words in discussions of welfare, are taken out of their normal setting and put to use in accounts of new activities, relationships, social policies, administrative structures, and so on. We may know perfectly well how to employ these words for everyday tasks, but be less happy when we employ them on special duties. No doubt sometimes special uses simply call for technical or legal stipulative definition. But it seems to us that this is not always the case. There are occasions on which discussion of welfare would be best advanced by conceptual analysis, by an examination of, for example, the nature of welfare, respect, dignity, indifference, interests and charity.

In part four of this section we introduce, but do not develop, the related theme of explanation. In part five we consider the implications of the accounts of identification and explanation using examples of welfare talk taken from some well-known texts.

The second section of our introduction uses the essay by Professor T.H. Marshall to trace some connecting themes to be found in the readings. These include questions concerning welfare, the right to welfare, a welfare society, possible moral foundations of a welfare society and community. Identifying these, being able to say what these things are, will clearly be an important contribution to talk about welfare.

A

1 Conceptual clarification

Discussion of welfare has reached sufficient proportions to enable us to identify a field of discourse, though it can be indicated only in outline. This introduction, and the essays and extracts it introduces are concerned with a preliminary exploration of certain general and certain specific problems that arise in discussions of welfare.

Our interest in this collection centres on general questions of identification - what is welfare, what sort of a right is a right to welfare and so on. The following quotations from welfare writing indicate the persistence of problems of identification in welfare talk. How, we may ask, is it possible to identify an activity from the following (italics added);

> The basis of public relief *is* partly the race instinct of sympathy, partly reasoned benevolence, religious belief and ethical philosophy, partly a deliberate measure of social protection, partly a socialized form of mutual insurance against misfortune and accidental misery, to whose fund all citizens contribute, and by which all who need are entitled to profit (Henderson, 1902).

> The care of the poor, sick, and abnormal members of human society *is* part of politics with a social orientation (Hnik, 1938).

> Social services *represent* a compromise between compassion and indifference, just as they reflect our dispositions both to remember and to forget our social obligations (Pinker, 1971).

We believe that now is an opportune time to try to bring into collaboration the methods and insights of contemporary analytical philosophy and the whole business of talking about welfare. Of course, conceptual analysis is not the whole of philosophy, and though we concentrate on it we do not want to suggest that other philosophical methods and insights can make no contribution to welfare discourse. The methods of phenomenological philosophy might contribute to accounts of inter-personal relationships, for example.

We have collected essays, some by professional philosophers and others not, covering a range of concepts and beliefs which figure prominently in discussions about welfare. In this way we hope to draw attention to an area of common interest to students of social administration, social work and social policy; and students of social and moral philosophy. The essays and even sections of our Introduction may be found to vary in level of difficulty according to the reader's academic background. Students of social administration and social policy will be more familiar with the essays say, by T.H. Marshall, R.M. Titmuss and David Donnison. They may be less sure of the relevance for their own study of the essays say, by G.H. Von Wright, Maurice Cranston, R.S. Downie and

Elizabeth Telfer, John Benson and part 3 of our Introduction. Students of social and moral philosophy will, no doubt, be more at home using the latter essays and less so using the former. However, both groups of students may take heart from the fact that the essays and extracts have been chosen as contributing to philosophical discussion of welfare in a serious but *readable* manner.

Discussions of welfare (a welfare state, a welfare society, even the welfare lady), the descriptions and evaluations of formal and informal help, contain far more conceptual and theoretical problems than is commonly realised, even by the more sophisticated of the welfare talkers. Philosophical analysis, we shall argue, is more richly effective, even in the realm of practice, than, for example, the common and dismissive charge of an exclusive and therefore sterile concern with 'mere words' suggests. We would argue that this view is misguided as follows.

It is very difficult to imagine an exclusive concern merely with *words*. The novelist and the poet, and indeed writers in general, cannot truly be said to have such a concern, even though they give words much of their attention. Neither may the grammarian, studying the sounds, inflexions, and constructions used in a language, nor the philologist studying the structure and development of language may be seriously so accused. A language is more than words. Perhaps the man whose researches show that there are four hundred four-letter words in the English language might with some truth be said to have had an exclusive concern with words, but thus occupied in compiling lists of words, he is not engaged in philosophical analysis.

Contemporary analytical philosophy in general aims at the clarification of concepts. Since the examination of concepts can only be carried out by considering the use of words, the contemporary analytical philosopher *may* be said to be concerned with *the use of words*, though not with words merely.

We may think of concepts very roughly, and thus debatably, as expressed by the uses of general words or descriptions, words or descriptions used to refer to a number of things. For example, such words or descriptions as 'horse', 'colour', 'tribe', 'rainbow', 'rational being', 'social service' and 'rapacious monster with the face and body of a woman and the wings and claws of a bird'. To clarify a particular concept is to understand better what it is to be a thing referred to by the use of a general word or description (words or descriptions), to be a thing of that sort. You may know enough about the use of the word 'therapist', say, to know that, for example, Jungian analytical psychologists are therapists, but not know enough about the use of the word, 'therapist' to say, for example, whether or not the word is correctly used to refer to social workers. In so far as your concept of a therapist is unclear, you do not know how the word 'therapist' is used, and, we may say, thus far you do not know what a therapist is. And, of course, if you do not know what a therapist is, you do not know who or what is a therapist. In our illustration, you do not know whether social workers are therapists. Clarification of the concept of a therapist might provide you with grounds for denying that social workers are therapists, and thus you would better understand what it is to be a thing referred to by the use of a general word or description (words or descriptions), to be a thing of that sort.

We said that we may think of a concept as the uses of general words or descriptions, but it is important to remember that more than one general word or description may have the same use.

The *same* concept may be expressed by the uses of different words, or descriptions. Let us suppose that 'therapist' is used to refer to 'a person providing a curative service'. Because the same concept may be expressed by the uses of different words or descriptions, it does not follow from the fact that someone does not know how a particular word or description is used that he does not have a clear concept of whatever is in question. He might know the use of another general word or description which expresses that concept. His ignorance of the use of a particular word does not justify the conclusion that he does not know what it is to be a thing of that sort, that he does not know what are, and what are not, things of that sort. Suppose, for example, I say to you of a mutual acquaintance, 'Pevsner is a marvellous therapist', and you reply 'I don't know about that, but he certainly provides a first class curative service.' In this case you do not know the use of the word 'therapist', but you do nevertheless know what it is to be a thing of that sort. You refer to things of that sort using the description 'person providing a curative service'. In such cases conceptual clarification is not required. It may be that we need to see and say some such thing as 'Ah, you use "therapist" as

I use "provider of a curative service",' but otherwise, no difficulty arises concerning the identification of things of the sort in question.

We said that in cases in which the same concept may be expressed by the use of more than one word or description, it does not follow from the fact that someone does not know how a particular word or description is used either that he has an unclear conception of whatever is in question, or that he does not know what it is to be a thing of that sort. However, where the person does not know how *any* general word or description used to signify things of the sort in question is used, the person does not merely have an unclear conception of whatever is in question, he has none; nor does he know what it is to be a thing of that sort. In our immediately preceding illustration the thing in question could be identified only because one person in the dialogue, though not knowing how the particular word 'therapist' is used, knew at least how *some* general word or description used to signify things of the sort in question is used. We shall later use some of the work in Professor P.F. Strawson, to emphasise the importance of their being, for every thing, *some* general word or description used to signify things of that sort, and shall consider the implications, in a given case, of there being no such general word or description.

We can distinguish three kinds of difficulty in connection with general words or descriptions used to signify a subject: (i) there is some general word or description used to signify things of the sort in question, but the use of that general word or description is unclear to at least one, but not both, parties to the discussion; (ii) there is some general word or description used to signify things of the sort in question, but its use is unclear to *both* parties to the discussion; (iii) the kind of case in which the use of no general word or description to signify things of a sort purported to be in question is clear to anyone. In the first two kinds of case, conceptual unclarity and difficulty in identifying things of the sort in question, go hand in hand. In the third kind of case conceptual unclarity, we shall later argue, goes hand in hand with impossibility of identifying things of the sort in question, goes hand in hand with there being no sort of things in question.

In practice it is difficult to distinguish these kinds of case. Listening to, or reading, a discussion of a certain idea we often suspect a case of the first kind, where the use of the general word or description used to signify the item in question is unclear to at least one party to the discussion - ourselves. That this is a case of the first kind and not of either of the other kinds is indicated when another party to the discussion is able to clarify the use of the general word or description. Thus the use of the word 'therapist' might be clarified for someone uncertain of its use within a staff conference. A case is of the second and not of the third kind where the use of the general word or description, though initially unclear to both parties to a particular discussion, may become clear to both for example, by their being referred to other discussions in which the general word or description in question is used. For example, members of a Local Authority Social Services Committee might, in discussion of local community care provision, discover themselves unclear about the technical use of the general term 'community care'. Their problem, however, may be resolved by an examination of policy statements by Central Government. Where this general kind of procedure is not efficatious, we may have a case of the third kind. In all three kinds of case, discussion in a sense can proceed, with clarification unconsidered or not attempted. Discussion can continue in the sense that people can go on talking. In another and more important sense, in all three kinds of case, discussion cannot proceed: we have not begun and cannot begin to communicate with others about the subject of our discussion, for we have not identified any item as the subject of our discussion. All three kinds of case are common in discussions of welfare. In our Introduction and in the essays collected, attention is focused upon conceptual clarification in relation to identification, and so upon important philosophical problems concerning communication in discussion of welfare.

Of course, conceptual clarification is not achieved, like the age of 18, once and for all. A notion of *adequate* conceptual clarification, however, will allow room for the varying needs to be clear and to identify things as of a certain sort. The adequacy of a conceptual clarification, like the adequacy of a legacy, must be judged relative to the demands made of it. A certain legacy might be adequate for the purpose of buying a hamper, but not for buying a house. Similarly the degree of conceptual clarity necessary in praying for 'the aged' may be less than is necessary in discussion of pensions for 'the aged'. This idea of adequacy of clarification will be taken up later. At this point we simply stress the relation between conceptual clarification and identification. This relation makes philosophical investigation of this kind important in the realm of practice.

Alan Keith-Lucas (1953) makes the following point in connection with social work.

> As social work becomes increasingly professionalised, the theories of social needs and goals developed by the profession become more and more esoteric, and consequently less easily understood and less susceptible to the control of public opinion. Because the practice of social work has increasingly become a governmental function affecting the lives and rights of millions of individuals, because the client group is increasingly in the hands of highly trained specialists whose theories are not easily understood or checked by public opinion, it has become more important than ever to examine critically the presuppositions underlying modern social work practice - if only to bring them to the light of day, where those concerned with the rights of people may be aware of the issues involved.

Keith-Lucas's concern to discover the implications for human rights contained in social work practice, and, we might add, a concern to discover the implications for human rights contained in *theories* offering accounts of social work practice, a welfare state, a welfare society etc., supports our view that philosophical investigations of this kind are important in the realm of practice. In general, where the presuppositions of a social theory are not already understood, they may be exposed through conceptual clarification of that theory.

General words and descriptions often appear, of course, within statements which we not only want to understand, but whose truth or falsity we wish to determine. But, as Professor David Raphael, (1970) says,

> in order to know whether a belief is tenable, and in particular whether it involves any inconsistencies, either within itself or between it and other accepted beliefs, it is necessary to understand just what the belief is and what it implies. We need to know clearly what is meant by the terms used in it.

Thus, an understanding of the uses of words, and in particular, we have argued and shall argue further, the uses of general words or descriptions is necessary before we can say a belief is *tenable*, i.e. could be true, let alone is true. This general point, which applies to beliefs of all kinds, is a further ground for asserting that the methods and insights of contemporary analytical philosophy will be usefully employed in talking about welfare. The distinctions drawn in philosophical analysis may be more or less complex, but without them, as Professor Raphael has said, 'we are likely to talk and act confusedly in social and political affairs and are liable to follow blind alleys in social and political science' (1970, p. 17).

Raphael (1970) points out that the clarification of concepts has three related purposes, analysis, synthesis, and improvement of concepts.

> By analysis of a concept I mean specifying its elements, often by way of definition; for example, one can analyse or define sovereignty as supreme legal authority, specifying the three essential elements which make up the concept. By synthesis of concepts I mean showing the logical relationships whereby one concept implies or is implied by another; for example, one can show a logical relationship between the concept of a right and that of an obligation by pointing out that whenever A has a right against B, that implies that B has an obligation. By improvement of a concept I mean recommending a definition or use that will assist clarity or coherence; for example, one can recommend, as I do, that the concept of sovereignty should be used *only* of the legal authority, and not of the coercive power, of a State (pp. 12-13).

The purposes of analysis, synthesis, and improvement go together and constitute the general aim of clarification of concepts which we have argued is the main focus of a form of philosophy which should play an important part in discussions of welfare.

In the chapter cited, Raphael suggests that in the main tradition of Western philosophy the clarification of concepts was pursued until very recently only as a necessary aid to another aim, *the critical evaluation of beliefs*. Conceptual clarification, as we have seen, may help us determine the tenability of a belief and its consistency within itself and between it and other accepted beliefs, but though unclarity and inconsistency are grounds for not adopting a belief, necessary truths apart, clarity and consistency are not grounds for positively *adopting* a belief. Until very recently, says Raphael, philosophy has been thought of as contributing not only to our understanding of a belief, but also to the debate leading to our adoption or rejection of a belief. According to Raphael, the philosophical activity of the critical evaluation of beliefs is the attempt to give rational grounds for accepting or rejecting beliefs which we normally take for granted without justification. There seems to be no reason why critical evaluation of beliefs might not extend also to the examination of the rationality of grounds given for accepting or rejecting beliefs not normally taken for granted. We hope to indicate, later in this introductory essay and in our selection of the essays and extracts which follow, that both the philosophical activity of the clarification of concepts and that of the critical evaluation of beliefs have an important place in talking about welfare.

On the account given, conceptual clarification is required in connection with a belief or set of beliefs expressed in the terms (words or phrases) of a field of discourse. We are concerned with the field of social welfare discourse which contains technical, would-be technical and 'everyday' terms. Conceptual clarification is required when, for example, the would-be technical terms of that belief or set of beliefs are explained in a way which does not permit us to know whether it is tenable, and in particular whether it involves any inconsistencies, either within itself or between it and other accepted beliefs. Conceptual clarification is also required if it is left unclear precisely which of the terms of the belief or set of beliefs are intended to be technical. These conditions may themselves go unnoticed because the terms in question, would-be technical or otherwise, have a familiar everyday use or uses. This familiarity may be retained when a term is transferred to or employed within a more (or less) precise field of discourse, but when such a transfer occurs we may forget the important task of explaining changes in use. And, of course, difficulties may arise even in connection with terms transferred to the more restricted field of discourse which suffer no change in use but continue to have their everyday use. The everyday uses of such terms may themselves require conceptual clarification.

These difficulties of language can easily be illustrated from the field of welfare if we begin to list some of the terms frequently used within its discussions - stigma, rights, community, love, integration, need, help, self-determination, second class citizen, welfare, community. As R.B. Brandt, for example, states in his essay (the second in the present collection): 'The term "welfare" seems to carry a meaning, in ordinary talk about the welfare of individuals, different from what it carries in many recent discussions in which it appears in the expression "social welfare"'. Or again, in the case of rights, Maurice Cranston, in an essay re-printed here, argues that the journey from the relatively well-defined territory of traditional human rights (to life, liberty and a fair trial) to the new land of universal social and economic rights (such as the right to unemployment insurance, old age pensions, medical services, and holidays with pay,) is a journey from sense to nonsense. Moreover, it is, in his view, dangerous nonsense since the circulation of a confused notion of human rights hinders the effective protection of what are correctly seen as human rights. With these and other terms we unconsciously move between technical, would-be technical and everyday usage, neglecting the fact that each of these perspectives offers its own way of elucidating the term in question. John Benson in an essay in this collection identifies three senses of the word 'community'. These senses

> even if not very clear, are pretty clearly different. Of course, their areas of application overlap, but this is just where the danger lies, for though the word may apply in two or all of its senses to the same thing, it does so by virtue of different criteria and says very different things depending on the criteria which are held to justify the application.

Another particularly acute problem for discourse in social welfare is that the terms of the discourse commonly have both descriptive and evaluative meaning: where the term is both used to name or describe some object or state of affairs *and* to evaluate it. Professor R.M. Hare, in his book 'The Language of Morals', has developed this distinction between descriptive and evaluative sorts of remark, using simple examples to highlight the logical point. 'Examples of the first sort of remark are "This strawberry is sweet", and "This strawberry is large, red, and juicy". Examples of the second sort of remark are "This is a good strawberry" and "This strawberry is just as strawberries ought to be"' (1952, p. 111). Both sorts of remark, says Hare, can be, and often are, used for conveying information of a purely factual or descriptive character. This may be less obvious about an evaluative remark, but, using Hare's example, if our hearer knows what sorts of strawberries we are accustomed to call 'good' (knows what is the accepted standard of goodness in strawberries), as Hare says, he undoubtedly receives information from our evaluative remark. He will complain that we have misled him if he subsequently discovers the strawberry to be small, green, and hard rather than juicy (cf. pp. 112-13).

However, an evaluative remark can be used to express a thought which a descriptive remark cannot be used to express. 'It is a thought which has something to do with choosing or being inclined to choose' (p. 105). An evaluative remark has a commendatory force which a descriptive remark does not possess. Thus, to say, 'This strawberry is just as strawberries ought to be', is to commend and express an inclination to choose this strawberry, while to say 'This strawberry is sweet' is not.

The similarity and difference between these two sorts of remark may now be brought together. We commend and are inclined to choose this strawberry, say, precisely because this strawberry comes up to our standard of goodness in strawberries, it satisfies the description we would give of a good object of this sort. Thus an evaluative remark may both commend and supply information about the object in question: it has both evaluative and descriptive meaning.

The fact that a person, or set of people, commend, are inclined to choose, or perhaps 'behave preferentially' towards a certain member of a class 'is not in itself a necessary or sufficient condition for saying that it is a good member of the class; it is only the most important of the many things that might make us want to say that they *think* that it is a good member' (p. 109). Evaluative remarks express the speakers conventional or unconventional evaluations, and, of course, different speakers may commend or be inclined to choose different members of a class.
Hare points out, in connection with the word 'good' that

> the evaluative meaning is constant for every class of object for which the word is used. When we call a motor car or a chronometer or a cricket bat or a picture good, we are commending all of them. But because we are commending all of them for different reasons, the descriptive meaning is different in all cases (p. 118).

The description which a motor car must satisfy before

we shall be inclined to choose it, is quite different from what a cricket bat must satisfy for us to be inclined to choose it. And, we might add that the associated descriptive meaning may not only be different in relation to objects in different classes, it may also be different for different people or groups of people in relation to objects in *the same* class. Thus, your criteria for a good holiday or a good lecture may not be ours.

Evaluative remarks are thus often controversial. Further, since the criteria of application employed by the speaker may differ from those which the hearer would employ in making the evaluative remark in question, evaluative remarks commonly require conceptual clarification. The descriptive meaning of the evaluative remark may need to be made explicit. It is arguable that the terms listed as frequently used within discussions of welfare: stigma, rights, community, love, integration, need, and so on, all have evaluative as well as descriptive meaning, and thus may figure in evaluative remarks about welfare. The fact that the term 'social work' commonly has both evaluative, and descriptive force, is one of the serious complications in any attempts to evaluate the activity: 'this is social work' and 'this is good social work' are characteristically interchangeable. In any case, evaluative remarks form a significant segment of controversial discussions of welfare. Their discrimination, and making explicit the descriptive meaning in each case where this is required, are important philosophical contributions to be made to discussions of welfare. And, as Keith-Lucas reminded us, so also is the exposure and critical evaluation of the principles of evaluation implied by evaluative remarks.

In this collection of readings we approach such discussions through the published work of academic theorists. This is not to suggest that social administrators, etc., have no views on their professional activities different from those discussed by academics in this field. Conceptual clarification may very well be required over a far larger set of beliefs than arise in published academic discussion for there are almost as many professional social administrators, policy-makers and social workers as there are amateur philosophers! However, our *introduction* is effected through academic discussion first, because such discussion may be expected to be more rigorous, leaving us less mileage to cover to the goal of conceptual clarification, and second, because the beliefs of professional social administrators, etc., in the absence of published academic empirical work on the subject, do not form a discernible set to which students of social and moral philosophy might be introduced, as is the case with published academic beliefs. Of course, there is a third party whose views might very well be worthy of philosophical attention: those whose welfare is in question, patients, clients, or service users. However, like the beliefs of welfare administrators and workers, the beliefs of those whose welfare is in question, in general do not yet constitute a discernible set from which philosophical analysis can begin. (1)

Raphael draws the following analogy which we might use to indicate what might be expected from the collaboration we hope to encourage.

> The clarification of concepts is like cleaning the house. When you have cleaned the house, there is not much to be seen for your work. You have not acquired any new possessions, though you will have thrown out some things that are not wanted and are just a nuisance. What you have at the end of it is a tidier house, in which you can move around more easily and in which you can find things when you need them (1970, p. 16).

For those who weary of conceptual clarification the news is bad. As Raphael adds, 'the analogy is apt in another respect also. Cleaning the house is not a job that can be done once and for all'. Old questions recur and new questions arise because society is a living thing. We have argued that the consequent scope for regular conceptual clarification raises what are not matters of 'mere words' and, for our field of interest, matters which constitute the basic stuff of welfare.

Some of the difficulties that arise in consideration of these conceptual matters have, as we shall note later, been acknowledged in the published work of academic social administrators, but the significance of these difficulties, as we shall also argue, has not been sufficiently appreciated. First, however, it is necessary to review some philosophical considerations that arise in any attempt to talk, which includes, of course, any attempt to talk about welfare, welfare activities, and in general all items which are subjects in welfare discussion. We shall also review some philosophical considerations that arise in any attempt to describe any such items as human activities.

2 Talk and welfare talk

We shall argue that every subject of welfare discussion must be capable of a certain sort of description, and that every human welfare activity must be capable of a certain sort of explanation. Discerning these necessities very usefully structures the philosophical tasks already delineated. They are the goals of conceptual clarification. We shall begin with a general review of some of the complexities in description and explanation, using simple illustrations. We shall then re-trace this ground using a philosophical theory of identification as a means of establishing why in general terms description and explanation are of central importance.

We may ask of any item 'What is it?' We may ask anyone engaged in any activity 'What are you doing?' In each case we are seeking a general name or description which distinguishes the subject as the thing it is. But it is no good using a name for something unless one knows who or what is referred to by the use of the name. What Professor P.F. Strawson has said of proper names is also true of general names, 'a name is worthless without a backing of descriptions to explain its application' (1959, p. 20). When we ask the questions 'What is it?' and 'What are you doing?', we are seeking a *description* which distinguishes the subject as the thing it is. Such a description may be more or less detailed, and, if the item is an activity, may include a description of the method adopted in carrying on or carrying out the activity. Thus, in answer to our first question, 'What is it?', a man in The Plough and Harrow might say, for example, 'It is a cribbage board', or perhaps, if this answer was not enlightening, 'It is a board used to keep the points score, in the card game cribbage, by placing pegs in certain holes in the board.' In answer to our question, 'What are you doing?' the same man might offer any one of a range of types of possible answers. He might say, 'I am drinking', or perhaps 'I am raising my glass to my mouth', or again, 'I am drinking by raising my glass to my mouth.'

We may also ask anyone engaged in any activity the question, 'Why are you doing what you are doing?' seeking a purposive explanation of the activity. An activity may be explained in this way by reference to something beyond itself: an activity may be a means to an end distinct from the activity itself. Thus, indifferent to snooker, one might play to keep fit, and explain one's playing snooker by referring to this end. But activities need not be thus explained. An activity might be what we call 'an end in itself'. One might play snooker for its own sake, and explain one's playing simply by saying 'snooker's got everything!' The man in The Plough and Harrow might drink for its own sake, but carry out preliminary activities merely as means to an end distinct from the preliminary activities themselves. Thus in answer to our question he might say 'Try it and you'll understand', or perhaps, 'I adopt the method of raising my glass to my mouth because I have found it promotes drinking rather better than the method of lowering my mouth to the glass.'

It is important to note in connection with human activities that the questions 'What are you doing?' and 'Why are you doing what you are doing?' are distinct, but also that the answers to these questions are not entirely independent. It may be granted that knowing what I am doing may not put you in a position to say why I am doing it. For example, knowing that I am saving money does not tell you that I plan to buy a house. You might guess my plan, but you might equally have guessed, in this case mistakenly, that I plan to go on holiday. It may also be granted that knowing why I am doing what I am doing may not put you in a position to say what I am doing. For example, knowing that I am doing what I am doing in order to buy a house does not tell you that I am robbing banks. Again, you might guess my method, but you might equally have guessed mistakenly that I am saving from my salary. Cases like these, and there are many of them, arise because what I am doing is often a means to more than one end, and why I am doing what I am doing, my end, is often attainable by more than one means. Nevertheless, the answers to our two questions are not entirely independent, for what I am doing is not in fact a means to *every* end, but only to some ends, and why I am doing what I am doing, my end, is not in fact attainable by *every* means (to some end) but only by some. Thus, for example, knowing that I am saving money could not lead you reasonably to suppose that I plan to go to bed early tonight, but might lead you reasonably to suppose that I plan to buy a car. And this is because saving money is not a means to the former end, but is a means to the latter end. Similarly, knowing that I plan to buy a house could not lead you reasonably to suppose that I am watching a football match, but might lead you reasonably to suppose that I am taking out endowment insurance. And this is because the former is not a means to the end of buying a house, while the latter is. Problems of description and explanation, then, are related.

To say that every subject of welfare discussion must be capable of a certain sort of description, and that every human welfare activity must be capable of a certain sort of explanation is not to deny, of course, that descriptions and explanations of these sorts (which we have not yet specified) are subject to many other kinds of appraisal. Descriptions and explanations may be unacceptable on various grounds. Some descriptions don't fit; some explanations aren't convincing. We do not want to deny the possibility of offering a description of the sort in question or an explanation of the sort in question which is unacceptable on *some* criteria of appraisal. We wish simply to make two assertions. First, it must be possible, for every subject of welfare discussion, to supply a description satisfying certain specifiable criteria of appraisal, and second, it must be possible, for every human activity (and so for every welfare activity), to supply an explanation satisfying certain specifiable criteria of appraisal. Both assertions must be supported by specifying the criteria to which we refer, by specifying the type of description and the type of explanation we have in mind. We shall do this in support of the first assertion by using some of the work of Professor P.F. Strawson. We have so far characterised descriptions of the sort in question simply as 'a description which distinguishes the subject as the thing it is'. To put it formally we shall now set our first assertion in its descriptive metaphysics. Naturally, we have attempted to put forward the general criteria to which we refer, as clearly as possible, but the views introduced in this discussion may also be usefully considered in the context of their original homes, references to which are supplied. Technical terms assumed in the original work to be understood, and not explained here, are explained in 'The Encyclopedia of Philosophy', editor-in-chief Paul Edwards (Macmillan, 1967).

3 Identification

We set our first assertion in its descriptive metaphysics because we are concerned with descriptions as means of identification. Through the detailed introduction of a theory of identification, we examine the conditions of the possibility of identification. We are then provided with criteria by which to assess terms employed in talking about welfare *as* means of identification. To admit that problems of identification arise in our welfare talk and to urge greater care with our means of identification, leaving a theory of identification aside, is not enough - for without a theory of identification we are not in a position to say that these terms are means of identification.

We have said that the development of means of identification of the sort in question is one of the goals of conceptual analysis. Our inclusion of this piece of descriptive metaphysics reflects our view that this goal should be presented as fully as possible, so that it might be better understood. We thus provide non-philosophers with an opportunity to consider theoretical problems concerning descriptions and explanations with which they are familiar, at a more general level. We return to the familiar descriptions and explanations in part five of section A, but the theory of the present section is also explicitly related to pieces of welfare discourse.

The subjects of welfare discussion are what Strawson has called 'individuals'. 'An individual is anything whatever; i.e. anything which can in principle, in any way whatever, be distinguished, as the single thing it is, from all other items under different presentations or descriptions or in different manifestations' (Strawson, 1971, p. 199). Usually when we talk about *individuals* we are talking about single human beings, as opposed perhaps to their societies or their families. The word 'individual' is being used in this way, for example, when it is argued that private markets in welfare erode the freedom of the 'individual' (Titmuss, 1948). It is important to notice, particularly in a discussion of welfare, that Strawson is using the word 'individual' in a way which recognises as *individuals* rather more than individual human beings. For Strawson an individual is *anything whatever,* so that not only is Aunt Fanny an individual, but so is her colouring, her living-room carpet, the fly on the end of her nose, etc., etc., so is anything whatever. Further, it should be remembered that when Strawson says 'An individual is anything whatever; *i.e.*, anything which can in principle, in any way whatever, be distinguished, as the single thing it is, from all other items under different presentations or descriptions or in different manifestations' (italics ours), what follows the 'i.e.' is not a *qualification* of his first statement, but an *explication* of it, making the same point more explicit by adding more detail. He is not allowing that there might *be* some thing which *cannot* in principle, in any way whatever, be distinguished, as the single thing it is, from all other items under different presentations or descriptions or in different manifestations. An individual is anything whatever, and everything is an individual; everything can in principle, in some way or other, be distinguished as the single thing it is, from all other items ... and so on. On Strawson's account, to *be* an individual is to be something in principle in some way or other, distinguishable as the single thing it is, from all other items ... etc. On this account the *existence* of an individual is neither more nor less than its discriminability and identifiability as the single thing it is, from all other items under different presentations or descriptions or in different manifestations (cf. Strawson, 1971, p. 200). On this account, discriminability and identifiability is a necessary and sufficient condition (2) of existence as an individual, of being something.

Discrimination and identification are possible only within a language; we cannot, for example, discriminate or identify anything without signifying the sort of thing it is, and this we do, and must do, within a language. Suppose, for example, that I want to pick out my pencil in order that you might pass it to me. I can only do this within a language, picking out what is of interest by specifying, perhaps amongst other things, what sort of thing it is. I might say, for example, 'Pass me the *pencil* by your left hand.' Thus, on this account we may say that an individual *owes* its existence to its being specifiable within a language in a way which discriminates and identifies it. Following Strawson, we may say that individuals owe their existence to a *style of specification* the terms of which embody or imply in their meaning principles for distinguishing, counting and identifying individuals (cf. Strawson, 1971,

p. 195, p. 200). In the example just given, in which the individual in question was designated by the use of the description 'the pencil by your left hand', the individual is specified in a style the terms of which embody in their meaning a principle or method for distinguishing, counting, and identifying individuals. The term 'pencil' embodies in its meaning just such a principle; if we know what 'pencil' means, then we know one method for distinguishing, counting and identifying individuals.

If I said 'Pass me the *thing* by your left hand', the individual in question, if any, is designated by the use of the description 'the thing by your left hand'. In this case the individual, if any, is specified in a style the terms of which do *not* embody in their meaning a principle or method for distinguishing, counting, and identifying individuals. The term 'thing' does not embody in its meaning any such principle. Everything is a thing, so the term 'thing' distinguishes nothing. To know what 'thing' means is not thereby to know at least one method for distinguishing, counting, and identifying individuals. In this case, so far as it has been specified, my request cannot be satisfied, you cannot pass to me what I want you to pass to me because I have not specified any individual in the required style; I have not picked out anything which you might pass to me. This is why, from the point of view of the hearer of the request, we said, 'the individual in question, *if any*'; because the style of specification does not embody in its meaning any principle or method for distinguishing, counting, and identifying individuals, the hearer is in no position to know that an individual *is* in question.

Suppose at a public meeting I stand up and say 'Scotland will receive no special benefits and may suffer severe coastal pollution as a result of the discovery of oil under the North Sea'. In this example, the individual in question is designated by the use of the proper name 'Scotland'. The individual is *not* specified in a style the terms of which embody in their meaning a principle or method for distinguishing, counting, and identifying individuals. However, the individual in question *is* specified in a style the terms of which *imply* in their meaning just such a principle or method.

As Strawson says, two linguistic means of identification are available. We can use descriptions or names or both. But, to repeat, it is no good using a name for an individual unless one knows who or what is referred to by the use of the name; a name is worthless without a backing of descriptions which can be produced on demand to explain its application (cf. 1959, p. 20). In our example, the name 'Scotland' would not succeed in picking out an individual if the audience did not know some such description as 'the most northerly country in the United Kingdom', which they might use to pick out a certain individual. And they use this description to pick out a certain individual because it is a description the terms of which embody in their meaning a principle or method for distinguishing, counting, and identifying individuals; if we know what 'country' means, then we know one method for distinguishing, counting, and identifying individuals - individuals of the sort of which that named 'Scotland' is an example. Thus, the identification of an individual by the use of a proper name is possible if and only if the speaker and hearer know some description of the individual the terms of which embody in their meaning a principle or method for distinguishing, counting, and identifying individuals. When this condition is satisfied, the speaker can use a proper name to pick out the individual in question and the hearer can identify the individual picked out. Our earlier example of a case in which the individual, if any, is specified in a style the terms of which do not embody in their meaning a principle for distinguishing, counting, and identifying individuals, the case in which I say 'Pass me the thing by your left hand', may also serve as an example of a case in which the individual, if any, is specified in a style the terms of which do not *imply* a principle or method of the required sort.

Examples of styles of specification the terms of which embody or imply in their meaning principles for distinguishing, counting, and identifying individuals can, of course, also be found in welfare discourse. When we talk about rent rebates, nuclear families, meals on wheels, presenting problems and methods of referral, the individual in question is specified in a style the terms of which embody in their meaning a principle or method for distinguishing, counting, and identifying individuals. If we know what 'rent rebate' means, for example, then we know one method for identifying individuals. Suppose at another public meeting I say 'Shelter must become politically aggressive.' In this example the individual in question is designated by the use of the proper name

'Shelter'. The individual is *not* specified in a style the terms of which embody in their meaning a principle for identifying individuals, but *is* specified in a style the terms of which *imply* in their meaning just such a principle or method. The name 'Shelter' would not succeed in picking out an individual if the audience did not know some such description as 'the voluntary organisation devoted to providing accommodation for the homeless', which they might use to pick out a certain individual because it is a description the terms of which embody in their meaning a principle of the required sort. The term 'voluntary organisation' embodies such a principle in its meaning.

Examples of styles of specification the terms of which neither embody nor *imply* in their meaning a principle or method for distinguishing, counting, or identifying individuals are more controversial. Sayings such as 'things will improve substantially if we are returned to office', where 'things' purportedly functions as a name, might be suggested. For, if this is all that has been said, it may well be the case that the speaker and hearers do not know some description the terms of which embody in their meaning a principle of the required sort, which can be produced on demand to explain the application of the name. They may not know *what* it is that it is being claimed will improve substantially. Of course, it may be that the speaker is using the name with a backing of one description of the required sort and the hearers mistakenly assume he is using the name with a backing of a different description of the required sort. But it may also be the case that the name is being used with *no* backing description of the required sort. In that case we do seem to have an example of a style of specification the terms of which neither embody nor imply in their meaning a principle or method for distinguishing, counting, and identifying individuals. An example from welfare talk can be found in Beales's attempt (1945) to describe 'the branches of social policy': 'They are *positive elements* in a world of public as well as private enterprise' (italics ours).

We might also suggest as examples of styles of specification of the kind at present in question, sayings such as 'The needy will receive special priority in future', where 'the needy' purportedly functions as a name. But in this case it would not be true to say that the speaker and hearers do not know *some* description the terms of which embody or imply in their meaning a principle of the required sort. 'The needy' is elliptical. It is an incomplete expression which requires completion, here clearly in the form of the noun 'people', yielding 'needy people' or 'persons in need'. Both the speaker and hearers know that the individuals in question are people, and the term 'person' embodies in its meaning a principle of the required sort - we do know how to count and identify people. On the other hand, knowing how to identify the *candidates* for neediness, we still don't know *which* people are to count as needy because the word 'needy' and the phrase 'in need' lack exact and rigid criteria of application; these expressions are *vague*.

It is important to bear in mind, then, that in the case of some styles of specification, it may not be enough, from the point of view of individuation, that the terms of the style of specification embody or imply in their meaning a principle for distinguishing, counting, and identifying individuals. Satisfaction of this latter condition may not be enough if we want to know *which* individuals are in question as opposed to *what sort*. If the expression used to ascribe a distinguishing characteristic to an individual of a known sort is vague, then though we know what sort of individual is in question, we shall not know which. We might therefore distinguish the following as two issues which may arise in connection with any style of specification of an individual. (i) Do its terms embody or imply in their meaning a principle for distinguishing, counting, and identifying individuals? (ii) Are any of its terms vague? We might go on to argue that both issues arise in connection with styles of specification employed within, as well as outside, the field of welfare. We might also argue that *both* are philosophical issues which should be of interest to anyone talking about welfare.

However, it might be suggested that these are not two distinct difficulties which might arise in connection with a style of specification, but one difficulty under different descriptions. In other words it might be suggested that for the terms of a style of specification neither to embody nor to imply in their meaning a principle of identification etc., is for those terms to be vague. Similarly, it might be suggested that terms which are vague fail to embody or imply in their meaning a principle of identification, etc. Consider our earlier examples of each type of case. In the case in which it was said that 'Things will improve substantially if we are returned to office', we have an example of a style of specification the terms of which neither embody nor imply in their meaning a principle for distinguishing, counting, and identifying individuals. 'Things' may also be said to be vague in the extreme; to say the least, it lacks precise criteria of application. In the case in which it was said (completing the incomplete expression used in the original example) that 'People in need will receive special priority in future', we have an example of a style of specification one of the terms of which embodies in its meaning a principle of identification etc., and another of the terms of which is vague: 'people' and 'in need' respectively. 'People' may also be said not to be vague, but to possess precise criteria of application; 'in need' may also be said neither to embody nor to imply in its meaning a principle of identification etc.

Against the view that there are here two distinct difficulties which might arise in connection with a style of specification, it might thus be suggested that we have here just one difficulty under two descriptions: for the terms of a style of specification not to embody or imply in their meaning a principle of identification, etc. *is* for its terms to be vague, to lack precise criteria of application. This rather complex problem needs more philosophical work. It is a significant problem for those of us talking about welfare, for if there are two distinct difficulties which might arise in connection with our styles of specification, then we need to be able to distinguish and identify examples as they arise. However, in this context the problem perhaps serves best as an example of an issue deep within philosophical territory which is nevertheless an issue which is an important consideration in talking about welfare. Whether there be one issue or two here, our present interest is in distinguishing styles of specification which supply a principle of identification, etc., from those which do not. The problem is relevant to our present interest, but we shall take it no further here.

We mentioned earlier another issue which might arise in discussion of any style of specification of an individual: are any of its terms evaluative? It is worth noting at this point that both terms which may be used to evaluate and terms which may not, may be more or less vague, or indeed not vague at all. The exactness or looseness of their criteria of application does absolutely nothing to distinguish evaluative from non-evaluative terms. As Hare says,

Words in both classes may be descriptively loose or exact, according to how rigidly the criteria have been laid down by custom or convention. It certainly is not true that value-words are distinguished from descriptive words in that the former are looser descriptively, than the latter. There are loose and rigid examples of both sorts of word. Words like 'red' can be extremely loose, without becoming to the least degree evaluative; and expressions like 'good sewage effluent' can be the subject of very rigid criteria, without in the least ceasing to be evaluative (1952, p. 115).

The discrimination of evaluative uses of general words or descriptions, as we stressed earlier, is an important task for the philosophy of welfare. However, evaluation must always be evaluation of something, of an individual, or individuals; the evaluative use of a general word or description must always be associated with some descriptive meaning. One can evaluate strawberries, sewage and social relationships, but one cannot simply evaluate. The identification of individuals is thus as important for the evaluative use of general words or descriptions as it is for the non-evaluative use. For this reason, then, our present interest lies in distinguishing styles of specification the terms of which embody or imply in their meaning a principle for distinguishing, counting, and identifying individuals, from those the terms of which do not. The essays we have brought together may be seen as contributions to the development of styles of specification of the required sort for a range of purported subjects of welfare discussion.

Adapting what Strawson has said elsewhere (1959) we may say that it is not merely a happy accident that we are often able, as speakers and hearers, to identify the individuals which enter into our discourse. That it should be possible to identify individuals of a given type seems a necessary condition of the inclusion of that type in our ontology (very roughly, by 'our ontology' we mean 'what our talk commits us to the existence of'). For what could we mean by claiming to acknowledge the existence of a class of individuals and to talk to each other about members of this class, if we qualified the claim by adding that it was in principle impossible for any one of us to make any other of us understand which member or members, of this class he was at any time talking about?

We may say, then, that every individual owes its

existence to a style of specification the terms of which embody or imply in their meaning principles for distinguishing and identifying individuals. Let us say, again following a suggestion put forward by Strawson, that an individual is specified in the required style when it is specified by an *adequately identifying designation*.

It will be recalled that Strawson's work was introduced as supporting and clarifying our assertion that it must be possible, for every subject of welfare discussion, to supply a description satisfying certain specifiable criteria of appraisal. Let us summarise our account so far. Given (i) that for every individual, that is, for everything, being specifiable by an adequately identifying designation is a necessary and sufficient condition of its being something, then (ii) being something entails being specifiable by an adequately identifying deisgnation; (iii) every subject of welfare discussion is something; therefore (iv) if our descriptive metaphysics is sound, every subject of welfare discussion must be specifiable by an adequately identifying designation.

Earlier we stressed the relation between conceptual clarification and, since the examination of concepts can only be carried out by considering the use of words, between clarification of the uses of words, general words, or descriptions, and the identification of things. What has just been presented is an account of the relation between the identification of individuals and the use of general words or descriptions the terms of which embody or imply in their meaning principles for distinguishing and identifying individuals. It is all very well, of course, to label as an 'adequately identifying designation' a style of specification the terms of which embody or imply in their meaning principles for distinguishing and identifying individuals, and to offer a clarification of this explanation. This still tells us very little about what we might call the 'mechanics' of distinguishing and identifying individuals; for the purpose of answering the question 'How do adequately identifying designations *in general* succeed in adequately identifying an individual?', the account so far given is inadequate. However, for our purposes, entry into such a discussion seems unnecessary. The account given is adequate for the purpose of distinguishing this style of specification. For our purposes we may simply draw attention to the fact that, as Strawson has pointed out, there are many

general terms under which individuals fall which embody
or imply in their meaning
> principles for distinguishing or picking out individuals which fall under them from other things,
> for counting or enumerating such individuals
> (though perhaps only under favourable circumstances) and for identifying such an individual
> encountered in one connexion or referred to under
> one description as the same item as one encountered
> in another connexion or referred to under another
> description (1971, pp. 195-6).

For individuals in general such general terms as fish, shoe, postcard, book, gazumping and cooking and such descriptions as raising one's glass, breaking and entering and turning over a new leaf, embody in their meaning principles for identifying individuals. Such terms as Atlantis and Tricky Dicky imply in their meaning principles for identifying individuals. For individuals which are the subjects of welfare discourse we have mentioned such general terms as rent rebate, nuclear family, and method of referral and might mention such descriptions as admitting into care and doing a domiciliary visit, as embodying in their meaning principles for identifying individuals. Such terms as Shelter and Oxfam imply in their meaning principles for identifying individuals.

Strawson, we can now note, regards the requirement that an adequately identifying designation should at least embody or imply a general term of the kind described as too stringent. He says
> Let us call terms which clearly satisfy that description 'clearly individuating terms'. There
> are other terms which, in one way or another fall
> short of being clearly individuating, yet are
> such that if a designation of an individual
> brings that individual under one of these terms,
> that designation is to count as adequately
> identifying (1971, pp. 196-7).

One example of a term falling short of being clearly individuating, says Strawson, is the kind of case in which the criteria of identity to be associated with the term are in dispute.
> This does not mean that there are no such criteria;
> only that the criteria are, so to speak, adjustable,
> depending on the purposes for which we wish to use
> the notion or the place we wish to give it in our
> theories. What we have here is the case where the
> meaning of the term is unsettled or disputed, but
> where any settlement of it would yield a clearly
> individuating term (1971, p. 197).

Strawson names the class of terms which fall short of being clearly individuating yet may be adequately identifying 'the class of variably individuating terms'. Admitting the existence of this class of variably individuating terms and that they are to count as adequately identifying, means that point (ii) in our summary given earlier (p. 26) must now be interpreted as the view that being something entails being specifiable by a clearly individuating term. For individuals which are often, though not exclusively, the subject-matter of welfare discussion, we may suggest as examples of variably individuating terms of the kind described charity, poverty, need, community and welfare. Of course, there will be cases where the criteria of identity to be associated with a term come to be disputed when we *change* the purposes for which we wish to use the notion or the place we wish to give to it in our theories. In other cases, such as a dispute may arise even though there are no such changes. The criteria of identity commonly associated with the term may be argued to make it unsuitable for the purposes for which we wish to use the notion or the place we wish to give it in our theories. If the term is to be retained in effect the criteria of identity to be associated with the term are in dispute. - In each case the meaning of the term is unsettled or disputed, but any settlement of it, we assume, would yield a clearly individuating term. It is a central aim of the series of which this collection is a member, to provide a forum for discussion of the variably individuating terms we employ, sometimes fatally insensitive to the fact that they are variably individuating, in talking about welfare. Strawson defines individuating terms in general as the logical sum of clearly individuating terms and variably individuating terms (1971, p. 198). We shall follow Strawson (cf. 1971, pp. 198-9) and say that any specification of an individual which embodies or implies an individuating term under which the item is presented as falling, is an adequately identifying designation.

We have now given a more precise account of the sort of description which we asserted earlier it must be possible to supply for every subject of welfare discourse: it must be possible to supply an adequately identifying designation for every subject of welfare discourse.

4 Explanation

Our second assertion, that it must be possible for every human activity (and so for every welfare activity) to supply an explanation satisfying certain specifiable criteria of appraisal, must now be substantiated. Having introduced the work of P.F. Strawson in supporting our first assertion, we shall introduce some of the work of Professor R.S. Peters in supporting our second assertion. For a fuller treatment of points used here, chapter I of his book (1958) should be read. We have so far characterised explanations of the sort in question simply as 'a purposive explanation of the activity'. This characterisation must now be amplified.

As Peters says,

the general question 'Why did Jones do that?' is capable of being asked and answered in a variety of different ways. The particular formula employed in asking the question usually dictates the sort of answer which is expected and which counts as an explanation. The paradigm case of a human action is when something is done in order to bring about an end. So the usual way of explaining action is to describe it as an action of a certain sort by indicating the end which Jones had in mind. We ask what was his *reason* for doing that or what was the *point* of it, what *end* he had in mind. If we ask why Jones walked across the road, the obvious answer will be something like 'To buy tobacco....' Even in this simple sort of explanation in terms of a man's reason for doing something there are, as a matter of fact, concealed assumptions. We assume, for instance, that walking across the street is an efficient way of getting to the tobacconist. This counts as an explanation not simply because Jones envisaged walking across the street as a means to getting the tobacco, but because it really is a means to getting it. We assume, too, that a man who has this information will act on it if he wants some tobacco. We assume that men are rational in that they will take means which lead to ends if they have the information and want the ends (1958, pp. 3-4).

He goes on,

but it is not only norms of efficiency and consistency that are implicit in the concept of 'his reason'. There are also norms or standards of social appropriateness. After all, Jones might

> have crawled or run across the road. But 'to get
> some tobacco' would be a very odd answer to the
> question 'Why did Jones *run* across?' Yet running
> would be quite an efficient way of getting across
> the road. It would, however, be socially odd as
> a way of crossing the road to get some tobacco.
> *Man is a rule-following animal*. His actions are
> not simply directed towards ends; they also con-
> form to social standards and conventions, and
> unlike a calculating machine he acts because of his
> knowledge of rules and objectives (1958, p. 5).

This purposive, rule-following, model of human actions, as Peters says, is the model in terms of which most of our explanations of human actions are couched and our predictions of people's behaviour presuppose it. It is this sort of explanation which we claim may be offered for every human action; every human activity may be accommodated within this purposive rule-following explanatory framework.

To make this claim is not to deny that people sometimes invent reasons for actions or that people sometimes delude themselves into thinking that the reasons they offer for their actions are operative reasons. As Peters says, we draw a distinction between *his* reason for doing so-and-so, and *the* reason why he did it (1958, pp. 8-9). And in some cases to offer an explanation in which *the* reason is opposed to *his* reason is to offer an explanation of a different sort from the purposive rule-following sort of explanation distinguished. In some cases, to give *the* reason why a person does something is to give a *causal* explanation. More generally, causal explanations are offered

> when there is some kind of *deviation* from the
> purposive rule-following model.... In such cases
> it is as if the man suffers something rather than
> does something. It is because things seem to be
> happening to him that it is appropriate to ask
> what made, drove, or possessed him to do that.
> The appropriate answer in such cases may be in
> terms of a causal theory (1958, p. 10).

Drawing this distinction between cases of doing something and cases of suffering something regarding only the former as cases of genuine action, we may concede that the latter sort of cases may be sufficiently explained in terms of causes, but argue that the former sort of cases may not. A *sufficient* explanation, of genuine action, can only be given in terms of the rule-following purposive model. Again, this is not to deny that there will be many causes in the sense of *necessary* conditions, but these do not add up to a sufficient explanation in the case of a genuine action. (5) Our second assertion may thus be expressed as the assertion that it must be possible to accommodate every genuine human activity within the purposive rule-following explanatory framework. Within the field of welfare, it must be possible to accommodate the genuine activities of, for example, policy-makers, executives, and the clientele, within the purposive rule-following explanatory framework.

We may sum up the preceding discussion by repeating our two assertions: (i) it must be possible, for every subject of welfare discussion, to supply an adequately identifying designation of that subject; (ii) it must be possible, for every human activity (and so for every welfare activity) to supply an explanation accommodating it within the purposive rule-following explanatory framework. We have supported the former assertion in greater detail. We do not want to suggest either that problems of explanation are less significant than problems of identification, or that they can be dealt with quite separately. It may be true in general that adequate explanations presuppose the adequate identification of those whose purposes they are and of whatever is to be explained, but the identification of some individuals may involve reference to their purposes or use (e.g. a social policy, a medical social worker, a reader, buying, tuning and sieving). The emphasis in our exposition upon problems of identification simply reflects our current interest.

5 Identification and explanation in welfare

Our collection of essays is designed to facilitate an examination of the adequacy, as identifying designations, of descriptions and definitions so far put forward of activities which are the subject-matter of welfare discourse. We also wish to facilitate consideration of the accommodation of the activities in question within a purposive rule-following explanatory framework by an examination of the adequacy of current designations of the objectives of the activities in question. Neither the essays collected here nor our introduction to them put forward final adequately identifying designations of the activities and objectives of interest, nor are these activities finally accommodated within a purposive explanatory framework. Our aim is not at this point to settle issues, even if we could, but to emphasise a number of underrated issues from the discussion of which both students of social administration, social policy and social work, and students of social and moral philosophy may benefit. We have collected together essays which may be regarded as undertaking the first essential step towards such designations and such an accommodation, the clarification of the use of terms of our field of discourse, and in particular of the terms in which current designations and accommodations are couched. (6)

The collection also facilitates an examination of what might be called 'justifications' in welfare discourse. Earlier, following Raphael, we suggested that the philosophical activity of the critical evaluation of beliefs has an important place in talking about welfare. Raphael (1970, p. 4) links critical evaluation to justification, adding that, 'I use the word "justification" to mean the giving of rational or justifying grounds either for accepting a belief or for rejecting it'. As Raphael uses 'justification' it might include examining purposive explanations of human activities as grounds for accepting or rejecting a belief about what some individual or group is doing. But it is important to stress that it might also include examining the moral principles to which a belief commits one. Welfare talk, often explicitly but also sometimes implicitly involves commitment to moral principles. These essays contribute to our consciousness of implicit moral commitment and to the examination of the principles to which we might be committed.

We are now in a position to consider further the implications of our assertions that it must be possible, for every subject of welfare discussion, to supply an adequately identifying designation of that subject, and that it must be possible, for every human activity (and so for every welfare activity) to supply an explanation accommodating it within the purposive rule-following explanatory framework. In the discussion which follows we shall deal specifically with activities, but it should be remembered that our first assertion applies to more than activities. It applies, for example, to those acting, persons or things acted upon, the context or setting of activity, and so on.

We recognised earlier that the same concept might be expressed by the uses of different words or descriptions. We may now recognise that the same item might be designated by more than one adequately identifying designation. Suppose the item in question is an activity. It is not a condition of doing (as opposed to suffering) something that one can supply *every* adequately identifying designation of what one is doing or one's method of doing it. One can imagine, say, a sausage-linker asked by a neighbour 'What do you do for a living?' unable to supply *every* possible specification in the required style either of the activity or of the method he adopts to carry it out daily. Such inability might be explained in various ways. The man might lack the necessary vocabulary, for example. Nor is it a condition of doing something that one can supply *every* possible accommodation of what one is doing within the purposive rule-following explanatory framework. Our sausage-linker might be as weak on such explanations as he was supposed to be on adequately identifying designations, and his weakness might be similarly explained. The fact that individual activities owe their existence to the possibility of their being signified by an adequately identifying designation is quite consistent with its being true that a man might both engage in an activity and be unable to supply *every* adequately identifying designation of it, and, we added, be unable to supply every accommodation of it within the purposive rule-following explanatory framework. And this latter is as true of men engaged in activities concerned with welfare as it is of sausage-linkers. It doesn't follow from the fact than an individual social worker, for example, is unable to supply every specification of the required sort for social work or for his way of doing social work, that he cannot do his job.

However, the fact that it must be possible, for every subject of welfare discussion, to supply an adequately identifying designation of that subject, entails that *some* such designation of it can be given by anyone for whom it is a subject. This is *not* consistent with its being true that a man might both engage in an activity (the activity thereby being a subject for him, the subject of his attention say) and be unable to supply *some* adequately identifying designation of it. A man cannot engage in an activity he is unable to identify. (7) And if no adequately identifying designation can be supplied by anyone, then no man might engage in the putative activity, for there is no activity in question. Again the fact that it must be possible, for every human activity, to supply an explanation accommodating it within the purposive rule-following explanatory framework, entails that *some* such explanation of it can be given by anyone for whom it is an activity. This is *not* consistent with its being true that a man might both engage in an activity and be unable to supply *some* purposive explanation of it. A man cannot engage in, actively take part in, what is not, for him, a genuine activity. And if no purposive rule-following explanation can be supplied by anyone, then no man might engage in the putative activity, for there is no genuine activity in question.

In connection with our first assertion then, the important implication is that if an activity cannot be described in the required manner, then it is not something, and hence not something a man might do. Lack of an explanation of the required sort compounds the felony. Not only is the putative activity not *something* a man might do, it is not something a man might *do*. As regards activities concerned with welfare in particular, we may, therefore, say that if no descriptions or explanations of the required sorts can be supplied by anyone, then the putative activities (8) concerned with welfare are neither possible activities, nor possible human activities. Expressed in relation to every putative subject of welfare discussion, the important implication is that if a putative subject cannot be described in the required manner, then it is not something, it is no more than a putative subject. We are not talking about anything and there is nothing to say.

Since a vast number of people and agencies are regularly *said* to be engaged in activities concerned with welfare, one might assume that adequately identifying designations and purposive explanations of their activities have been given, adequate in the context of the political, moral, or perhaps professional discussions in which these things are said. As we suggested earlier, an examination of current literature on activities concerned with welfare at the very least exposes the innocence of the assumptions that such designations and explanations have been *clearly* given. (9) An examination of current literature makes the same point as regards putative subjects of welfare discussion which are not activities.

Writers on welfare have, naturally, noted both that these are difficult matters and that they are unresolved. These points have usually been made in connection with activities, activities described by Kathleen Slack, in a way which has a touch of irony in the present connection, as aiming 'to advance and secure the welfare and well-being of the citizen in particular and general respects' (1966, pp. 73-4). That is, in connection with welfare activities designated by such phrases as 'social service' and 'welfare state'. Professor David Marsh states (1970, p. 1) that 'even now, in the 1970's, there seems to be no real consensus of opinion as to what is a welfare state and what are the principles and practices of a state which entitles it to be given this label.'

Moreover, says Marsh, 'in Britain it would seem that most people believe we have a welfare state because we have a wide range of social services, yet if one asked the man-in-the-street to define what he means by the social services, he would probably find great difficulty in giving an adequate definition' (1970, p. 1). Marsh, unfortunately, does not clarify his use of the phrase 'an adequate definition', but his remarks support our case if we assume that as regards human activities, including socially organised activities, an adequate definition is provided when an adequately identifying designation and a purposive rule-following explanation are given.

Those writers who have noted the absence of descriptions and explanations of the required sort for such activities or organisations specifically concerned with individuals as are signified by such phrases as 'social services' and 'welfare state' have, in general, not gone on to offer the perspicuous and consistent descriptions and explanations required. Marsh, for example, concludes his discussion of the evolution of the concept of a welfare state by asserting a welfare state to be 'one in which there are conscious and deliberate policies for ensuring at least a minimum standard of life at all times for everyone, and, as far as possible, equality of opportunity for everyone to achieve the best out of life, commensurate with aptitude and ability' (1970, p. 21). This 'definition' is inadequate, we would argue, because it fails to put us in a position to distinguish such individuals and fails to accommodate them within a purposive rule-following explanatory framework. Too much is unsaid. What criteria do we or ought we to employ in assessing the standard of life in a state? How do we or ought we to distinguish impaired opportunities from missed opportunities? Are conscious and deliberate government policies *ensuring* my opportunity to achieve all that is best out of life consistent with my achieving all that is best out of life, in particular the development of self-determination? On what grounds and on what kind of grounds does or ought the state to act in relation to a man's opportunities? Are all aptitudes and abilities to be encouraged equally? Do all aptitudes and abilities contribute equally to 'the best in life'? And, of course, amongst the many remaining questions, what is welfare? Other sections of Marsh's book do something towards satisfying the need to accommodate social services and welfare within a purposive rule-following explanatory framework, but the requirement of an adequately identifying designation remains unsatisfied.

Penelope Hall noted (1952, p. 3) that the term 'social service' is 'relatively modern, having come into general use with the multiplication of public and voluntary provisions to further the well-being of members of the community which is one of the outstanding characteristics of our times', it is a term which is 'sometimes used rather vaguely, and universal agreement has not yet been reached as to which services should be classified as "Social"'. However, Miss Hall suggested that if there is not universal agreement, there is at least *general* agreement in the description of welfare activities labelled 'social service'. 'The generally accepted hall-mark of social service is that of direct concern with the personal well-being of the individual' (1952, p. 3). More optimistic than Marsh, Miss Hall nevertheless provided a description of social services which is not perspicuous enough to be an adequately identifying designation. Again, too much is unsaid. What constitutes 'direct concern'? What is personal well-being? Nor does her account accommodate social services within a purposive explanatory framework. What implications, for example, does 'direct concern' have for the liberty of the individual, which is often held to be a part of personal well-being?

Kathleen Slack provides a very useful survey of descriptions and explanations of a welfare state in Concepts of the Welfare State (1966, ch. 4), many of which are, as adequately identifying designations and purposive rule-following explanations, unsatisfactory. As she says, a major problem in discussions of a welfare state is that

> like the social services, there is not consensus of opinion about its precise aims, or characteristics. It is clear that antagonist and protagonist have not the same concept in mind. The Welfare State means or conveys different things to different people. In these circumstances agreement about the value or disvalue of the Welfare State cannot easily, if ever be reached. The student can but examine what has been said and done and make up his own mind (1966, p. 62).

If the situation with regard to these key terms is as Kathleen Slack describes it, we have two cases of variably individuating terms and so of adequately identifying terms. If matters were worse, the student would not be in a position to follow Miss Slack's advice. The student may make up his own mind about the value or disvalue of the welfare state only when the subject of his value-judgment is signified by an adequately identifying designation and accommodated within a purposive rule-following explanatory framework.

In the essay The Subject of Social Administration (1968, p. 21) Titmuss says

> the study of welfare objectives and of social policy ... lies at the centre of our focus of vision. We may bring to this focus, singly or in combination, the methods, techniques and insights of the historian, the economist, the statistician, the sociologist, or, on occasion, some of the perspectives of the philosopher.

In our view the occasion for some of the perspectives of the philosopher is when there is no consensus of opinion about the characteristics or aims of an activity, for one source of such a lack of consensus is, as we said earlier, inadequate clarification of descriptions and explanations of our subject-matter. Until each of two men can offer an adequately identifying designation of the item which is his subject, it makes no sense to say either that they are talking about the same thing or that they are not. Until each can also offer a purposive rule-following explanation of the item which is his subject it makes no sense to say either that they are talking about the same human activity or that they are not. The root of a lack of consensus about the characteristics and aims of an activity may lie in inadequate identifying designation and purposive rule-following explanation of that activity.

In the pursuit of adequately identifying designation and perspicuous purposive rule-following explanation we must bear in mind the following point made by Aristotle in connection with the pursuit of clarity in offering an account of 'the good and the chief good' of human activities.

Our discussion will be adequate if it has as much clearness as the subject-matter admits of, for precision is not to be sought for alike in all discussions, any more than in all of the crafts. Now fine and just actions, which political science investigates, admit of much variety and fluctuation of opinion, so that they may be thought to exist only by convention, and not by nature. And goods also give rise to a similar fluctuation because they bring harm to many people; for before now men have been undone by reason of their wealth, and others by reason of their courage. We must be content then, in speaking of such subjects and with such premisses to indicate the truth roughly and in outline, and in speaking about things which are only for the most part true and with premisses of the same kind, to reach conclusions that are no better. In the same spirit, therefore, should each type of statement be received; for it is the mark of an educated man to look for precision in each class of things just so far as the nature of the subject admits; it is evidently equally foolish to accept probable reasoning from a mathematician and to demand from a rhetorician scientific proofs ('The Nicomachean Ethics', Book 1, Chapter 3, 1094b11-27, trans. Ross, 1925).

As Penelope Hall puts it, 'some vagueness is inevitable, and may even be desirable, in a sphere in which growth and change are continually taking place' (1952, p. 3). Bearing these points in mind, adequately identifying designations and clear purposive rule-following explanations should nevertheless be pursued, for in their pursuit we may discover how much clearness is as much clearness as the subject-matter admits of and, in a sphere in which growth and change are continually taking place, in what way our subject-matter grows and changes.

B

This section of our essay introduces the works that follow partly through a critical review of the first

essay we reprint, Professor T.H. Marshall's The Right
to Welfare. Marshall's essay is chosen not because
its key concepts or beliefs stand in greater need of
clarification or critical evaluation than those of
any other essay. Rather, Marshall's is an essay in
which a writer on welfare does not merely recommend
the perspectives of the philosopher, but adopts them
and offers a philosophical analysis.

In The Right to Welfare Marshall at least touches
upon most of the areas of discussion represented by
other essays. As well as being a useful vehicle for
the introduction of other contributions, the essay is
a contribution in its own right.

We now proceed to draw in some of the lines which
link the areas of interest represented by the essays
and extracts for, as we shall see, we are presented
with a cluster of problems. To use another analogy,
what we have here is a problem family most easily
seen to be a problem family, and not just a number of
individual problems, by their being gathered together.
We also believe that the problem family in question is
more likely to be understood when it is considered as
a family. A collection is a setting in which family
relationships and problems can be respectively clarified and, hopefully, resolved.

From the point of view of clarification, Marshall
begins his essay with salutary intentions.

> Let me say first, by way of definition, that I am
> using the word 'welfare' in the broad sense given
> to it in the term 'Welfare State', and not with
> the more specialised meaning of the services pro-
> vided by Welfare Departments.

This method of distinguishing different senses of a
word requires comment. Marshall's distinction between
the 'broad sense' and a 'more specialised meaning'
suggests his point to be that welfare takes many forms
and that there is a use of 'welfare' which signifies
all or most of those forms and another use which
signifies only some of them, those catered for by
Welfare Department services. We would not deny
either that welfare takes many forms or indeed that
Welfare Department services do not cater for all of
these forms, but what is questionable is that it
follows that 'welfare' has more than one sense. To
use the agreed facts as a method of distinguishing
different senses of the word 'welfare' is to assume
this case to fall under the general rule that if there
is more than one sort of X, then there is more than one
sense of 'X'. This general rule and its application

in this particular case stand in need of support. There is more than one sort of laughter and satirical magazines do not cater for all of these sorts, but we would surely not want to say that 'laughter' has more than one sense. We may object more strongly to the rule and so to its application in any case along the following lines. We must distinguish the use of the phrase 'there is more than one sort of X' from the use of the phrase 'there is more than one sort of thing called "X"'. Use of the latter phrase allows the possibility of more than one sense for 'X'. Thus we might say 'there is more than one sort of thing called "tall"': men and stories. (10) Use of the former phrase does not allow the possibility of more than one sense for X since every different sort of X is an X and may be distinguished as such using the same adequately identifying designation. It follows from the fact that there is more than one sort of X that there is some adequately identifying designation which distinguishes every different sort of X. This does not follow from the fact that there is more than one sort of thing called X. Every sort of laughter is a sort of laughter, but not every sort of thing called 'bank' is a sort of establishment for the custody of money, some things called 'bank' are a sort of sloping margin.

Another and independent objection may be developed against Marshall's method in practice. This objection may be most clearly developed in connection with the use of the word 'welfare' in the phrase 'the welfare services', used to refer to the services provided by Welfare Departments. In this use 'welfare' has the grammatical role of adjective qualifying the noun 'services' so that services of a certain sort are mentioned. The suggestion is that we may say quite precisely what services are provided by Welfare Departments. On this assumption, and the assumption that welfare services in this sense of 'welfare' are all and only those services provided by Welfare Departments, we may say quite precisely what services are welfare services in this sense of 'welfare'; we may draw up a list. But in doing this we shall have done no more than clarify a use of 'welfare services' as a noun-phrase: to name those services provided by Welfare Departments; we shall not have clarified the use of the adjective 'welfare' in that noun-phrase, for we shall not have said what sort of services the services provided by Welfare Departments are.

Similarly, one might try to list state welfare provisions and claim to have given an account of the sense of 'welfare' in or associated with the name 'Welfare State'. But the claim would be ill-founded. One would do better to offer the criterion or range of criteria by which one selected the provisions in question, an adequately identifying designation of *welfare* provision in a state given this label.

The essays The Concept of Welfare by R.B. Brandt, The Good of Man by G.H. Von Wright and Alienation and Self-Realisation by Kai Nielsen, reprinted in this collection, discuss criteria of personal and social welfare. One very common conception of personal welfare is that on which personal welfare implies realising one's potential, developing one's capacities to the full. Kai Nielsen examines this 'murky doctrine'. Marshall's attempt to isolate the use of 'welfare' in which he is interested assumes that we already know how 'welfare' is used in referring to the services provided by Welfare Departments and in labelling a Welfare State. Far from himself distinguishing two uses of 'welfare' Marshall assumes the existence of two distinct uses and our ability to distinguish them. We have suggested that the rule supporting Marshall's assumption about the existence of two distinct uses is dubious, and, as Marsh and Hall noted, our ability to distinguish uses may also be reasonably doubted. Brandt and Von Wright attempt to distinguish uses of 'welfare' systematically, and this is the essential groundwork preliminary to adequately identifying designations of a welfare service and a Welfare State.

Marshall continues the preliminaries: 'When I speak of rights, I include everything from legal rights, through social rights to moral rights, though I shall be concerned chiefly with the first two'. We naturally feel the absence of an account of how these three sorts of rights are to be distinguished, and in particular, we should like to know where rights to welfare fall.

> Any legal right there may be in the context of welfare must have an indirect or mediate character, being a right to those benefits which may be expected to produce welfare and which, on the average, will do so.

In the context of welfare, 'The ultimate object' of legislators and courts of law 'is something beyond the scope of legislative or judicial action'. Marshall conceives of welfare as an end to which legislation can supply only what is, on the average, the means to it. Rights to welfare which are legal rights are, says Marshall, rights to means rather than to welfare itself. At this point welfare is akin to happiness for Marshall, both are ends beyond the scope of legislative or judicial action. One 'could not give the citizen a legal right to sue for damages on the grounds that he was ... unhappy', though one might well give him a legal right to what was, on the average, the means to it. Discussions of happiness as an end and of the relation between welfare and happiness are taken up by Von Wright and by Nielsen.

On the other hand, says Marshall, 'it has been consistently argued that there can be no legal right in the fullest sense to a benefit the award of which is subject to discretion'. So it may be suggested that there cannot be a legal right even to the means of welfare, for as Marshall says,

> almost any benefit or service that is really designed to satisfy a particular individual need must include an element of discretion. For the assessment of needs in an individual case, and of the measures that are best suited to meet it, involves an act of personal judgment.

This view stands in need of development.

Prima facie an element of discretion would not seem to prevent a right from being a legal right, and to suggest that this is so would seem to be to adopt too simple and mechanical a view of the operation of the law. Discretion introduces a flexibility which Marshall seems to equate with an uncertainty which is foreign to legal response. Discretion

> as positive, personal and beneficent can only be fully realised in a 'welfare society', that is to say a society that recognises its collective responsibility to seek to achieve welfare, and not only to relieve destitution and eradicate penury.

In such a society an element of discretion does not undermine the certainty of benefit. In a 'welfare society' sanctions which are not legal sanctions effectively sustain rights that are not enforceable by litigation, for in such a society 'the public, the politicians, and the administration fully accept the legitimacy of the claims, take them seriously and give them a high degree of priority'. Against this 'background of welfare-consciousness' welfare benefits, even if we accept that they are not a legal right, are awarded as a right, rather than as a favour.

Two other issues connected with welfare rights discussed by Marshall are taken up by essays which are included in this collection. We may introduce the essay Human Rights, Real and Supposed, by Maurice Cranston, by examining a criticism made by Marshall of the Beveridge plan 'for universal, unconditional benefits attached to compulsory contributory insurance'. Beveridge

> did not see that national social insurance is no longer a system for fulfilling obligations derived from 'impulses of common humanity' by meeting a need that is common to all human beings, the need for the means of subsistence. It is a fiscal arrangement devised by the citizens of a particular society to adjust the distribution of the income of that society in a manner considered most conducive to the welfare of all. It is a mutual benefit arrangement of a special kind, which to some extent favours the weaker at the expense of the stronger, and the rights it confers are not rights rooted in the nature of man as a human being, but rights created by the community itself and attached to the status of its citizenship.

Marshall does not explain what sort of rights and obligations may be said to be 'derived from impulses of common humanity'. Nor does he give an account of what it is for a right to be 'rooted in the nature of man as a human being'. It seems to us that Marshall is here referring to what have traditionally been called 'human rights' and Cranston's essay provides a useful systematic introduction to this notion in the context of a distinction between legal and moral rights which Marshall uses and Cranston draws.

We said earlier that Marshall does not give an account of his distinction between legal, moral, and social rights. Rights 'derived from impulses of common humanity' are, it seems, what Marshall would call moral rights. He says later in connection with welfare services for old people and the mentally handicapped, 'the motive that inspires the services rendered to these people is compassion rather than interest', so that these rights to welfare are each 'bound to be more dependent ... for its driving and sustaining force on the fact that it is a moral right'. Sympathy would seem to be the source of morality according to Marshall. Moreover, he thus allows that welfare rights may be legal rights and that they may be moral rights. The notion of a social right is not explained but 'a right created by the community itself and attached to the status of its citizenship' would seem to be a reasonable suggestion. Since Marshall describes the right to national social insurance as a right of this kind, if this account is accepted, then Marshall also allows that welfare rights may be social rights. As we said earlier, it has not been shown that these are exclusive categories of rights. Reference to welfare rights as rights created by the community itself and attached to the status of its citizenship sets welfare rights once more within the context of a welfare society. The essays mentioned earlier in this connection discuss social rights based upon public morality and the concept of a community within which such rights are sustained.

The instruments of state welfare policies such as health regulations, health visitors and health education are, says Marshall,

> there to promote welfare by stressing a duty even more than a right, for your body is part of the national capital, and must be looked after, and sickness causes a loss of national income, in addition to being liable to spread.

It might be argued that to justify welfare rights on grounds referring to the economic interests of the nation, or of oneself, is to confuse economic exchange with what Titmuss (1970) has called 'the gift relationship'. It is at least to suggest that welfare rights and duties may also be economic rights and duties. Throughout the essay, rights are conceived as serving interests. This perspective may be enriched if we bear in mind that public morality may take into account more than a principle of maximisation of welfare, and particularly economic welfare. We might regard extreme inequality, for example, as morally unjustified even if it promotes economic welfare. The chapter Respect for Persons and Public Morality by R.S. Downie and Elizabeth Telfer sets a Utilitarian outlook in the context of a public morality which recognises the demands of equality, liberty and fraternity. Downie and Miss Telfer go on to argue that 'the importance attached to the three principles of utility, equality and liberty can be explained only if we say that the principle of respect for persons is assumed'.

Marshall's discussion of a 'background of welfare-consciousness' sheds a little light on the distinction

between a welfare state and a welfare society. The
implication is that in a welfare state there is what
might loosely be described as an official background
of welfare-consciousness, there are welfare policies
and machinery to administer those policies. In a
welfare society, welfare-consciousness extends beyond
the official domain, to the public at large. The
essay Welfare State and Welfare Society by Professor
R.M. Titmuss, which we include, is an attempt to
illuminate this important distinction.

If welfare rights are not, or are not only legal
rights, but are moral or social rights too, it will
be useful to consider the concept of welfare in relation to moral and social principles. Such a consideration will itself contribute to the elucidation of the
notion of 'a welfare society'. In the welfare society
described by Marshall, which has developed 'socially
acceptable selective services aiming to discriminate
positively, with the minimum risk of stigma, in favour
of those whose needs are greatest' (Titmuss, op. cit.)
the principle of respect for persons may be expected
to be of some considerable significance. It seems to
us that the notion of a welfare society is a rather
overworked and underelucidated one which might fruitfully be developed in this context.

There is a serious danger, in our discussion of the
notions of a Welfare State and a Welfare Society, of
suggesting that the public morality which supports
such social arrangements is straightforwardly Utilitarian. We are in danger of saying that a Welfare
State and a Welfare Society aim at the greatest
happiness for the greatest number or that actions are
right in proportion as they tend to promote happiness,
wrong as they tend to produce the reverse of happiness, or some other version of a Utilitarian morality.
Again, Professor R.S. Downie and Elizabeth Telfer, in
Respect for Persons and Public Morality, remind us
that the Welfare State and the Welfare Society may be
conceived within a public morality which supports
other principles as well as the principle of Utility.

The principle of respect for persons is often
explicitly and crucially used in discussions of the
ways in which clients of social services should be
treated. Professor W.G. Maclagan (1960) has argued
that an understanding of the principle may be gained
through an examination of the concept of friendship:
an examination of this concept offers a better route
to an adequate characterisation of the principle than
an examination of the concept of justice. Now

'friendship' also features, in its own right as it were, both amongst the possible models for social work practice and amongst more general descriptions and even explanations of social policy. It is not without significance, for example, that one of the chapters on social policy we reprint here is entitled 'Who is my Stranger?' In this chapter Titmuss suggests that the lag of supply behind demand in blood-giving can be seen, in the words of Professor M. Mauss, as a 'refusal of friendship'. The notion of friendship is left relatively undeveloped by Titmuss, and its necessary development, in our view, requires the kind of treatment attempted by Maclagan.

The concept of friendship seems to be closely related to those of fellowship, neighbourliness, and fraternity mentioned by David Donnison in his 'Liberty, Equality and Fraternity' which we reprint. Donnison attempts to invigorate both discussion of social policy and some 'traditional' political theory by a judicious mixture of the two. He distinguishes, however, only certain kinds of fraternity, and his view that

> A free world will be full of conflict: it cannot be a fellowship of friends, ruled by love, because the search for friends soon degenerates into the exclusion of enemies, the suppression of conflict and, ultimately, rule by hate,

alerts us to the importance of distinguishing matters of fact (here, actual tendencies) from matters of logic (here, the logic of the concept of a fellowship of friends, ruled by love). The degeneration of a fellowship of friends may in fact always have taken place, along the lines described, but no such degeneration is implied by the concept and so a free world might conceivably be without conflict, a fellowship of friends ruled by love. Indeed it might be argued by some that a fellowship of friends, guided by the principle of respect for persons, would be well equipped to resist degeneration to the point of the exclusion of enemies, for enemies (ignoring other animals, viruses, etc.) are persons. The principle of respect for persons is set in the context of public morality in general and of the values of equality, liberty and fraternity in particular, in Professor R.S. Downie and Elizabeth Telfer's Respect for Persons and Public Morality. In this chapter Downie and Telfer, but also elsewhere Downie, discusses the relation between fraternity and the concept of community. Downie (1971, p. 44) draws our attention to F. Tönnies

distinction between a *Gesellschaft* and a *Gemeinschaft*. The distinction, says Downie, can be explained if we translate it
> as one between an organisation or an association, such as a business or other commercial or official enterprise, and a community, such as may be found in a country district which has traditional ties with the soil. In a commercial association the individuals involved have nothing in common other than their interest in a specific commercial aim. If that aim is once achieved then there is nothing left holding the group together. A community, by contrast, is held together by many bonds, which are likely to be deep and complex.
>
> But any organisation, however commercially orientated, is always liable to become more than a mere association of persons for a specific objective. The members will tend to have a single meeting-place, to adjourn for coffee after their discussions, to have an annual party, to have a small library, to give their surplus funds to a certain charity, etc. All these additional interests are liable to be added almost imperceptibly to the basic commercial objective, and they all constitute growing points for a *Gemeinschaft*.

Thus Downie identifies through a concept of community that aspect of social morality he wishes to identify by means of the concept of fraternity. R.M. Titmuss's Who is my Stranger? provides discussion and evidence of this kind of community. Professor John Benson's essay The Concept of Community details different senses of 'community' and attempts to answer the question what is it that makes a relationship a human social relationship, what is it for a collection of individuals to have a 'common life'. His answer, suggesting that we think of society as a network of roles and that men share a 'common life' in so far as there exists among them a consensus about the various roles that individuals can occupy, leads him to comments which put Tönnies distinction in a new light: the sharp dichotomy can be misleading. Amongst other things, says Benson, 'we may be persuaded to think of any large-scale society as a mechanical contrivance, hostile or at best indifferent to human values, and having nothing to do with genuine human relationships'

Welfare provision is delivered in the context of a community in the sense of a collection of individuals having a 'common life'. It is not necessarily only delivered when such a community is a *Gemeinschaft*.

In The Function of Social Work in Society Peter Leonard reminds us of the range of possible conceptions of social relationships, social work and society. It may be that the consensus model of society, in which society is conceived as 'a system of interacting parts which are cemented together by a common set of values' fits poorly the actual context in which we deliver welfare provision through social work agencies.

Alan Keith-Lucas's The Art and Science of Helping makes interesting reading, particularly following Leonard's discussion. We have all confidently said that social work, amongst others, is a helping profession. The conjunction of these two papers helps us to see that what constitutes *helping* depends upon one's conception of social relationships and society. Leonard shows us a range of conceptions which have different implications for what it is to help a client. Keith-Lucas develops an account of helping which is not offered as one among many and which can be read as an attempt to marry more than one conception of social relationships and society. At one point Keith-Lucas reminds us that many clients 'refuse to admit their real need ... demand help from us on their own terms ... find ways of neutralising our help', suggesting *both* that client's and social worker's perceptions of what Leonard calls 'social reality' are in conflict, *and* that *really*, which hopefully the client will in time have the courage to recognise, there is consensus. A helping profession, it seems, can give its clients what they want and at the same time impose on them what they don't want.

Keith-Lucas includes an account of empathy. It is 'an act of compassionate understanding. It says "I can understand how you feel, and feel it with you in a limited way, but I don't feel that way myself."' In Knowing by Living Through, Dorothy Walsh discusses in more detail the nature of self-knowledge and understanding others. In On not being Judgmental Ian T. Ramsey takes up another theme introduced by Keith-Lucas. According to Keith-Lucas 'the helping relationship must be one in which negative feelings can be expressed without fear of blame, anger, sorrow or loss of face'. Ramsay provides us with a careful analysis of such 'acceptance' through consideration of what a 'judgmental' attitude may involve. (11)

NOTES

1 Social workers' views appear in, amongst others, the journal of The British Association of Social Workers, 'Social Work Today'. The views of some of those whose welfare is in question are recorded in John E. Mayer and Noel Timms 'The Client Speaks', London, Routledge & Kegan Paul, 1970.
2 A brief explanation of the terms 'necessary condition' and 'sufficient condition' is provided by G. Wallace and A.D.M. Walker at the foot of p. 2 in their collection 'The Definition of Morality', London, Methuen, 1970.
3 That there may be two distinct issues here was suggested to us by Professor Strawson.
4 Those who feel deprived by the omission of a discussion of what we called the 'mechanics' of successful designation might usefully read the Introduction to Wallace and Walker's 'The Definition of Morality' (especially pp. 1-4), and Strawson (1970) especially pp. 194-9.
5 Peters's *argument* for the insufficiency of causal explanations as explanations of genuine action should be examined.
6 See Slack (1966), ch. 4.
7 This is of course a logical rather than a psychological point. Our sausage-linker might very well engage in the activity of sausage-linking and be unable, because too embarrassed, to identify that activity for someone else. Our point is that it must be the case that he is able to identify it, even if, in particular circumstances, he can't bring himself to do it.
8 Since an item lacking an adequately identifying designation cannot be identified, when we talk in such circumstances of 'the activity', 'activities', 'it', or of 'the item', we are not signifying an individual, but are rather signifying what is, as it were, a would-be individual, a putative individual. Talk of putative individuals does not commit us to their existence, i.e. their discriminability and identifiability.
9 It seems fair to say that in the context of theory *construction* in this field, adequately identifying designations and purposive rule-following explanations cannot reasonably be expected to be *clearly* given. This may be our aim, but descriptions and explanations of the required sorts must first be *developed*. However, we would argue that a

distinctly philosophical contribution might be made to their development, by way of conceptual clarification and critical evaluation of the set of beliefs which constitute the theory. Further, while descriptions and explanations of the required sorts are still in the process of development, what we possess is not a theory about certain individuals within the field of welfare, but merely a theory *in the course of construction* about putative individuals.

10 On the other hand, use of this phrase does not preclude the possibility of just one sense for X. Thus we might say 'there is more than one sort of thing called "popular": music and mother's cooking', but not mean to suggest that 'popular' has more than one sense.

11 Many of the articles are taken from books and contain references to other parts of their original: e.g. chapters by Von Wright and Cranston. These then are not references to other parts of this collection. They remain to give the reader access to extended and related discussion in the original sources.

1 The right to welfare

T. H. Marshall

Twenty years ago the Welfare State was a novelty, and there was much that could be said, in general terms, about the genesis and the nature of the rights to which it gave effect. Today all this can be taken for granted, and anybody who is bold enough to broach the subject afresh will be expected to try to dig deeper and to look more closely into the details of the picture. It is difficult for him to say anything that is worth saying without getting involved in matters that are either technical or controversial, or both, and these are apt to demand more space for their proper treatment than I have at my disposal here. So I shall be content to concentrate on the highlights of the scene, as I see it, and to indicate the paths along which one's thoughts would travel, if one were to pursue the subject further.

Let me say first, by way of definition, that I am using the word 'welfare' in the broad sense given to it in the term 'Welfare State', and not with the more specialised meaning of the services provided by Welfare Departments. And when I speak of rights, I include everything from legal rights, through social rights to moral rights, though I shall be concerned chiefly with the first two.

It is tempting to dismiss at once the idea that there can be a legal right to anything as nebulous, as subjective and as personal as welfare. My dictionary, having made the obvious remark that it means the 'state of faring or doing well', can find nothing better to add to this than 'freedom from calamity, etc.: enjoyment of health, etc.: prosperity', and one cannot have a legal right to *et cetera's,* or even, for that matter, to prosperity. Welfare, as I have suggested elsewhere, is a compound of material means and

immaterial ends; it is located somewhere on the axis
which runs between the poles of wealth and happiness.
Now it may well be that the wealth of nations and the
greatest happiness of the greatest number are the
proper preoccupations of social scientists and politicians, but you could not give the citizen a legal
right to sue for damages on the grounds that he was
one of the greatest number but was nevertheless unhappy. Any legal right there may be in the context
of welfare must have an indirect or mediate character,
being a right to those benefits which may be expected
to produce welfare and which, on the average, will do
so. But we still have to ask whether there can be
rights *of some kind* to the thing itself - to welfare,
and how the concept of such rights may influence social
policy. For it is beyond question that it has influenced and does influence policy. As we watch legislators framing statutes and courts of law pronouncing
judgments, all in a perfectly proper and practical way,
we can see that what they are doing is deeply coloured
by the knowledge that their ultimate object is something lying beyond the scope of legislative or judicial
action. The constitution of one of the States of the
American Union contains a clause to the effect that
the Counties within the State 'shall provide as may be
prescribed by law for those inhabitants who, by reason
of old age, infirmity, or other misfortune, may have
claims upon the sympathy and aid of society. (1)
That expresses the dilemma very neatly. Somehow the
law has got to prescribe to what acts our sympathy is
to move us.

The dilemma became apparent when the poor laws
gave statutory force to the obligation of society to
look after its destitute members. An eminent American
judge defined this obligation when he said in 1873,
perhaps a trifle over-optimistically, that 'the relief
of the poor, the care of those who are unable to care
for themselves, is among the unqualified objects of
public duty. In obedience to the impulses of common
humanity, it is everywhere recognised. (2) But did
the duty to care for the poor, even when 'unqualified',
imply a right of the poor to be cared for? In England
the answer was an equally unqualified 'No'. The
pauper was a person deprived of rights, not invested
with them. The duty to relieve him was admitted, but
its source did not lie in any rights possessed by the
person relieved. He was the *object* of the action
taken, just as he had previously been the *object* of
charity. The 'impulses of common humanity', one could

say, were considered to be a matter between the people and their conscience, just as the impulses of charity belonged to the moral welfare of the charitable. And this was reflected in the legal doctrine. The duty to relieve the poor, says Sir Ivor Jennings (writing about the Poor Law of 1930), was 'a duty owed to the public and not to the poor person himself'. Consequently no action could be brought by the poor person to whom relief was denied, and any negligence of an official in his treatment of the poor was an offence, not against the pauper, but against the public who employed him to look after paupers. (3)

In some other countries, notably in Scandinavia and the United States, there was evident a desire to recognise the pauper as something more than an object, and to regard him, in fact, rather as the *subject* in the case, that is to say as a person who could be a source of rights and therefore of obligations. And this led, at times, to the very brink of an admission that the poor had a legal right to receive what the society had a legal obligation to give them. In a survey of the social services of the Northern Countries published in 1953 the chapter on Assistance opens with the statement that 'Assistance from the community as a legal right of the citizen in need is barely a century old.' And it appears that the term 'legal right' did appear for a period in Norwegian legislation, but was rather quickly dropped. It was replaced early in the present century both in Norway and in Sweden by a classification of basic minimum relief as 'mandatory assistance', and anything given over and above that as 'optional assistance'. This meant, in effect, that the poor person had an undeniable right to 'mandatory assistance', for it was expressly stated that relief was 'mandatory' whatever the cause of the need. But technically the right was not a legal one, because no legal remedy was attached to it; the pauper could not sue for his relief, he could only appeal. (4) The difference is that a legal remedy takes the matter to an independent court which judges the issue strictly in terms of the law; an appeal normally takes the matter to a higher level in the same system of authority, where it is decided by somebody who acts, not judicially, but administratively.

Edith Abbott (1940) summed up the position in the United States by saying that 'every American poor law for the past century and a half has given the person who is in need a "right to relief"'. The quotation marks indicate that special significance was given to the phrase, and she goes on to explain that there was much discussion of the issue whether the right was 'legal' or not. The verdict, it seems, was that it was not. This is so, in spite of the fact that the existence and nature of the right were a constant subject of litigation. The Courts were asked to decide who the poor were, which of their needs could and should be relieved and, of course, in which local government area their right was effective. The so-called 'seed and feed' cases illustrate this. In one of the American States crops had been destroyed by locusts. The farmers were facing destitution. The local authorities decided to provide them with means to get food to eat and corn to sow. They were taken to Court for this and the judge decided that it was legitimate to provide corn to eat, but not to provide corn to sow. Lack of seed-corn was not destitution. This judgment was subsequently reversed, on the grounds that, without seed-corn, they would have become destitute next year, and that prevention was better than cure. More generally, it was a matter of dispute whether a man could be a pauper if he still possessed land, even if the land was producing nothing. Another case raised issues both of settlement and of redress for negligence. A man was suffering from frozen feet, and applied for care. The County pushed him out, disputing his settlement. He was chivied along until eventually both his feet had to be amputated. He wanted to sue the original County for damages, but was denied the right to do so. And the County which treated him wanted to sue it for expenses, but, though it was warmly praised for saving the man's life, it could not recover from the local authority which had defaulted, and which was hotly rebuked for doing so. (5)

What one notices about the Court cases cited in profusion by Edith Abbott is that they are nearly all negative in character. They are initiated by a local authority or by one or more tax-paying citizens in order to prove that, in this particular case, there is no obligation to give relief and no right to receive it. When action has been taken with the opposite end in view - to assert a right or to condemn a violation of it, this has been done on the initiative of private citizens or voluntary bodies who, as Elizabeth Wickenden put it, 'were crusading for social justice in the highest tradition of the law'. (6)
The number of such cases has increased in recent years, as the 'war on poverty' has gathered strength. This does not mean, however, that the poor are on the

way to winning a legal right to relief. For, it has been consistently argued, there can be no legal right in the fullest sense to a benefit the award of which is subject to discretion. In support of this one may quote high American and British authority. The American so-called 'Ruling Case Law' on the subject held that 'the extent of relief, and its character, as well as the necessity therefor, are left to the discretion and judgment of the officers charged with the care of the poor', (7) and that precludes a legal claim by the beneficiary. And Beveridge, in his book 'Insurance for All and Everything' (1924), insisted that a benefit must be classed as assistance rather than insurance if its receipt 'depends in any way upon the discretion of some authority', and it is therefore 'given not as a right but as a favour'. (8) The point is clear and the distinction just, but its significance requires closer examination. This will lead us to consider two things, the concept of need and the relation of rights to duties.

The question is whether discretionary aid deserves the inferior status that has generally been ascribed to it. It has, I think, earned this reputation largely owing to its association with various forms of 'means test'. This has encouraged the view that the essence of discretion is that it gives somebody the power to refuse or to reduce the benefit. But this is quite false. In the first place a means test is not usually discretionary in Beveridge's sense, because it is applied by the officials concerned according to a schedule set out in regulations based on a statute. This was true, for example, of non-contributory Old Age Pensions. It was true to a less degree of unemployment assistance between the wars. According to Ronald Davison, 'no attempt was made to enforce rigid uniformity' on the Public Assistance Committees. But approximate uniformity was achieved except in ten or a dozen places, with Labour Committees, where the instructions for calculating private income were ignored. He describes these as 'rebellious areas'; their rebellion consisted in using more discretion than was permitted. When subsequently the Unemployment Assistance Board was set up, it actually encouraged in its officers 'a generous interpretation of the regulations and a use of their discretionary powers which seemed to be beyond anything revealed in the original plan'. And it is significant that the Board also made the most of its discretionary powers in another direction, namely to develop its welfare services. (9) It would almost seem that in the course of these few years the idea of discretion as a brake on generosity and a safeguard against extravagance had yielded place to a conception of it as a positive, not a negative, instrument of policy, to be used to increase the services rendered to those whose need for them was most pressing.

The truth is that almost any benefit or service that is really designed to satisfy a particular individual need must include an element of discretion. For the assessment of needs in an individual case, and of the measures that are best suited to meet it, involves an act of personal judgment. This is true not only of the decision how much cash income a family requires to satisfy its right to welfare, or of the organization of care for the aged, but also of the provision of an education suited to the talents of a student and of the doctor's diagnosis of an illness and his prescription of treatment. That is why the right to such benefits and services cannot be fully legal. You may sue a doctor for gross negligence, but not simply for refusing to prescribe the treatment you asked for, nor can you take legal action against an examining body for giving you lower marks than you consider you were entitled to. But discretion exercised in this way does not make a right inferior in quality to other rights. On the contrary, it is from some points of view superior, because the question asked in each case is not 'What do the regulations say must be done?', but 'What action is most likely to produce the desired result?' The 'means test' is transformed into a 'needs test', and the desired result becomes identifiable with 'welfare'. No doubt many Poor Law Guardians in the old days would have claimed that they used their discretionary powers in this spirit, but the claim could not be generally sustained for a moment. It would be nearer the truth to say that this notion of discretion as positive, personal and beneficent can only be fully realised in a 'welfare society', that is to say a society that recognises its collective responsibility to seek to achieve welfare, and not only to relieve destitution or eradicate penury.

The inferiority of discretionary assistance was emphasised in the Beveridge plan for universal, unconditional benefits attached to compulsory contributory insurance. He insisted that insurance benefits were given 'as of right' whereas assistance was not, and that assistance, therefore, 'must be felt to be something less desirable'. (10) His argument bred confusion in the public mind. For his aim was to guarantee to everybody a 'national minimum', or subsistence income at a flat rate. Now a guaranteed subsistence income is one way of meeting the obligation accepted by all societies to satisfy the basic needs of their members, an obligation arising, as the American judge said, from 'impulses of common humanity'. But Beveridge's plan took no account of needs at all, chiefly because to do so would involve applying a means test and this, he thought, would impair the right. He did not see that the right to 'mandatory assistance' can be made quite firm, even if it is not strictly speaking legal or, in his sense, unconditional. More important, he did not see that national social insurance is no longer a system for fulfilling obligations derived from 'impulses of common humanity' by meeting a need that is common to all human beings, the need for the means of subsistence. It is a fiscal arrangement devised by the citizens of a particular society to adjust the distribution of the income of that society in a manner considered most conducive to the welfare of all. It is a mutual benefit arrangement of a special kind, which to some extent favours the weaker at the expense of the stronger, and the rights it confers are not rights rooted in the nature of man as a human being, but rights created by the community itself and attached to the status of its citizenship. The plan adopted, therefore, takes account, not only of the national income and the demands made upon it, but also of the structure of the society and the position of the individual in it; so it is now customary for benefits to be related in some measure to individual earnings. To speak of modern social insurance as a means of waging war on want is misleading. It is better described as an apparatus by which the income of workers is spread over the periods when they can no longer work. This increases the total sum of welfare enjoyed in a life-time, and the social right to this welfare is converted into a legal right to the maintenance of income at whatever level the society may determine, after considering what is fair and appropriate in relation to the general standard of living attainable with its collective income.

I have referred several times to the difference between rights that are legal and rights that are less than legal. There is no doubt at all that in the past this difference mattered a lot; but does it matter now? In other words, granted that, in the strict legal sense, 'there can be no right without a remedy', can there, in another sense, be a remedy without a right? Are there other sanctions that can equally effectively sustain the rights - or claims - that are not enforceable by litigation? Once again, as in the case of the positive, personal and beneficent use of discretionary powers, the answer is, I think, that such a remedy can exist in a 'welfare society'. It can exist if the public, the politicians and the administration fully accept the legitimacy of the claims, take them seriously and give them a high degree of priority. Against this background operate various forces, latent and manifest, which constrain all those on whom the implementation of the claims depends to carry out their duties honestly, impartially, consistently and in accordance with the intentions of the legislation on which the service is based. In addition to the ever-growing latent force of tradition, there is the manifest force of rules and principles, sustained by publicity, accountability, supervision and, finally, the right of appeal. This right has been recognised in all the countries to which I have referred. It invokes, as I said, not the judicial decision of a court of law, but generally an over-ruling decision by a higher instance in the administrative structure, or by some special tribunal set up for the purpose. Such is the Appeal Tribunal established by the National Assistance Act, and in recent years it was hearing an average of some eleven or twelve thousand appeals annually. The number is very small in proportion to the total volume of cases dealt with under the National Assistance Board, but it helps to keep alive the idea that the granting of assistance is not an act of grace, but the satisfaction of a right, even if not strictly a legal right.

But the right of appeal is of little use if the background of welfare-consciousness is not present, as is apparent if one looks at what has been happening in many parts of the United States. Elizabeth Wickenden cites several cases to illustrate the arbitrary way in which some of the administrators of public assistance behave, such as the imprisonment of five recipients of relief for failure to cut brush in eight feet of snow, the claim made by a caseworker that she could decide 'whether a legal resident of New York would be "better off" in North Carolina', the decision to treat a woman who has an illegitimate child while on relief as automatically guilty of child neglect, and so forth.   The theme of her paper was that use should be made of every possible opportunity of invoking the law in defence of the rights of the poor, and it is clear that this was necessary precisely because the other kinds of sanctions which guarantee the enjoyment of social rights were not fully operative. (11)

Another reason for making the award of benefits discretionary lies in the relation between rights and duties. The point is a very simple one. If you concede to a poor person an absolute, unconditional right to relief, the question then arises how to deny him the right to become poor if he so wishes. The obligation of the community to relieve destitution must somehow be matched by a duty of the individual not to become destitute, if he can help it. That is why the emphasis in the early poor laws was on the punishment of idle vagabonds and on setting the poor, both adults and children, to work. As it became increasingly difficult to do either of these things, an easy substitute was found in reliance on the deterrent character of relief to keep the undeserving away. In conditions of full employment and a rising standard of living the temptation to indulge in voluntary penury has lost any force it ever had, and, though difficult cases may still sometimes arise, the problem is not one of real importance.

I have been speaking so far of the relief of poverty and of social insurance, and I have left myself little space to discuss the social and welfare services. So I must confine myself strictly to the highlights, as I see them. First, then, we find that here there is a much more intimate blending of rights and duties, and that it takes a different form. It is not that the discharge of a duty - the duty to work - gives entitlement to the right, but that the exercise of the right is at the same time a duty. This is most obvious in the case of education. For education is not only something to which every citizen has a right; it is a process by which citizens are made. As such it is something that every society must promote in its own interest, and every society that can afford to do so, and can produce the necessary teachers, makes education up to a certain level compulsory. For the individual, education at this level is simply a part of the social environment into which he is born and by which he is absorbed. Even above that level, right up to the university, education is of such vital importance for the health and prosperity of a nation, that it is regarded as something of which the individual has a duty to avail himself, to the extent that his natural abilities warrant. So the government is as much concerned to persuade children to stay at school, to take examinations, and to go on to technical colleges and universities, because society needs them, as it is to provide additional educational facilities because young people want them and claim that they have a right to them.

It is just as important for a society to have a healthy population as to have an educated one, so the right to health, like the right to education, is blended with duties. Public health is in large measure a form of public discipline, and the element of obligation spreads from environmental to personal health, from one's duty to one's neighbours to one's duty to one's dependants and one's duty to oneself. Health regulations, health visitors and health education are there to promote welfare by stressing a duty even more than a right, for your body is part of the national capital, and must be looked after, and sickness causes a loss of national income, in addition to being liable to spread. But at the same time the State applies pressure to its citizens in their own interests, which it feels able, in some respects, to interpret and translate into action better than they can themselves. Though we may boggle at Rousseau's idea that citizens in a democracy 'will be forced to be free', we can accept more easily the view that they may be induced to be healthy.

The important thing to note here is the difference between these rights to education and health, as conceived in the twentieth century, and the rights of the citizen as envisaged in the eighteenth and nineteenth, of which the right to property was the prototype. Locke and others maintained that they were 'natural rights', inherent in the individual and not created for him by the society of which he was a member. Even when this extreme view was not accepted, the rights to property and personal freedom were seen as the basis of the individual's power to assert and protect himself against his fellowmen and the State - the power, in the last resort, to isolate himself by converting his home into his castle. The modern rights to education and health are, on the contrary, not merely recognised by all as being social in origin, but are part of the mechanism by which the individual is absorbed into society (not isolated from it), and simultaneously draws upon and contributes to its collective welfare.

The case of the welfare services, in the technical administrative sense, is different. It cannot be said that society needs happy old people in the same way that it needs a healthy and educated population. Nor would it suffer any grave loss if the mentally handicapped were not assisted (at considerable cost in time and money) to make the most of their limited capacities. The motive that inspires the services rendered to these people is compassion rather than interest. And though compassion (or 'the impulses of common humanity') may create a right, having almost the force of law, to minimal subsistence, it cannot establish the same kind of right to the benefit of services which are continuously striving to extend the limits of the possible, and to replace the minimum by the optimum. So this particular right to welfare is bound to be more dependent than the others for its driving and sustaining force on the fact that it is a moral right. And that is why its champions have had, and are still having, so hard a struggle to win for it full recognition on the only terms they can accept. Furthermore, those in need of these welfare services are minority groups, set apart from the general body of normal citizens by their disabilities. The principle of universality which is a characteristic feature of the modern rights of citizenship does not apply, and the right cannot be reinforced, as in the case of education and health, by a corresponding duty to exercise it. The most one can say is that the handicapped have a moral duty to try to overcome their misfortunes as far as in them lies.

Every right to receive implies an obligation to give. It is, perhaps, not too fanciful to suggest that, whereas in the relief of the poor (in its early days) the obligation was that of one human being to another, and in the case of social security and the health and education services it is the obligation of the State to its citizens, or of the society to itself, the obligation to promote the welfare of the old, the ill-treated and the handicapped rests on one's duty towards one's neighbour. It is natural, therefore, that welfare services of this last kind should be generally regarded as involving a local, or neighbourhood, responsibility.

In conclusion there are two points that need to be stressed. First, a right to receive certain benefits or services does not necessarily imply the right to receive them free of charge. It means only that the rendering of the service should not be conditional on the ability to pay. The cost of the service may be met by pre-payment out of taxes, rates or insurance contributions, or may be recovered, in part at least, by levying *ad hoc* charges in proportion to the ability to pay, ranging from the full cost of the particular service received down to nothing at all. The choice of financial arrangement is a matter of importance, and the decision will vary according to the nature of the service concerned. But these are questions secondary to the existence of the right itself.

Secondly, welfare is only to a very limited extent the product of social services or of social policy. Its roots lie deep in the social and economic system as a whole. Its realisation and enjoyment depend, therefore, on a number of other rights, which I have barely mentioned, including those to property and personal freedom, to work and to justice. The national wealth is produced and distributed by men exercising these rights within the framework of national institutions, and national wealth is the material source of national welfare. Sometimes in the course of history it has seemed that the crucial point was production and that, if production throve, distribution could be left to take care of itself. At other times it has been the inequalities of distribution that have impressed men's minds and caused some people to urge that these must be corrected even if production suffered in the process. Very broadly speaking the former view prevailed in the early nineteenth century and the latter was prominent in the early twentieth. Today the emphasis is once again on production. This is not because distribution is considered to be unimportant or able to look after itself, but rather because the machinery for correcting the major inequalities has been established and been functioning for a long time. This machinery is far from perfect and nobody is entirely satisfied with it. But it is there, and with it general acceptance of the ends which it is designed to achieve. So today efforts to increase the supply of homes, hospitals, doctors, schools and teachers are seen to be getting nearer to the root of the problem than attempts to improve the apparatus through which access to these sources of welfare is distributed, while great stress is laid on the need to raise the output of goods and services of all kinds. For success in this will not only increase the sum total of welfare, but also greatly ease the problem of rectifying defects in its distribution, and the work on the welfare apparatus is quite certain to go on. If new resources are created, the pressure to spread the benefits is likely, in the long run, to be irresistible.

It follows that the claim to, and the clamour for, welfare are one aspect of the now general expectation that social and economic progress will be continuous and that the standard of living will keep on rising. And nothing is clearer than that this expectation can be realised only if the people who entertain it are ready to work for it. Their right to welfare is the right to their fair share of the individual enjoyment of the fruits of their collective labour.

NOTES

Based on a lecture delivered at the University of Keele on 12 February 1965.
1 Edith Abbott, 'Public Assistance', vol. I, p. 5.
2 Ibid., p. 74.
3 W.I. Jennings, 'The Poor Law Code' (1930), p. lxxvi.
4 George R. Nelson (ed.), 'Freedom and Welfare', pp. 448-55.
5 Abbott, op. cit., pp. 20-2.
6 Elizabeth Wickenden, 'The Legal Needs of the Poor' (paper given at a Conference in Washington in November 1964).
7 Abbott, op. cit., p. 9.
8 W.H. Beveridge, 'Insurance for All and Everything', pp. 6-7.
9 R.C. Davison, 'British Unemployment Policy since 1930', pp. 22 and 69.
10 'Beveridge Report', para. 369.
11 Wickenden, loc. cit.

2   The concept of welfare

Richard B. Brandt

One area in which the moral philosopher might say something useful for the thinking of economists is that of welfare economics - not by improving formalizations or criticizing proofs as to conditions necessary or sufficient for an optimum situation, much less by suggesting what particular state of society would be optimal. Rather, he can do this by pointing out some distinctions (e.g., explaining why assigning 'social welfare' a certain meaning obscures important points), by suggesting how some terms used by economists can profitably be defined, and by questioning some assumptions which seem to lie behind the thinking of some economists.

The following discussion is aimed along these lines. The main goal of the argument will be to produce helpful definitions of 'increase the welfare of an individual' and 'increase social welfare.' But the logical points and distinctions introduced in the course of the discourse may be of more interest to the economist and can be accepted on their merits irrespective of one's appraisal of the main definitions. My discussion will draw upon recent work in 'philosophical psychology' and moral philosophy, but it would be misleading, in view of controversies among philosophers, to suggest that it represents any 'agreed results' of philosophical inquiries.

THE WELFARE OF INDIVIDUALS

The term 'welfare' seems to carry a meaning, in ordinary talk about the welfare of individuals, different from what it carries in many recent discussions in which it appears in the expression 'social welfare.' Hence, it will be useful to begin by examining the meaning of 'welfare' in our more familiar discourse about the welfare of individuals. Since I shall argue later that a useful concept of social welfare *involves* the concept of individual welfare, it behooves us to be clear about the latter notion before we try to define the former.

The 'Shorter Oxford Dictionary,' among others, equates the meaning of 'welfare' with that of 'good fortune, happiness, or well-being; prosperity.' This proposal is hardly helpful for our purposes. For if clarification of 'welfare' is needed, it is equally needed for the terms 'well-being' and 'good fortune.' The other two terms are at least somewhat more explicit, although for 'prosperity' one may wonder whether money income, real income, or something else is meant. But in the case of these two terms it is mistaken to assert an equivalence of meaning with 'welfare.' It is untrue that a person's welfare increases if and only if his prosperity increases, for, to cite an example, we should say that a person's welfare was enhanced by a happy marriage, although such a marriage need not contribute to one's prosperity. 'Happiness' is rather closer; but we should not want to say that a person's welfare is increased *only* if, and *to the extent that,* his happiness is increased. There is room for reasonable doubt about this last point, partly because 'welfare' is a somewhat vague term; the reader will be in a better position to judge at a later stage.

A different reason for objecting to the Oxford proposal is that it undiscriminatingly mixes terms of entirely different kinds. 'Well-being' and 'good fortune' appear to be value-words and probably do not designate anything observable (probably are not parts of an 'empiricist language'); whereas 'happiness' and 'prosperity' are not value-words and, with reservations about vagueness, are parts of an 'empiricist language.' Since it is helpful to place these distinctions in clear focus, in view of their importance for the confirmation of judgments containing these terms, let us pause to formulate the concepts of 'empirical language' and 'value-judgment' (or 'value-word').

Let us consider the notion of an 'empiricist language.' (1) Such a language may be explained or defined in terms of its vocabulary. First, it includes words for the concepts of logic - those essential for discourse and argument about any subject matter - and in particular words like 'all,' 'some,' 'the,' 'if ... then ...' (and including 'if it *were* the case that ... then it *would be* the case that ...'), 'not,' and 'or.' Second, it includes terms for *observable* properties and relations, such as 'red,' 'between,' 'painful,' and 'joy.' There are debates about which terms should be classified as observation terms, but for the present this rather technical epistemological point may be ignored. Third, it includes all terms synonymous with any complex of terms formed from the vocabulary already admitted. Fourth - and here we get into deeper water - it includes other terms (like 'electron') which are tied to terms of the second and third classes by virtue of appearing in laws or rules in which terms of the other classes also appear. Such laws or rules are often said to accomplish a 'partial definition' of terms of this fourth type. Rudolf Carnap has argued that this fourth class is very large indeed, in science, but we need not pursue this question.

Whether a statement belongs to an empiricist language in this sense is an important matter. For any statement in an empiricist language is open to assessment by the methods of empirical science, whereas this is not possible for any statement which does not belong to an empiricist language.

If we overlook some points of vagueness, it is clear that 'happiness' and 'prosperity' belong to an empiricist language; the same is true for 'welfare' *if* its meaning were equated with that of these terms. (I.D.M. Little has doubted this claim about 'happiness' in contexts of talk of 'increasing the happiness of the community'; explanations are needed if we are to use the term in such a context.)

Let us turn now to the concepts of 'value-judgment' and 'value-word.' Some writers classify a judgment as a value-judgment if and only if it *cannot be formulated in an empiricist language*. If this proposal were acceptable, we could drop 'value-judgment' as a *second* conceptual tool, and get along with the first one alone. But the proposal is too broad. Statements in books on theology, or on metaphysics, or even inductive logic (statements containing 'probable' or 'well-warranted') appear not to be formulable in an empiricist language, but it would be odd to say that they necessarily express value-judgments. Moreover, some philosophers ('naturalists' in value theory) hold that value statements *do* belong to an empiricist language, and we do not wish to prejudge this issue by linguistic legislation. (Even if we did, we should not succeed in settling any important issue, for the question could still arise whether judgments to the effect that 'It is a good thing that ...' were value-judgments in that sense.) I believe, then, that we should adopt a neutral definition of 'value-judgment' which at least begs no important questions. I propose the following, while conceding that it needs to be spelled out more elaborately than is possible here. Let us say that a judgment is a value-judgment if, and only if, it entails or contradicts some judgment which could be formulated so as to involve any one of the following terms, in its ordinary sense, in an essential way: (i) 'is a good thing that' (or 'is a better thing that'), (ii) 'is morally obligatory,' (iii) 'is reprehensible' and (iv) 'is morally praiseworth.' If one wishes to use 'value-judgment' more narrowly, so as to distinguish it from specifically ethical or moral judgments, one could define it by reference to just the *first* of the foregoing phrases. Now a 'value-word' or 'value-phrase' is one the occurrence of which in a statement marks the statement as a value-statement expressing a value-judgment. 'Is a good thing that' is a clear case of a value-phrase.

If we ask whether, by this criterion, judgments about the welfare of individuals are value-judgments, the correct answer appears to be affirmative. For take the phrase, which is the important one for the economist, 'is on a *higher level of welfare*.' The statement, 'X is on a higher level of welfare if he is in situation S rather than S′' appears to imply or even mean the same as 'X is *better off* in S than in S′, if we abstract from all questions of moral obligation and the rights of others'; and the same for, 'If we abstract from all questions of moral obligation and the rights of others, it is a *better thing* for X to be in S than in S′.' If this is correct, then such judgments are value-judgments in our sense, and 'welfare' appears to be a value-word. The same is not, however, true of 'happiness.' From 'X is happier in S than in S′' it does not appear to *follow* that he is necessarily better off. This is shown by the fact that it is not inconsistent to think that knowledge is better than ignorance, and therefore, that, whereas a person might be happier in S than in S′, he is worse off because he is more ignorant in S (perhaps he is happily half-witted in situation S). 'Happiness,' then, is not a value-word - which is an additional reason for denying that it is synonymous with 'welfare.'

So far, then, our tentative conclusion about 'welfare' is (i) that it is a value-word and (ii) that it does not mean the same as either 'prosperity' or 'happiness.' Since we have defined 'value-word' (and 'value-judgment') in a neutral way, so as not to commit us on the question whether value-words belong to an empiricist language, we are not yet committed to any conclusion about whether welfare-judgments can be confirmed by the methods of science.

It might seem that the next order of business, then, must be to state the outcome of the enormous philosophical literature on the meaning and function of value-words in general and then to attempt to map the place of 'welfare' among value-words (viz., map the logical relations to other value-words) as all of these are used in ordinary speech.

This undertaking would be all very well for the authors of a dictionary, but I do not believe it would be very profitable for economists or philosophers. (2) The fundamental reason for this is that value-words, in their ordinary use, are very vague, and the authors of value-statements do not have any definite meaning in mind when they make them. Moreover, there is some reason to think that what meaning they have varies a good deal from one person to another, the extent depending largely upon the cultural history of the individual. What is called for, in contrast to laboring with ordinary usage, is that we *assign* some definite meaning to these terms, doubtless within the rough and vague limits prescribed by present usage, and that we do so for definite, statable, and relevant reasons. This holds, I believe, for the term 'welfare.'

It may seem that the job of picking a useful and relevant meaning for 'welfare' is a wholly amorphous one, too indefinite to qualify as a job at which one could either succeed or fail. But let us see. In fact, it will be possible to be quite brief, although at the outset we must consider some facts which may seem extraneous to our concern about 'welfare.'

Let me begin by pointing out that there are a great many choices or decisions which an individual has to make when we think he is free to attend only to his own welfare – when no moral obligations to others are involved and no considerations of the rights of others arise. An example of such a choice, in normal circumstances, is which profession to prepare for, whether law, or teaching philosophy, and so on. Another and humbler example is whether to enter this drugstore for a breakfast egg or to seek the same in the cafeteria across the street. Let us consider only choices of this sort.

Suppose there is such a choice to be made. The

agent may be in doubt what to do. Or, having made the choice, he may be in doubt whether he did not 'make a mistake.' If there is this element of doubt or puzzlement, the question arises whether one possible choice may be defended, supported, or justified, as compared with others. It is obvious that people *do* engage in some sort of reflection which they think sometimes results in a justification of a choice, to their own satisfaction.

About this process of reflection, we can sensibly raise two questions: is there any particular kind of consideration or reflection which in practice thoughtful people in general find weighty or conclusive support or justification of this sort? And, if so, is it possible to give an account, universally persuasive to thoughtful people, of *why* attention should be given this kind of consideration, in guiding one's conduct? (3)

I believe there is a particular kind of reflection which thoughtful persons do find weighty, and for good reasons. Something close to it was indicated by John Stuart Mill, when he said that the only way to find whether something is desirable is, in the end, to find whether people do desire it. A more adequate account is, roughly, to say that a choice is considered justified, and with good reason, if it is shown that it is one which the agent, if he were 'rational,' would prefer to any alternative open to him. Or, to spell out the term 'rational' just a bit, a choice is considered justified, and with good reason, if it is shown that the agent would prefer it to any other open to him at the time, if he were in a normal frame of mind and believed correctly all the facts relevant to the choice and had them vividly before his mind. To say this is still so brief as to be cryptic: I shall, therefore, proceed now to spell out what I mean by 'prefer,' and by 'rational'; and I shall sketch the reasons which may be given for saying that one should pay attention to one's rational preferences in making one's decisions.

But first let me acknowledge that other proposals have been made about how to justify one's choices, some of them highly implausible and unrealistic. One of these I shall discuss at some length in a moment: it is the by no means implausible proposal that a choice is justified, for the limited type of context we are discussing, if and only if it would (or probably would) maximize the net enjoyment or satisfaction of the agent.

Let me now explain the concept or rational preference,

and then the alternative proposal. After I have done this, we shall be in a position to consider what meaning may fruitfully be assigned to 'increases the welfare of an individual.'

Preference

What is it to 'prefer'? First, it is convenient to say that what we prefer is always *that one situation be the case* rather than that another be the case. Thus, we may prefer *that* Jones be elected mayor rather than that Smith be elected. We often *say* we prefer *things*, say chocolate to vanilla. But we can always rephrase such remarks in our standard vocabulary; e.g., we can say that we prefer *that* we be savoring chocolate than that we be savoring vanilla.

Now, what I mean by 'X would *prefer* that p to that q' (e.g., that he do A rather than that he do B) is 'X would *want* that p *more* than that q' or else 'would have less of an *aversion* to p than to q,' if the alternatives were before him as possibilities. It is perhaps obvious that it does not follow, from the fact that X *chooses* that p rather than that q, that he *wants* that p more than that q. For a person may *select* a cake from a plate of cakes offered him, when he does not prefer (want more) that one to any other cake on the plate, simply because he is busy talking with someone. Moreover, people often act impulsively without attending carefully to what they most want. Further, people can make mistakes about what they want: a person can think he wants a good character, when in reality he simply has an aversion to a bad reputation. Since what a person does is more closely related to what he thinks he wants than to what he does want, there is a further reason why what one does may not be an indicator of what one most wants or prefers.

But what then is it to *want* that p? This is a more elusive concept than might appear at first, as anyone will know who when making a difficult decision has tried to follow the advice 'Do what you most *want* to do!' It seems quite clear that wanting something is not a simple introspectible datum like a tickle. The exact logic of the concept of wanting is a difficult matter, (4) but I believe the central portion of the concept of wanting is captured in the following propositions, relating wanting to observable events:
(a) If, given that X had not been expecting p but now suddenly judged that p would be the case, X would feel

joy, then X wants p.   (b) If, given that X had been expecting p but then suddenly judged that p would not be the case, X would feel disappointment, then X wants p.   (c) If daydreaming about p is pleasant to X, then X wants p.   (d) If X wants p, then, under favorable conditions, if X judges that doing A will probably lead to p and that not doing A will probably lead to not-p, X will feel some impulse to do A.   (e) If X wants p, then, under favorable conditions, if X thinks some means M is a way of bringing p about, X will be more likely to notice an M than he would otherwise have been.   (f) If X wants p, then, under favorable conditions, if p occurs to the knowledge of X, without the simultaneous occurrence of events X does not want, X will be pleased. (5)

It seems plausible to suppose that evidence for wanting p more than q is provided by occurrence of the events cited in a more intense form, in connection with judgments about p, than with judgments about q.

If the foregoing conception is well taken, then what a person wants is fixed by what he has to *think about* in order for these effects to occur.

I have suggested that there is not a simple relation between what a person wants and the choices he makes. For very similar reasons there is not a simple relation between what a person wants (or wants more or less) and the bets he will lay.   It would, of course, be unreasonable to deny that betting behavior is strong evidence about the relative strength of wants.

Rational preference

I have suggested that preference may be called 'rational' when it meets certain conditions.   Let me explain these more fully.

When we prefer one event p to another q, it is always because we think (at least take for granted or believe) that these events have different properties. (These could be just the properties defining what it is to be a 'p' or a 'q' occurrence.)   For instance, we may prefer the profession of medicine because we think the life of a physician, as compared with that of a philosopher, is one of more contact with other persons or one which produces more definite and tangible results.   This fact points to one possible way of criticizing a preference: that of showing that the beliefs on which it is based are incorrect, or even unintelligible.   It also points to a second possible way: that of showing that the beliefs on which it is based are incomplete, that there are further facts such that if the agent had thought about them, he would have preferred what he did either more or less. It seems, then, that one condition of a fully justified preference could be this: that it is based on all true beliefs about the object in question which would tend to move the agent one way or the other. I propose calling a preference 'rational' only if this condition is met.

There is a second and closely related condition. Sometimes in a sense we *know* all the pros and cons relevant to a preference, but we do not have them *all before our mind*. Sometimes when we think of one feature of an alternative, we feel drawn toward it; when we think of another feature, we feel repelled. This raises the question: what would we prefer if we could get *all* the relevant features before our mind with full vividness - as vividly as if we could actually perceive them all? I propose to call a preference fully 'rational' only when it is as it would be if this condition were met.

There is a third defect from which a preference may suffer. It may be formed, and be capable of being formed, only in a peculiar mood or frame of mind. Some features of something may appeal to us more in some frames of mind than others, for instance, under the smart of a wound to our pride. So, again, I propose to call a preference 'rational' only when this defect is absent - when the preference is one that would be framed in a state of mind undistorted by temporary mood or emotion or by some temporary craving.

I suggest that we call a preference for p over q a *rational* preference *if, and only if,* these three conditions are met.

We should notice that the question whether a person rationally, in this sense, prefers p to q is one that in principle can be answered by empirical means, by the person and also within limits by other people (assuming they can get information about his wants and aversions) - of course, in some cases by no means easily; for answering requires finding the actual properties of p and q, correct beliefs about which would tend to move a person if he had them.

When thoughtful people have an important decision to make and are in some doubt what to do, I believe that in fact they try to see whether their tentative preference is rational in this sense. If they are convinced it is, they are satisfied with a corresponding decision. The reader is invited to introspect, to determine whether or not this is the case.

But is there any reason, which will be universally persuasive to thoughtful people, why they should guide their conduct by this sort of reflection? (i) For one thing, there is not really a serious alternative, if one is going to be reflective about choices, to paying attention to what we *want* to do. This will be clearer after we have considered the major alternative. (ii) *If* we aim to make it a policy to do what we most want to do, presumably the policy will be to do the thing we most want of the *actual* alternatives open to us, as they really are, and not the thing we most want among mere caricatures of the alternatives. And to this end we need knowledge of the relevant facts before us. (iii) It is sensible to pay attention to 'normal' preferences since we have to live with our decisions. It would be imprudent to favor the fleeting preference of a moment in making a decision we may long dislike and regret. To this it may be replied that no reason has been given why we now should take an interest in whether we shall regret something; but at any rate we can say that it is arbitrary to favor only the preference of the present moment and also that in fact most persons do take an interest in whether they will regret a decision later, when they reflect that they are the very same person who will have to endure the later regrets.

I have already acknowledged that there are other possible systems for appraising choices of the limited kind under consideration. I shall discuss a closely related method in a moment. But there are some quite different ways. A person might think he should choose only what conforms with the 'purpose' of the universe, or with God's will. Conceivably reasons might be given for using such a method (although I suspect such reasons would reduce to the method already described). I do not see how we can rule out, in advance, all such possibilities as being absurd. But we also need not worry about them until they are formulated and we know what they are. What we can say now is that up to the present no comparably supported method (aside from the one to be discussed next) has been produced (6) and that a choice which meets the conditions described has met the known possible objections which might seriously be raised against it.

Pleasure, happiness, and satisfaction

There is one possible way of supporting or justifying one's choices (in cases where no questions arise about moral obligation or the rights of others), which is different from the one just outlined, and which has some plausibility. This is the familiar view that an agent's choice is justified if, and only if, it will (or probably will) result in maximizing the agent's pleasure, happiness, or satisfaction. This conception has appealed to many economists and philosophers influenced by the utilitarian tradition.

We can simplify discussion without loss by construing the proposal in terms of maximizing the agent's net long-run *pleasure*, dropping out explicit reference to happiness and satisfaction. At least we can do this if we construe 'pleasure' broadly enough so as not to imply merely sensory pleasure but to include such enjoyments as that of reading a book and if we construe 'displeasure' broadly enough so as to include such displeasures as those of anxiety and embarrassment in addition to physical discomforts.

It might be objected to this simplification that it distorts and reduces the plausibility of the proposal. But this can hardly be correct, for it appears that we can define 'happiness' in all its various senses in terms of 'pleasant.'

For instance, 'I was happy all evening until he said ...' means the same as 'I was enjoying myself this evening until he said ...' or 'I was having a perfectly pleasant evening until he said ...' It is often asserted, however, that 'happiness' is not a sum of pleasures. In this statement, 'happy' is being used in a different and somewhat narrower sense. To be happy in this sense is to be pleased, or at least not discontent, with one's achievements or prospects with respect to one's major goals in life. Indeed, some recent work suggests that people call themselves 'happy' if they are pleased, or at least not discontent, with achievement, or prospects, with respect to what they consider their most important goals. So we might define 'is happy' in this sense as meaning 'does not feel any unpleasant emotion at the thought of where he is or is getting with respect to certain major aims in life' and perhaps also 'goes about his work with a pleasant cheer and zest.' In other words, when one is happy in this sense, one's life is not marred with unpleasant emotions when one reflects on certain matters and by and large one's activities are pleasant. If we conceive 'happiness' thus, then it is true that a sequence of sensual pleasures does not amount to happiness; but it is also true that happiness is nothing other than the enjoyment (or absence of displeasure) resulting from being able to take an optimistic view about progress toward important goals. There are doubtless other senses of 'happy' which we should recognize; and we must remember that the term is a rather vague one. There is no reason to believe, however, that such other senses cannot be explained in terms of 'enjoys' and 'pleasant.'

Much the same is true of 'satisfaction.' Suppose a person says he gets much satisfaction out of the progress of his former graduate students in the academic world. What he means is no more than that reflection on the success of certain former students is pleasant. Explanations of other uses of this term will readily come to mind.

With these preliminaries out of the way, the question is this: might we regard a choice as sensible (in the limited context described above), if it will (or probably will) maximize one's net long-run pleasure, as contrasted with being in conformity with one's rational preference? It will help us adjudicate this question if we consider briefly the nature of pleasure or pleasantness, about which there has recently developed a considerable literature. (7)

The first thing to be noted is that what is pleasant is always some conscious state, or activity, of a person. Things that are pleasant are things like dozing in the sun, listening to a symphony, reading a novel, or hearing good news.

It follows that on this second theory the class of 'ultimate reasons' justifying a choice is narrower than on the first theory. The reason for this is that people actually *want* other things besides their own conscious states or activities. Of course, people do want enjoyment and do have an aversion to pain, anxiety, and other unpleasant states. But there are other things they want: such as to get a manuscript in better shape, to have a daughter happy in her marriage and financially secure after her parents' death. Some writers have thought that what a person desires is always some state (or, more particularly, some pleasant state) of himself; but by any reasonable criterion for identifying what a person desires (such as the criteria sketched above), people desire some things which cannot be described as states of themselves. It is true that if one's manuscript gets in better shape, one will feel 'happier' about it, and if one's daughter is happily married and provided for, one will feel less unpleasant anxiety about her. But these states of one's self are obviously not the targets of one's desire. For this reason it is quite natural and unconfused for people to ask themselves whether it is sensible to sacrifice personal enjoyments in order to achieve something important; this is a real alternative and some people prefer one course, some another. Of course, it may be that one can *rationally* want something only to the extent that getting it will make one happier; but the rational-preference theory leaves open the possibility that this is not the case. And it is surely not obvious that a 'rational' want would be only for some pleasant state of one's self.

A second feature of pleasure is important for our purposes. What precise kind of state or activity is a 'pleasant' one? On this the experts are much less fully agreed. Some suppose that 'pleasure' consists in relaxation-feelings or bright pressure-feelings, but others find it impossible to introspect such feelings when they are enjoying themselves. Others have held that 'pleasure' is always a case of activity in which one is absorbed or to which one attends without effort, but this description hardly fits what is happening when one is dozing in the sun, and one wonders how such writers would describe how one feels when the dentist is drilling. I think myself that the property which most clearly belongs to all pleasant states and activities is simply that *at the time the person wants them to continue for their own sakes* (which is consistent both with not *thinking* that one wants them to continue, and also with *not wanting* to continue them, *everything considered,* in view of consequences or of other things one ought to be doing). And, for one experience to be *more* pleasant than another, is for the person to want to continue it, more intensely, for itself. We should notice that things as diverse as playing a game and having a certain kind of sensation may be pleasant in this sense. (8)

If I am right in this, then pleasure is a *species* of wanting: it is wanting some *present* state or activity to *continue, for its own sake*. Incidentally, one can want a state or activity to continue at the time, but afterward wish it had not. Whether one wants something, and how much, seems to be partly a function of the state of one's glands, so that there may be some inconstancy in what one wants, perhaps even in what one rationally wants. (*If* there is, there may be a limit to the consistent direction we can get for action from appeal to our rational preferences.)

I can now explain why I believe that the traditional hedonist view of how choices (for our limited context) are to be appraised should not be substituted for the 'rational-preference' proposal. The major reason is simply that to adopt the hedonist view amounts to an arbitrary decision in favor of conscious states or activities which one wants at the time one has them. It is true that we want these, both at the time and often beforehand, but what is so sacrosanct about them so that all other wants must be dismissed? If a person, after careful reflection, finds that he wants some things (to make an important discovery or the security of his children) more than states of personal enjoyment, it is not clear that there is any persuasive ground for abandoning these desires (as there is for abandoning desires which we would not have except in depressed moments). Of course, the rational-preference proposal leaves open the possibility that a rational want is never directed at anything but a pleasant state of consciousness or a pleasant activity. The rational-preference proposal, therefore, leaves open the possibility that the hedonist is right in his conclusion. But to adopt it at the outset as a method of appraisal is to opt arbitrarily for a special sort of want: for wants directed at the continuance of some state or activity of the self at the time.

There is a second difficulty in the proposal. In order to make rational decisions by the hedonist standard, one must compare enjoyments of certain duration and intensity, for magnitude, with enjoyments of different duration and intensity. But this is impossible: we can compare the intensities of different experiences (strength of wanting to continue at the time), but we cannot compare intensities with durations. We *can* make the comparisons necessary for decision, however, if we take the notion of preference as basic. We can prefer to endure, say, a certain stretch of pain of a given intensity for the sake of a different stretch of enjoyment of a given intensity. (It does not follow from this that there is *more enjoyment* in the preferred experience.) So it appears that the hedonist can make judgments he needs to make, only if he falls back on the preference standard after all. (He can refuse to do this if he admits that there is no rational answer to questions about conduct which could be answered only by comparisons of the sort described.)

Levels of individual welfare

Thus far I have argued that one might support a choice by showing that it conforms with one's 'rational preference' in a sense explained. I have suggested that thoughtful people do appraise actual or possible choices in this manner and that there are reasons which would dispose a thoughtful person to pay attention to his rational preference in deciding what to do. Further, I have suggested that there is no other mode of appraising choices which has a comparable claim on conduct for those cases in which moral obligations and the rights of others are not involved.

We must now revert to the original question what meaning can usefully be assigned to 'welfare' or 'on a higher level of welfare.'

It might be argued that we do not have to 'assign' any meaning here, for it is clear that what we *already* mean, in English, by these terms is such that 'X is on a higher level of welfare if p rather than if q' just means 'X rationally prefers that p to that q' in the above-defined sense of 'rationally prefers.' (And the same for, 'X is better off if p than if q.') At one time I inclined to this view myself, but I believe that 'better off' and 'welfare' are too vague for this suggestion to be correct. Therefore, if 'welfare' is to have a meaning of the kind indicated, it must be an assigned one.

What purpose should guide our assignment of meanings? We need not aim to preserve the vagueness of ordinary language. We need, rather, to have meanings so assigned that things which are important to say can be said clearly and unambiguously. Further, we need terminology related to choice and conduct which enables us to raise and distinguish all the questions it is important to raise, in view of our total understanding of the human scene. And, if I am right in thinking that there is a preferred method for resolving doubts about choices and for appraising choices, we shall need some terms indicative of the status of a choice with respect to the application of this method.

What meaning, then, all these points considered, should we assign to 'is on a higher level of welfare'? One possibility is simply to use it as a synonym for 'prefers.' However, we already have a perfectly good term for this concept. Further, in ordinary speech we often contrast preference with welfare (a person may prefer what is bad for him). I suggest, then, that we are keeping reasonably close to the ordinary associations of 'welfare,' and are at the same time assigning a useful meaning to the term, if we decide to use 'X is on a higher level of welfare if p than if q' to mean 'X rationally prefers p to q.'

If we adopt this definition, it follows that one person might be put on a higher level of welfare by the very same kind of occurrence that will put another person on a lower level. It also follows that a person's own rational desires are decisive for his own welfare and that the desires of others are not - however much another's wish for him may be more reliable as an indicator of his rational desires than his own actual wishes are. If X conforms to what others want him to do, when their wants are rational, he is adding to *their* welfare, not necessarily to his own. Also, if X wants his son's happiness (rationally), then his son's happiness really does raise X's level of welfare, the extent depending upon how much X wanted it.

Some propositions appear to be true about the rational wants of all persons; but whether they are logically or only empirically true, I shall not discuss. Among them are the following: (i) If a person rationally wants both p and q, and is indifferent between them, he will rationally prefer a given probability of getting p to a smaller probability of getting q. (ii) A person will not rationally prefer p to q on account of temporal position *alone*. (iii) Knowledge that an event will be pleasant for a person will always arouse, so far, a favorable rational interest in the event; and knowledge that it will be unpleasant will always arouse, so far, a rational aversion toward the event. (iv) The rational preferences of a person will be transitive.

Given the above definition, we shall want to specify that a good or service has *utility* for a person if he would rationally prefer to have it rather than not have it. To say that two goods have equal utility for a person will be to say that the person would be rationally indifferent between them.

If the foregoing definition is accepted, 'welfare' and 'utility' both belong to an empiricist language and at the same time are 'value-words' which can function essentially in the expression of a value-judgment.

SOCIAL WELFARE

The foregoing definitions do not commit us to any particular definitions of 'social welfare' or 'increases social welfare,' terms which appear frequently in the literature of welfare economics. Let us now consider what would be a useful way to construe these terms. Our results will enable us to appraise the status of the proposition 'The social welfare is increased by the change from S to S' if this increases the welfare of at least one person and the welfare of no one is diminished by the change,' a proposition which is viewed by some economists as an ultimate value-judgment. My conclusion will be that this proposition is true by definition.

Space limitations forbid considering various possible meanings that could be assigned to the above expressions. So let us go at once to the heart of the matter: the question what an economist might do, with good reason, to *support* advice he might offer to a public official as to some proposed rule or law. We could follow lines of thought similar to those pursued in the preceding section to justify saying that what one must do, in order to support a recommendation of a rule or law, is show that the rule or law is one *he (or others) would want adopted, if he (they) were rational (in the above-defined sense) and also were a person (persons) whose concern for others were equal to his (their) concern for self or family*.

I shall have to pass by the question what complications are raised by the possibility that two rational and sympathetic persons might disagree in their recommendations. I incline to think that in fact they *would* disagree to some extent, but I also believe there are some principles on which they (9) will necessarily agree - parallel to what was suggested for the case of individual welfare.

Now we could, with some sense, propose to assign to 'Rule A will *increase the social welfare* more than Rule B' the meaning 'If I [alternatively: anyone] were rational and sympathetic I [he] would prefer to have Rule A adopted rather than Rule B.' But in fact this would be inconvenient and misleading, for there are different fundamental reasons on account of which thoughtful people have wanted rules adopted - not only considerations of welfare, but also considerations of justice or equality. (Witness how people have favored equality of income when they have not argued that this would increase the total real income; or they have argued that it should be illegal to purchase ration tickets or to buy a substitute for military service, although they have not denied that such exchanges might increase total welfare.) Indeed, the difference between utilitarians and their critics has been that the utilitarians have said that in the end only increasing welfare is a relevant and forcible reason for adopting an institution, whereas their critics have denied this. In order to preserve at least the possibility of debating these controversial points, it is necessary to assign a meaning to 'increases social welfare' so that it is not *self-contradictory* to say 'If I [one] were rational and sympathetic I [one] would prefer to have Rule *A* adopted rather than Rule *B*, for reasons of justice, and despite the fact that Rule *B* would enhance social welfare more.'

How might we assign meaning to 'increases social welfare' so as to meet this condition in a helpful way? I see no alternative to a formulation equating 'increases social welfare' with 'increases the *sum* of individual welfare' where 'individual welfare' is explained as in the preceding section. It remains to be shown, of course, that the welfares of individuals, in that sense of 'welfare,' *can* be summed. But it is clear, at least, that if 'social welfare' is defined in this way, it follows that the social welfare is increased if the welfare of at least one person is increased and that of no one else decreased. It is for this reason that I suggested above that it is an analytic proposition, as we must construe 'increased social welfare,' that social welfare will be increased under these conditions. Thus, if this definition is adopted, part of welfare economics rests on the sound foundation of an analytic proposition.

It is well-known, however, that if we are to speak of the 'sum' of individual welfares and also in principle to be able to determine which of two laws increases the sum of individual welfares the more, certain other propositions must be true. Most important, we must be able to compare for size the prospective utility of one person or persons with the prospective disutility of some other person or persons, if a certain law is adopted. And, if we explain 'utility' as above suggested, this means that at least sometimes we must be able to affirm reasonably the following proposition: that *X wants A* more than *Y wants B*. (We are ultimately concerned with a comparison between the *rational* wants of *X* and *Y*, but that problem can be ignored for the present.)

Since the possibility of reasonably affirming propositions of this sort is so central to application of this (traditional) concept of 'social welfare' that I am suggesting, and since I happen to think that some economists take an unreasonably purist view about this matter, I shall conclude my remarks with some queries about the epistemology of these economists.

Since according to suggestions made above, the intensity of a person's wanting is measured by various things such as the disappointment he would feel if he did not get it, we may as well simplify our problem by asking simply whether we can know that one person has some conscious state (e.g., disappointment, pain) more intensely than does some other person.

One difficulty a noneconomist has in discussing this problem is that he does not know exactly what is behind the economist's conclusions. If the economist thinks we cannot have sufficient reasons for thinking other persons conscious at all, that is one thing. If, however, he thinks we have sufficient reasons for thinking other persons are conscious, and perhaps for asserting *some* things about their states of consciousness, that is another.

Let us begin with the second possibility. Presumably in this case the purist economist thinks that certain pieces of evidence are good and sufficient for making some assertions about the consciousness of others. Then our question must be: why draw the line here? Are the reasons you think adequate for these assertions not essentially of the same kind as those available for other affirmations? Suppose the purist economist thinks another person has at least three different colors in his visual field (he may say we cannot know what these colors are like). If this is asserted because it is necessary to explain the other's color discriminations, then one might go on to suggest that the other person's ability to predict that a proctoscopic examination will hurt *me* more than a mosquito bite is good reason for saying that the former hurts *him* more than the latter sort of thing. It is, perhaps, obvious how we might go on. Exactly what we should do is necessarily unclear, of course, until we have information about exactly what the purist is prepared to concede.

The purist economist may be much more radical, however. He may say we have no good reason for making any assertions about the conscious states of other persons, even for asserting that other persons are conscious at all. We should notice, incidentally, that it would not be to the point for him to say merely that we do not have *certain* knowledge about the experiences of others, for this would not disparage our grounds for statements about experiences of others in comparison with grounds for other assertions. If we grant that such knowledge is not certain, it may still be more nearly certain that the man having the proctoscopic examination is in pain than that there will not be a business recession next year. So let us suppose the purist is saying we have *no good and coercive* reasons for beliefs of this sort *at all*.

This position is an extreme one. What are the purist's reasons for adopting it? (One is inclined to say that these reasons are very likely to be more dubious than the reasons for regarding the man having the proctoscopic examination as being in pain.) Presumably the economist thinks that some *type of inference* is required for assertions about the experiences of other persons which is not required in the rest of science and is dubious. (He might go further: he might say we have no good reason for believing, unless it can be shown to *follow logically* from observations, that another person's experience is so and so. But to say this is to condemn all of science, for no law or theory in science anywhere follows logically from a description of the observations.) What kind of inference might this be? Perhaps the purist will reply: 'inference *by analogy*.' If he does, we must then ask him (a) what he *means* by 'analogical inference' (this term is used in many different senses) and (b) why he thinks that analogical inference in that sense is required for the present context. (10)

It is not unfair to demand that the purist produce *his* epistemology, for he is the one who is departing radically from common sense. The purist obviously does not believe his creed in practice: if his child were about to have an operation, he would not question the advisability of using an anesthetic or of giving morphine after the operation! Nevertheless, it is worthwhile to produce two positive reasons on the other side.

1 In physics it is thought proper to extrapolate laws confirmed for observable entities, to the unobserved (e.g., Newton's laws are extrapolated to the realm of microscopic entities). It is supposed that if postulates about the unobservables, plus these extrapolated laws, lead to correct predictions, the postulates and the extrapolation are justified. But the logic is the same for inferences about other minds.

We know in our own case (a) that we feel pain when having a proctoscopic examination, (b) that we seldom succeed in making witty sallies when in severe pain, (c) that we feel grief when we learn of the death of our mother, (d) that we find it hard to take an interest in things, or to act in a vivacious manner, when we feel severe grief, and (e) that the passage of time reduces the poignancy of grief. On the basis of this, we predict that a man having a proctoscopic examination will seldom come out with witty remarks and that the person whom we have just apprised of his mother's death will not behave vivaciously this evening although he probably will do so in a month's time. These predictions work out magnificently. Why, then, as compared with the physicist, are the extrapolations and assumptions wholly dubious? We use mentalistic assumptions in making a good many predictions about the behavior of others, and it is not clear how we would make them without mentalistic assumptions. The correctness of the predictions would seem to reflect glory on the assumptions, in principle just as in physics (although, of course, the predictions are non-quantitative and much more humble).

2 Other people succeed in making a good many correct assertions about *our* mental states. One's mother, when dropping iodine on the wound or in stripping back one's injured fingernail, says 'That must hurt badly!' How was she able to guess if she has never experienced pain herself? The books on psychology are very successful in predicting all sorts of visual illusions and various facts about the emotional life. How are the psychologists able to predict how things will look, or feel, if they are unconscious? Indeed, the very availability of a rich language for description of our mental life must be explained by the purist - and also how it was possible to teach us the use of this language. The minimal explanatory assumption appears to be that other persons are built very much along our lines and so there has been a point in the existence of such a language, and they have been able to teach it to us because, on the basis of their own experience, they have been able to know when we have experiences to which these terms properly apply.

Whether the purist in economics will want to deny the force of these lines of reasoning, I do not know. Perhaps he will wish to fall back on the less extreme position, described earlier, that it is only some kinds of information about others which we cannot claim with strong supporting grounds.

We need not deny that it is difficult to know whether an increase in the tariff on bicycles would do more harm than good. But I venture to suggest that some economists are locating the source of the difficulty in the wrong place; they are giving way to a penchant to attribute all our predictive ills to one disease - the philosophical problem about knowledge of other minds - instead of attributing them to the various difficulties of knowing exactly what will happen to various individuals, or classes of individuals, if the tariff were raised. If we knew exactly what difference to the *total conditions of living insofar as these are publicly observable* an increase in tariff would bring about, it seems doubtful to me that the impossibility of observing others' mental states would be much of a further problem. Indeed, if we even knew such a simple fact as that the total effect of a tariff increase would be that one hundred not very sturdy newsboys could not afford bicycles and must, therefore, spend one more hour each day delivering their papers on foot and also (on the credit side) that one man would be able to buy a third air-conditioned Cadillac, it is hard to believe that the purist would doubt that more harm than good was done. Unfortunately the effects of a change of tariff are so hard to predict in detail that we cannot well say just what people are doing, eating (etc.) given the change which they would not have been doing without it. But such effects are essentially knowable, if we wish to spend the time and money.

NOTES

1 For a discussion of the concept of an empiricist language, and some of its difficulties, see C.G. Hempel, Problems and Changes in the Empiricist Criterion of Meaning, reprinted, with afterthoughts, in A.J. Ayer, ed., 'Logical Positivism,' New York, Free Press, 1959. This paper includes a useful bibliography.
2 I have argued this at some length in 'Moral Philosophy and the Analysis of Language,' The Lindley Lecture for 1963, published by the Department of Philosophy, University of Kansas, 1963. I have discussed the varieties, and difficulties, of various theories about the meaning of value-words in ordinary language in 'Ethical Theory,' Englewood Cliffs, N.J., Prentice-Hall, 1959, chs 7 to 9.

3 It may be interesting to reflect on whether the accepted standards for inductive inference in science can be given support fundamentally different from that which can be given for choices.
4 See the discussion by R.B. Brandt and Jaegwon Kim, Wants as Explanations of Actions, 'Journal of Philosophy,' 60 (1963), pp. 425-35. For some differences between wants and aversions see Stephen Pepper, 'The Sources of Value,' Berkeley, University of California Press, 1958, ch. 10; and E.C. Tolman, 'Purposive Behaviour in Animals and Men,' New York, Appleton, 1932. See also Fritz Heider, 'Psychology of Interpersonal Relations,' New York, Wiley, 1958, chs 4 and 5.
5 These propositions are drawn from Brandt and Kim, 'Journal of Philosophy.' Some of them require refinement. I do not believe that at present we can give any satisfactory general explanation of 'under favourable conditions.' We shall wish to include as 'unfavourable' conditions such things as extreme fatigue, emotional excitement, and temporal remoteness of the event judged about.
6 I have discussed the merits of the theological proposal in 'Ethical Theory,' pp. 63-82 and 252-3.
7 See G. Ryle, 'The Concept of Mind,' London, Hutchinson's University Library, 1949, ch. 4; also his 'Dilemmas,' Cambridge University Press, 1954, ch. 4; and G. Ryle and W.B. Gallie, Pleasure, symposium, Aristotelian Society, supplementary vol. 28 (1954), pp. 135-64. T. Penelhum, The Logic of Pleasure, 'Philosophy and Phenomenological Research,' 17 (1957), pp. 488-503; and T. Penelhum, W.E. Kennick, and A.I. Isenberg, symposium, Pleasure and Falsity, 'American Philosophical Quarterly,' 1 (1964), pp. 81-100. C.W.W. Taylor, Pleasure, 'Analysis,' Supplement, 23 (1963), pp. 1-19. R.M. McNaughton, A Metrical Concept of Happiness, 'Philosophy and Phenomenological Research,' 14 (1953), pp. 172-83. A.R. Manser, Pleasure, 'Proceedings,' Aristotelian Society (1960-1961), pp. 223-38. B. Williams and E. Bedford, 'Pleasure and Belief,' symposium, Aristotelian Society supplementary vol. 33 (1959), pp. 57-92. R.B. Brandt, 'Ethical Theory,' pp. 304-07. P. Nowell-Smith, 'Ethics,' Harmondsworth, Penguin, 1954, ch. 10.

For interesting psychologists' discussions, see Fritz Heider, 'The Psychology of Interpersonal Relations,' New York, Wiley, 1959, ch. 5; J.G. Beebe-Center, 'The Psychology of Pleasantness and

Unpleasantness,' New York, Van Nostrand, 1932, pp. 394-413; and his Feeling and Emotion in H. Helson, ed., 'Theoretical Foundations of Psychology,' New York, Van Nostrand, 1951; P.T. Young, 'Emotion in Man and Animal,' New York, Wiley, 1943, ch. 7; Magda Arnold, 'Emotion and Personality' vol. I, New York, Columbia, 1960. Perhaps most interesting of all is K. Duncker, On Pleasure, Emotion, and Striving, 'Philosophy and Phenomenological Research,' 1 (1941), pp. 391-430.

8 An objection sometimes raised to this proposal is that we can tell directly, by inspection, whether we are enjoying something, whereas we would (it is supposed) have to stop and reflect in order to know that we want to continue some experience or activity for itself (assuming the correctness of the above account of 'wanting'). Various points may be made in reply to this. One is that we know, without elaborate reflection, that we would like to have a lot of things: an increase in salary, a trip to Europe, a drink of water, to find misplaced glasses. Another, is that it is not impossible to become conditioned to respond with 'Yes,' when stimulated by the question, 'Are you enjoying yourself?', when and only when we want some present state or activity to continue. Many analogous phenomena have been found in experiments on concept formation.

9 See my 'Ethical Theory,' chs 5, 6, and 11; also 'Value and Obligation,' New York, Harcourt, 1961, pp. 433-40; and 'Hopi Ethics: A Theoretical Analysis,' University of Chicago Press, 1954, ch. 16 and following.

10 It is possible some economists are influenced by the logical positivism or operationalism which was influential in the 1930s. They may then be saying that statements about the experiences of others are meaningless because in principle we cannot observe them. (We can, of course, observe our *own* mental events, and presumably other persons can observe *their* mental events.) But if he does, is he not condemning most of modern physics? Most of the assertions in the area of quantum mechanics, for instance, are about occurrences which in principle we cannot observe in the required sense.

3   The good of man

G. H. Von Wright

1

The notion of the good of man, which will be discussed in this chapter, is the central notion of our whole inquiry. The problems connected with it are of the utmost difficulty. Many things which I say about them may well be wrong. Perhaps the best I can hope for is that what I say will be interesting enough to be worth a refutation.

We have previously (Ch. III, sect. 6) discussed the question, what kind of being has a good. We decided that it should make sense to talk of the good of everything, of the *life* of which it is meaningful to speak. On this ruling there can be no doubt that man *has* a good.

Granted that man has a good - what *is* it? The question can be understood in a multitude of senses. It can, for example, be understood as a question of a *name*, a verbal equivalent of that which we *also* call 'the good of man'.

We have already (Ch. I, sect. 5) had occasion to point out that the German equivalent of the English substantive 'good', when this means the good of man or some other being, is *das Wohl*. There is no substantive 'well' with *this* meaning in English. But there are two related substantives, 'well-being' and 'welfare'.

A being who, so to speak, 'has' or 'enjoys' its good, is also said to *be well* and, sometimes, to *do well*.

The notion of being well is related to the notion of health. Often 'to be well' means exactly the same as 'to be in good, bodily and mental, health'. A man is said to be well when he is all right, fit, in good shape generally. These various expressions may be said to refer to minimum requirements of enjoying one's good.

Of the being who does well, we also say that it flourishes, thrives, or prospers. And we call it happy. If health and well-being primarily connote something privative, absence of illness and suffering; happiness and well-doing again primarily refer to something positive, to an overflow or surplus of agreeable states and things.

From these observations on language three candidates for a name of the good of man may be said to emerge. These are 'happiness', 'well-being', and 'welfare'.

The suggestion might be made that 'welfare' is a comprehensive term which covers the whole of that which we also call 'the good of man' and of which happiness and well-being are 'aspects' or 'components' or 'parts'. It could further be suggested that there is a broad sense of 'happiness', and of 'well-being', to mean the same or roughly the same as 'welfare'. So that, on *one* way of understanding them, the three terms could be regarded as rough synonyms and alternative names of the good of man.

The suggestion that 'the good of man' and 'the welfare of man' are synonymous phrases I accept without discussion. That is: I shall use and treat them as synonyms. (Cf. Ch. I, sect. 5; also Ch. III, sect. 1.)

It is hardly to be doubted that 'happiness' is sometimes used as a rough synonym of 'welfare'. More commonly, however, the two words are *not* used as synonyms. Happiness and welfare may, in fact, become distinguished as two concepts of different logical category or type. We shall here mention three features which may be used for differentiating the two concepts logically.

First of all, the two concepts have a primary connexion with two different forms of the good. One could say, though with caution, that happiness is a 'hedonic', welfare again a 'utilitarian' notion. Happiness is allied to pleasure, and therewith to such notions as those of enjoyment, gladness, and liking. Happiness has no immediate logical connexion with the beneficial. Welfare again is primarily a matter of things beneficial and harmful, *i.e.* good and bad, for the being concerned. As happiness, through pleasure, is related to that which a man enjoys and likes, in a similar manner welfare, through the beneficial, is connected with that which a man wants and needs. (Cf. Ch. I, sect. 5.)

Further, happiness is more like a 'state' (state of affairs) than welfare is. A man can become happy, be happy, and cease to be happy. He can be happy, and

unhappy, more than once in his life. Happiness, like
an end, can be achieved and attained. Welfare has not
these same relationships to events, processes, and
states *in time*.

Finally, a major logical difference between happiness
and welfare is their relation to *causality*. Considerations of welfare are essentially considerations of how
the doing and happening of various things will causally
affect a being. One cannot pronounce on the question
whether something is good or bad for a man, without
considering the causal connexions in which this thing
is or may become embedded. But one can pronounce on
the question whether a man is happy or not, without
necessarily considering what were the causal antecedents and what will be the consequences of his present
situation.

The facts that happiness is primarily a hedonic and
welfare primarily a utilitarian notion, and that they
have logically different relationships to time and to
causality, mark the two concepts as being of that which
I have here called 'different logical category or
type'. It does not follow, however, that the two concepts are logically entirely unconnected. They are,
on the contrary, closely allied. What then is their
mutual relation? This is a question on which I have
not been able to form a clear view. Welfare (the
good of a being) is, somehow, the broader and more
basic notion. (Cf. Ch. III, sect. 12.) It is also
the notion which is of greater importance to ethics and
to a general study of the varieties of goodness.
Calling happiness an 'aspect' or 'component' or 'part'
of the good of man is a non-committal mode of speech
which is not meant to say more than this. Of happiness I could also say that it is the consummation or
crown or flower of welfare. But these are metaphorical terms and do not illuminate the logical relationship between the two concepts.

2

By an end of action we shall understand anything, *for
the sake of which* an action is undertaken. If something, which we want to do, is not wanted for the sake
of anything else, the act or activity can be called an
end in itself.

Ends can be intermediate or ultimate. Sometimes a
man wants to attain an end for the sake of some further
end. Then the first end is 'intermediate'. An end,

which is not pursued for the sake of any further end, is 'ultimate'. We shall call a human act 'end-directed', if it is undertaken either as an end in itself or for the sake of some end.

What is an ultimate end of action is settled by the last answer, which the agent himself can give to the question, *why* he does or intends to do this or that. It is then understood that the question 'Why?' asks for a reason and not for a causal explanation of his behaviour. (Cf. Ch. IV, sect. 8.)

In the terms which have here been introduced, we could redefine Psychological Hedonism as the doctrine that every end-directed human act is undertaken, ultimately, for the sake either of attaining some pleasure or avoiding something unpleasant. The doctrine again that every end-directed human act is undertaken, ultimately, for the sake of the acting agent's happiness we shall call Psychological Eudaimonism. A doctrine to the effect that every end-directed act is ultimately undertaken for the sake of the acting agent's welfare (good) has, to the best of my knowledge, never been defended. We need not here invent a name for it.

Aristotle sometimes talks (1) as though he had subscribed to the doctrine of psychological eudaimonism. If this was his view, he was certainly mistaken and, moreover, contradicting himself. It would be sheer nonsense to maintain that every chain of (non-causal) questions 'Why did you do this?' and answers to them must terminate in a reference to happiness. The view that man, in everything he does, is aiming at happiness (and the avoidance of misery) is even more absurd than the doctrine that he, in everything he does, is aiming at pleasure (and the avoidance of pain).

I said that, if Aristotle maintained psychological eudaimonism, he was contradicting himself. (And for this reason I doubt that Aristotle wanted to maintain it, though some of his formulations would indicate that he did.) For Aristotle also admits that there are ends, other than happiness, which we pursue for their own sake. He mentions pleasure and honour among them. (2) Even 'if nothing resulted from them, we should still choose each of them', he says. (3) On the other hand, those other final ends are sometimes desired, *not* for their own sake, but for the sake of something else. Whereas happiness, Aristotle thinks, is *never* desired for the sake of anything else. (4) Pleasure, e.g. pleasant amusement, can be desired for relaxation, and relaxation for the sake of continued activity. (5) *Then* pleasure is not a final end.

I would understand Aristotle's so-called eudaimonism in the following light: among possible ends of human action, 'eudaimonia' holds a unique position. This unique position is *not* that 'eudaimonia' is the final end of all action. It is that 'eudaimonia' is the only end that is never anything except final. It is of the nature of 'eudaimonia' that it cannot be desired for the sake of anything else. *This* is, so Aristotle seems to think, why 'eudaimonia' is the highest good for man. (6)

It is plausible to think that a man can pursue, i.e. do things for the sake of promoting or safeguarding, his own happiness only as an ultimate end of his action. A man can also do things for the sake of promoting or safeguarding the happiness of some other being. It may be thought that he can do this only as an intermediate end of his action. The idea has an apparent plausibility, but is nevertheless a mistake. The truth seems to be that a man can pursue the happiness of others either as intermediate *or* as ultimate end.

The delight of a king can be the happiness of his subjects. He gives all his energies and work to the promotion of this end. Maybe he sacrifices his so-called 'personal happiness' for the good of those over whom he is set to rule. Yet, if this is what he likes to do, it is also that in which his happiness consists. To say this is not to distort facts logically. But to say that the king sacrifices himself for the sake of becoming happy and not for the sake of making others happy, would be a distortion. It would be a distortion similar to that of which psychological hedonism is guilty, when it maintains that everything is done for the sake of pleasure, on the ground that all satisfaction of desire may be thought intrinsically pleasant.

Can a man's *welfare* be an end of his own action? The question is equivalent to asking, whether a man can ever be truly said to do things for the sake of promoting or protecting his own good. It is not quite clear which is the correct answer.

On the view which is here taken of the good of a being, to do something for the sake of promoting one's own good, means to do something *because* one considers doing it *good for* oneself. And to do something for the sake of protecting one's own good means to do something *because* one considers neglecting it bad for oneself.

For all I can see, men sometimes do things for the reasons just mentioned. This would show that a man's welfare *can be* an end of his own action.

Yet the good of a being as an end of action is a very peculiar sort of 'end'. Normally, an end of action is a state of affairs, something which 'is there', when the end has been attained. But welfare is not a state of affairs. (Cf. the discussion in section 1.) For this reason I shall say that welfare, the good of a being, can only in an *oblique* sense be called an end of action.

Obviously, the reason why a man does something, which he considers good for himself, is not always and necessarily *that* he considers doing it good for himself. Similarly, the reason why a man does something, which he considers bad for him to neglect, is not always and necessarily *that* he considers neglecting it bad for himself. This shows that a man's own welfare is not always an ultimate end of his action. It also shows that a man's own welfare is not always an end of his action at all. It does not show, however, that a man's own welfare is sometimes an intermediate end of his action. Whether it *can* be an intermediate end, I shall not attempt to decide. If the answer is negative, it would follow that, when a man's own welfare is an end of his action, it is necessarily an ultimate end.

Sometimes a man does something because he considers doing it good for another being, and neglects something because he considers doing it bad for another being. It is obvious that another man's good can be the *intermediate* end of a man's action. The reason why the master takes heed to promote and protect the welfare of his servants, can be that he expects them to serve him more efficiently if they thrive and are happy. Then his servants' welfare is an intermediate end of the master's. It may be suggested that, when the end of a man's action is another being's welfare, then it is necessarily an intermediate end. This suggestion, I think, is false. We shall return to the topic later (Chapter IX), when discussing egoism and altruism.

Beings can be handled or treated as means to somebody's ends. This is the case, e.g. with domestic animals and slaves. Philosophers have sometimes entertained the idea that beings could also be treated as 'ends' or 'ends in themselves'. It is not clear what it means to say that a being, e.g. a man, is an 'end in itself'. But treating a man as an end in itself *could mean*, I suggest, that we do certain things because we consider them good for that man. In other words: whenever a being's good is an ultimate end of action, that being is treated as an end in itself. A man can treat other men thus, but also himself. That men *should be* thus treated is an interesting view of the nature of moral duty. We shall briefly talk of this in Chapter X.

In the next five sections of the present chapter we shall be dealing with various aspects of the concept of happiness and in the last five sections with questions relating to the concept of welfare.

3

Happiness, we said, is a hedonic notion. It is, of course, not *the same* as pleasure. Nor can it be defined, as has been suggested, as 'pleasure and the absence of pain'.

Moralists who have written about happiness have sometimes associated the notion more intimately with one, sometimes with another, of the three principal 'forms' of pleasure, which we have in this book distinguished. One could, accordingly, speak of three types of 'ideals of happiness' or of the happy life.

The first I shall call 'Epicurean ideals'. According to them, 'true happiness' derives above all from *having* things which please. 'Pleasure' need not here be understood in the 'grosser' sense of sensuous pleasure. It includes the enjoyment of agreeable recollections and thoughts, of good company, and of beautiful things. Moore's position in 'Principia Ethica' can, I think, be called an Epicureanism in this broad sense.

Can a man find happiness entirely in passive pleasure? i.e. can following an Epicurean recipe of living make a man completely happy? I can see no *logical* impossibility in the idea. If a man's supreme desire happened to be to secure for himself a favourable balance of passive pleasure over passive 'unpleasure', i.e. of states he enjoys over states he dislikes, and if he were successful in this pursuit of his, then the Epicurean recipe of living would, by definition, make him happy. It may be argued - from considerations pertaining to the contingencies of life - that the chances are strongly against his succeeding. It may also be argued - this time from considerations pertaining to the psychology of human nature - that very few men are such pleasure-lovers that the supreme thing they want for themselves in life is a maximum of passive pleasure. But the facts - if they be facts - that Epicurean ideals are risky and not very commonly pursued throughout a whole life, must not induce us to deny that a man - if there be such a man - who successfully pursued such ideals was genuinely happy and flourishing. To deny this would be to misunderstand the notions of happiness and the good of man and would be symptomatic, I think, of some 'moralistic perversion'.

The second type of ideals of the happy life probably comes nearer than the Epicurean ideals to something which the classical writers of utilitarianism had in mind. It seems to me true to say that the utilitarians thought of happiness, not so much in terms of passive pleasure, as in terms of satisfaction of desire. Happiness, on such a view, is essentially contentedness - an equilibrium between needs and wants on the one hand and satisfaction on the other.

Yet one of the great utilitarians - protesting against unwanted consequences of a view which he was himself, though not wholeheartedly, defending - made the famous dictum, 'It is better to be a human being dissatisfied than a pig satisfied'. I am not a utilitarian myself. But I would like to protest, in a sense, against Mill's remark. The ultimate reason why it is not good for man to live like a pig, is that the life of a pig *does not satisfy* man. The dissatisfied Socrates, to whom Mill refers, we may regard as a symbol of man in search of a better and therewith more satisfying form of life. If his cravings were all doomed to be nothing but 'vanity and the vexation of spirit', then to idealize the dissatisfied Socrates would be to cherish a perverted view of the good life.

If one adopts the view that happiness is essentially an equilibrium between desire and satisfaction, one may reach the further conclusion that the safest road to happiness is to have as few and modest wants as possible, thus minimizing the chances of frustration and maximizing those of satisfaction. This recipe of happiness I shall call 'the ascetic ideal' of life. (7) When carried to the extreme, this ideal envisages complete happiness in the total abnegation of all desire whatsoever.

Ascetism, in this sense, can be termed a *crippled* view of happiness. In order to see in which respect it is crippled, it is helpful to consider the contrary of happiness, i.e. unhappiness or misery. It would seem that there is a more direct connexion between unhappiness and dissatisfaction of desire than there is between happiness and satisfaction. Frustration of desire is a main source of unhappiness. Never or seldom to get that for which one is craving, never or seldom to have a chance of doing that which one likes to do, *this* is above all what makes a man miserable.

To call extreme asceticism a crippled ideal is to accuse it of a logical mistake. This is the mistake of regarding happiness as the *contradictory*, and not as the *contrary*, of unhappiness. By escaping frustration a man escapes unhappiness - provided, of course, that it does not befall him in the form of such affliction, which accident or illness or the acts of evil neighbours may cause him. The man of *no* wants, if there existed such a creature, would not be unhappy. But it does not follow that he would be happy.

The third type of ideals of the happy life which I wanted to mention here, seeks happiness neither in passive pleasure nor in the satisfaction of desire, but in that which we have called active pleasure, i.e. the pleasure of doing that on which we are keen, which for its own sake we like *doing*. In the activities which we are keen on doing, we aim at technical goodness or perfection. (See Ch. II, sect. 12.) The better we are in the art, the more do we enjoy practising it, the happier does it make us. Therefore, the more talented we are by nature for an art, the more can the development of our skill in it contribute to our happiness.

It may be argued - chiefly against Epicureanism I should think - that the pleasures of the active life are those which are best suited to secure the attainment of lasting happiness. It is more risky to be, for one's well-being, dependent upon things we *have* or *get* than upon things we *do* (or *are*). That is: it is more risky to seek happiness in passive than in active pleasure. There is probably a great deal of truth in the argument. But it would certainly be wrong to think that the road to happiness through an active life were completely risk-free.

4

The factors which determine whether a man will become happy, we shall call 'conditions' of happiness. Of such conditions one may distinguish three main groups. Happiness, we shall say, is conditioned partly by 'chance' or luck, partly by innate 'disposition', and partly by 'action'. 'Action' here means action on the part of the individual concerned himself. That which is *done to* a man may, for present purposes, be counted as chance-factors conditioning his happiness.

Illness can befall a man or he can become bodily or
mentally injured without any fault of his own. If such
misfortune assumes a certain permanence, it may affect
a man's happiness adversely. It may do so either as
a cause of pain or as a cause of frustration of desire
or because it prevents the victim from engaging in
activity which, for its own sake, he enjoys. However,
luck may also favour a man's good. The benefit a
person draws from good friends or good teachers or
financial benefactors has, partly if not wholly, the
character of luck. It is something which life has in
store for some men but not for others to make them
happier, independently of their own doings and pre-
cautions.

It is an aspect of that which we called the ascetic
ideal of life, that man is well advised to *make* himself
as independent as possible of chance and luck as conditions of his happiness. This he can try to do in
various ways: by hardening himself to sustain pain,
by withdrawing from political and social engagements,
or by not aspiring too high even in those activities,
which he enjoys for their own sake. The belief that
a man could make himself altogether independent of
external affectations of his good, is a conceit peculiar
to certain 'ascetic' and 'stoic' attitudes to life.
It overrates man's possibilities of conditioning his
happiness and peace of mind by assuming a certain attitude to contingencies.

The innate dispositions of happiness have to do
both with bodily health and with mental equipment and
temper. A man of weak health is more exposed to
certain risks of becoming unhappy than a man of good
health. A man of many talents has more resources of
happiness than a man of poor gifts. A man of good
temper and cheerful outlook will not let adversities
frustrate his efforts as easily as the impatient and
gloomy man. To the extent that such temperamental
dispositions can be developed or suppressed in a man,
they fall under those conditions of happiness which a
man controls through his action.

Human action, which is relevant to the happiness of
the agent himself, is of two types. Action of the
first type are things which the agent does, measures
which he takes for the sake of promoting or protecting
his happiness. Such action is 'causally' relevant to
his happiness. Action of the second type are things
which the agent does or practises for their own sake,
as ends in themselves, i.e. simply because he wants to
do or likes to do them and for no other reason.

Action in which a man delights one could call 'constitutive' of his happiness, 'parts' of his happiness.

Now it may happen that action, which is thus constitutive of a man's happiness, *also* affects his happiness causally. It may affect his happiness promotingly, but also affect it adversely. For example: a man is immensely fond of playing various games. He plays and enjoys playing them all day long. In so doing he neglects his education and his social duties and maybe his health too. Thus the very same thing, which is constitutive of his happiness, may, by virtue of its consequences, accumulate clouds of unhappiness over the agent's head, while he is rejoicing in this thing. This possibility is responsible for the major complications, which are connected with a man's own action as a conditioning factor of his happiness and welfare generally.

5

When is a man happy? It is obvious that a man can be truly praised happy, even though many painful and unpleasant things have happened to him in the course of his life. But not if he never had any pleasures. What must the preponderance of the pleasant over the unpleasant be, if he is still to be called happy?

Here it is helpful to consider the states which we call gladness and sadness. They occupy a kind of intermediate position between happiness and unhappiness on the one hand, and pleasure and its contrary on the other hand. It may be suggested that pleasant and unpleasant experiences and activities are constitutive of gladness and sadness in a manner similar to that in which states of joy and depression are constitutive of happiness and unhappiness. A man can be glad although he has toothache, and he can be a happy man even though he chances to be very sad for a time. But he could not be glad if he had no pleasures to compensate such pains as he may have at the time of his gladness; and he cannot be happy if he is not *on the whole* more glad than sad. But we cannot tell exactly what must be the balance.

Pleasure, joy, and happiness are things of increasing degrees of permanence and resistance to changes. Something can please a man without cheering him up, and cheer him up without making him happy. Something can be a terrible blow to a man and make him sad, but whether it makes him unhappy is another matter.

Consider, for example, a man whom we praise happy and who is hit by a sudden blow of bad luck, say, the loss of a child in an accident. He will experience painful agonies and extreme sadness. 'News of the disaster made him dreadfully unhappy', we might say, thinking of these emotional effects on him. If, however, we were to say that the news made him *an unhappy man,* we should be thinking not only, or maybe even not at all, on those emotional effects, but on effects of a less immediate showing and of a longer lasting. If we can say of him some such things as, 'For years after he was as paralysed; none of the things, which used to delight him, gave him pleasure any longer', or 'Life seemed to have lost meaning for him, - for a time he even contemplated suicide', then the accident made him *unhappy* as distinct from merely *sad*. But whether things, bearing on the distinction, can be truly said of the man, is not to be seen in an inkling.

Analogous things can be said about changes in the reverse direction. A piece of news, say of an unexpected inheritance, can make a man jump with joy. But whether it makes him *happy* as distinct from merely *glad* can only be seen from effects of a longer lasting and less obvious showing on his subsequent life.

Should we say 'the *whole* of his subsequent life'? I think not. Happiness is neither a momentary state nor is it a sum total to be found out when we close our life's account. A man can *become* happy, *be* happy, and *change* from happy to unhappy. Thus, in the course of his life, a man can be both happy and unhappy. And he can be happy and unhappy more than once. (See section 1.)

We could make a distinction between a happy *man* and a happy *life* and regard the second as a thing of wider scope. This would make it possible to say of somebody that he had a happy life although, for some time, he was a most unhappy man.

6

A judgment to the effect that some being is happy or is not happy or is unhappy we shall can an 'eudaimonic' judgment.

I think it is illuminating to compare the logic of the eudaimonic judgment to the logic of the statement 'This is pleasant'. Of the sentence 'This is pleasant' we said that it conceals a logical form. (See Ch. IV, sect. 6.) It suggests that pleasantness is a property which we attribute to some object or state, whereas in fact to judge something pleasant is to verbalize a relationship in which the judging subject stands to this thing. To judge something hedonically good is to manifest an *attitude*, one could also say, to certain things (activities, sensations, the causes of sensations). The logically most adequate form of the verbalization is therefore, it seems, the relational form 'I like this' or some similar relational form.

In an analogous sense the sentence 'He is happy' may be said, I think, to conceal a logical form. It suggests a view of happiness as a property which the happy individual exhibits - which shines forth from him. Whereas, in fact, to be happy is to be in a certain relationship. A relationship to what? it may be asked. A relationship to one's circumstances of life, I would answer. To say 'He is happy' is similar to saying 'He likes it', the 'it' not meaning this or that particular thing or activity but, so to speak, 'the whole thing'. One could also say, 'He likes his life as it is.'

On this view, if a man says of himself 'I am happy', he manifests in words an attitude which he takes, or a relationship in which he stands, to his circumstances of life. Happiness *is* not in the circumstances - as it were awaiting the judgment - but springs into being with the relationship. (Just as hedonic goodness does not reside in the taste of an apple, but in somebody's liking the taste of an apple.) To judge oneself happy is to pass judgment on or value one's circumstances of life.

To say 'He is happy' can mean two different things. It can mean that the man, of whom we are talking, is in the relationship to his circumstances which, if *he* were to verbalize his attitude, he could express in the words 'I am happy'. Then 'He is happy' is not a value-judgment. It is a true or false statement to the effect that a certain subject values certain things, i.e. his circumstances of life, in a certain way. We could also call it a statement to the effect that a certain valuation *exists* (occurs, takes place).

Quite often, however, 'He is happy' is not a judgment about that which *he is* at all, but about that which *we should be*, if we happened to be in his circumstances. 'He is happy' then means roughly, 'He *must be* happy, viz. considering the circumstances he is in.' Such judgments are often an expression of envy. To say with conviction, 'Happy is he, who ...' is usually to pronounce on that which we think would make ourselves happy.

We shall henceforth disregard the case, when the third person judgment 'He is happy' is only a disguise for our own valuations and thus really is a first person judgment.

7

On the view which I am defending here, judgments of happiness are thus very much like hedonic judgments. The third person judgments are true or false. In them is judged that so-and-so is or is not pleased with his circumstances of life. They are judgments *about* valuations - and therefore are no value-judgments. The first person judgments are not true or false. They *express* a subject's valuations of his own circumstances. They are genuine value-judgments, and yet in an important sense of 'judgment' they are no judgments.

Ultimately, a man is himself judge of his own happiness. By this I mean that any third person judgment which may be passed on his happiness, depends for its truth-value on how *he himself* values his circumstances of life. This is so independently of whether he verbalizes his attitude in a first person judgment or not.

In *a* sense, therefore, a man's own verdict 'I am happy' or 'I am unhappy', should he happen to pass it, will be final - whatever we may think we should say, if we were in his circumstances. We must never make the presence or absence of circumstances, which would determine our own first person judgments of happiness, the *criteria* of truth of third person judgments.

What may make it difficult to see clearly this 'subjectivity' of the notion which we are discussing, is the fact that not every man is the best and most competent judge of his *prospects* of happiness. A man may strongly want to do something, think his life worthless if he is not allowed this thing. But another, more experienced man, may warn him that, if he follows his immediate impulses, he will in the end become a most miserable wretch. The more experienced man may be right. But the criterion, which proves him right, is *not* the mere fact that certain things - illness, destitution, and what not - befall this other man as a predicted consequence of his folly and wickedness. The criterion is that these consequences make that other man unhappy. If our fool accepts the consequences with a cheerful heart, the wise man cannot insist that he must be right. He cannot do so on the ground, say, that those same consequences would have made him, or most people, miserable. Nor can he pretend that the lightsome fellow is 'really' unhappy, though unaware of his own misery.

But cannot a man be mistaken in thinking that he *is* happy? In a sense he can *not*, but in another he *can*. 'He says he is happy, but in fact he is not' can express a true proposition. But does not the truth of this proposition entail that the person who professes to be happy is lying? And is this not uninteresting? The answer is that, beside uninteresting lies, there exist profoundly interesting lies in the matters, which we are now discussing. First person judgments of happiness can be insincere, and insincerity may be regarded as a species of lying.

The same, incidentally, holds good for first person hedonic judgments too. A youngster may profess to like the taste of tobacco, which in fact he detests, just for the sake of showing off. He may even make himself believe this, in some involved and twisted sense of 'believe'. A polite man may say he likes the taste of a wine merely to please his host. The insincerity of such first person judgments may be relatively easy to unmask.

In the case of first person judgments of happiness and misery, the problem of sincerity is most difficult - both psychologically and conceptually. I shall not here try to penetrate its logical aspects, which I find very bewildering. (I am not aware of any satisfactory discussion of the topic in the literature.) I shall make a shortcut through the difficulties and only say this much in conclusion:

However thoroughly a man may cheat himself with regard to his own happiness, the criterion of cheat or insincerity must be that *he* admits the fraud. A judgment is insincere when the subject 'in his innermost self' admits that it is not as he says it is. If his lips say 'I am happy' and he is not, then in his heart he must already be saying to himself 'I am not happy'. He, as it were, does not hear the voice of his heart. These are similes, and I am aware of the temptation to misuse them. (They are the same sort of similes that are used and misused in psychoanalysis - the similes of the subconscious, the superego, etc.) What I mean by them could perhaps be said most plainly as follows: the fact that first person judgments of happiness can be insincere must not be allowed to conflict logically with the fact that, whether a person is happy or not depends upon *his own* attitude to his circumstances of life. The supreme judge of the case *must be* the subject himself. To think that it could be otherwise is false objectivism.

8

Judgments of the beneficial and the harmful, i.e. of that which is good or bad for a man, involve two components. We have called them the 'causal' and the 'axiological' component. (See Ch. III, sect. 5.) We must now say some words about each of them.

When something happens, i.e. the world changes in a certain respect, there will usually also be a number of subsequent changes, which are bound (by so-called 'natural necessity') to come about, once the first change took place. These subsequent changes we here call the 'consequences' of the first change. If the first change is of that peculiar kind which we call a human act, then the subsequent changes are 'consequences of action'. The change or changes upon which a certain further change is consequen (i.e. the consequence of which this further change is) we shall call the 'cause(s)' of this further change.

Most things which happen, perhaps all, would not have happened, *unless* certain antecedent changes had taken place in the world. These antecedent changes we shall call the 'causal prerequisites' or 'requirements' of the subsequent change. They are sometimes also called 'necessary causes'. The necessary causes may be, but need not be, 'causes' in the sense defined above.

These explanations are very summary. Not least of all considering the importance to ethics of the notion of consequences of action, it is an urgent *desideratum* that the logic of causal relationships be better elaborated than it is. We shall not, however, attempt this here. Only a few observations will be added to the above.

The notions both of consequences and of prerequisites and of causes of a change are relative to the further notion of a *state of the world*. Thus, e.g., a change which is required in order to effect a certain change in the world as it is to-day, may not be required in order to effect this same change in the world as it is tomorrow.

It is sometimes said that every event (change) 'strictly speaking' has an infinite number of consequences throughout the whole of subsequent time, and that for this reason we can never know for certain which all the consequences of a given event are. These statements, if true at all, hold good for some different notion of consequence, but not for the notion with which we are here dealing. Exactly what could be meant by them is not clear. Yet we need not dismiss them as nonsense. When, for example, something which happens to-day is said to be a consequence of something which took place hundreds of years ago, what is meant is perhaps that, if we traced the 'causal history' of this event of to-day we should find among its 'causal ancestry' that event of hundreds of years ago. Here the notions of causal ancestry and causal history could be defined in terms of *our* notions of cause, consequence, and prerequisite and yet it need not follow that, if an event belongs to the causal ancestry of another event, the first must be a cause or prerequisite of the second or the second a consequence of the first. For example: let event *b* be a consequence (in our sense) of event *a* and a causal prerequisite (in our sense) of event *c*. It would then be reasonable to say that event *a* is a 'causal ancestor' of event *c*, or that tracing the 'causal history' of *c* takes us to *a*. In some loose sense of the words, *a* may be said to be a 'cause' of *c* and *c* a 'consequence' of *a*. But in the more precise sense, in which we are here employing the terms, *a* is not (necessarily) a cause of *c*, nor *c* (necessarily) a consequence of *a*.

The causes and consequences of things which happen, are often insufficiently known and therefore largely a matter of belief and conjecture. Sometimes, however, they *are* known to us. The statement, should it be made, that they *cannot* ('in principle') be known either is false or applies to some different notions of cause and consequence from ours.

By knowledge of the causes and consequences of things which happen, I here mean knowledge relating to *particulars*. An example would be knowledge that the death of N.N. was due to a dose of arsenic, which had been mixed into his food. Such knowledge of particulars is usually grounded on knowledge of general propositions - as for example that a dose of arsenic of a certain strength will (unless certain counteracting causes intervene) 'inevitably' kill a man. Whether all such knowledge of particulars is grounded on general knowledge, we shall not discuss.

When in the sequel we speak of *knowledge* of the causes and consequences of things, or of known causes and consequences, 'knowledge' is short for 'knowledge

or belief' and 'known' for 'known or believed'. The
consequences which are known (i.e. known or believed)
at the time when the thing happens, we shall also call
foreseen consequences.

So much for the causal component involved in judgments of the beneficial and the harmful. We now turn to the axiological component. A preliminary task will here be to clarify the notions of a *wanted* and an *unwanted* thing.

9

The notion of a wanted thing, which I shall now try to explain, is not the same as that of an end of action. I shall call it the notion of being *wanted in itself*. How things which are wanted in themselves, are related to things which are wanted as ends of action, will be discussed presently. Correlative with the notion of being wanted in itself is the notion of being *unwanted in itself*. 'Between' the two falls a notion, which we shall call the notion of being *indifferent in itself*.

The notion of being wanted in itself is the nearest equivalent in my treatment here to the notion of *intrinsic value* in Moore and some other writers. Moore, when discussing the notion of intrinsic worth, often resorts to a logical fiction which, *mutatis mutandis,* may be resorted to also for explaining the meaning of a thing being wanted, unwanted, or indifferent 'in itself'.

This fiction is that of a preferential choice between two alternatives. A major difficulty is to formulate the terms of the choice correctly for the purpose of defining the axiological notions under discussion. (Moore's explanation of intrinsic value in terms of betterness of alternatives cannot be regarded as *logically* satisfactory - apart from questions of the meaningfulness of the very notion. (8)) Our proposal here of a solution to the problem is tentative only.

Assume you were offered a thing X which you did not already possess. Would you then rather take it than leave it, rather have it than (continue to) be without it? The offer must be considered apart from questions of causal requirements and of consequences. That is: considerations of things which you will have to do in order to get X, and of things which will happen to you as a consequence of your having got the thing X must not influence your choice. If then you would rather take X than leave it, X is *wanted in itself*. If you have the opposite preference, X is *unwanted in itself*. If you have no preference, X is *indifferent in itself*.

As readily noted, the ideas of the in itself wanted and unwanted, which we have thus tried to explain in terms of a fictitious preferential choice, are necessarily relative to a *subject*. Nothing is wanted or unwanted 'in itself', if the words 'in itself' are supposed to mean 'apart from any rating or valuing subject'. The words 'in itself' mean 'causal prerequisites and consequences apart'. A thing, which for one subject is a wanted thing, may be regarded as unwanted by another subject. A thing, furthermore, which is wanted *now,* may be unwanted at another time - the subject being the same. The notion of being wanted or unwanted in itself is thus relative, not only to a subject, but also to a particular time in the life of this subject.

Moore did not think that intrinsic value was relative to subject and time. In this respect his 'objectivist' notion of the intrinsically good and bad differs from our 'subjectivist' notion of the in itself wanted and unwanted.

It is important to note that from our definition of the in itself wanted, unwanted, and indifferent it does not follow that, if X is wanted in itself, then not-X (the absence of X) is unwanted in itself. That not-X is wanted, unwanted, and indifferent in itself corresponds on our definitions, to the following set of preferences:

Consider a thing X, which you have. Would you rather get rid of it than retain it, rather be without it than (continue to) possess it? The proposal must be considered apart from things which you will have to do in order to get rid of X and from things which will happen to you as a consequence of your having got rid of X. Then not-X is wanted in itself, if you prefer to get rid of X, unwanted in itself, if you prefer to retain X, and indifferent in itself, if you have no preference.

10

Anything which is an - intermediate or ultimate - end of action, can be called *a good* (for the subject in pursuit of the end). (Cf. above Ch. I, sect. 5 and Ch. III, sect. 1.) Anything which is an end of action, can also be said to be *a wanted thing*.

Also every thing, which is wanted in itself, can be called a good (for the subject to whom it is wanted). And every thing, which is unwanted in itself, can be called a bad (for the subject who shuns it).

Ends of action and things wanted in themselves thus both fall under the category 'goods'. Ends of action also fall under the category 'things wanted'.

The question may be raised, how ends of action and things wanted in themselves are mutually related. The question is complicated and I shall not discuss it in detail. It is reasonable to think that only things, which are attainable through action, *can be* ends of action. 'Craving for the moon' is not aiming at an end. But things other than those which are attainable through action, can be wanted in themselves - sunshine on a chilly day, for example. The only simple relationship between ends of action and things wanted in themselves, which I can suggest, is that ultimate ends of action are also things wanted in themselves.

Intermediate ends of action are either things wanted in themselves or things indifferent in themselves or, not infrequently, things unwanted in themselves. To get the in itself **unwanted** can never be an ultimate end of action, since the assumption that it is involves a contradiction. But to escape the in itself unwanted sometimes is an ultimate end of action. The unwanted is that which we shun, except when occasionally we pursue it as intermediate end for the sake of something else or suffer it as a necessary prerequisite of something coveted.

When a man gets something which is, to him, wanted in itself, without having pursued it as an end, we shall say that this wanted thing *befalls* him. Similarly, when a man gets something which is, to him, unwanted in itself and which he has not pursued as an intermediate end, we shall say that this thing befalls him.

The question may be raised whether a thing which befalls or happens to a man can appropriately be said to be 'wanted'. 'Wanted' in English has many meanings and must therefore be used with caution. Sometimes it means 'desired', sometimes 'needed', sometimes 'wished for'. When the wanted thing is an end of action, the nearest equivalent to 'wanted' is 'desired'. Perhaps things which happen to a man and which satisfy our explanation of the in itself wanted, should better be called 'welcome'. They are things we 'gladly accept' or are 'happy to get'. Often we just call them 'good'. When I here call them 'wanted', it is

by contrast to 'unwanted', which word is certainly
correctly used for shunned things that befall or
happen to a man.

11

Consider something, which an agent pursues as an ultimate end. Assume that he gets it. Attaining the
end is usually connected with a number of things as
its causal prerequisites and a number of other things
as its consequences. Of the things which are thus
causally connected with his end, some are perhaps
known and others not known to the agent. Some, moreover, may be known to him already at the time when he
pursues the end, others become known to him after he
has attained it. That is: their causal relationship
to the end is (becomes) known to him.

The thing which the agent pursues as an ultimate
end, is to him a good and something he wants in itself.
Of those things again which are causally connected -
either as prerequisites or as consequences - with his
attainment of the end, some are wanted in themselves
(by him), others are unwanted in themselves (by him),
others indifferent in themselves (to him). The sum
total of those things, which are unwanted in themselves, we shall call the *price,* which the agent has
to pay for the attainment of his ultimate end.

This notion of 'price', be it observed, includes
consequences as well as causal prerequisites. On
this definition of the notion, not only those things
which the agent has to endure, in order to get his
wanted thing, but also those which he has to suffer as
a consequence of having got it, count as part of that
which he has to *pay* for the good. One can define the
notion of a price in different ways - for other purposes. This is how we define the notion for present
purposes.

For anything which is wanted in itself, the question
may be raised: is this good worth its price? The
question can be raised *prospectively,* with a view to
things which have to be gone through as a consequence
of starting to pursue this good as an end, or it can
be raised *retrospectively,* with a view to things
already suffered.

To answer the question whether a certain good is
(was) worth its price, is to pass a value-judgment.
It is to say of something, a good, that it is better or
worse, more or less worth, than something else, its

price. How shall this value-judgment be properly articulated?

I think we must resort here, for a second time, to the logical fiction of a preferential choice. We said (in section 9) that things which we do not have, are wanted in themselves when, ignoring their causes and consequences, we would rather get them than continue to be without them, and unwanted in themselves when we would rather continue to be without them than get them. This question of taking or leaving, having or being without, we can also raise for things, *considering their causes and consequences*. A correct way of presenting the choice which we should then be facing, is, I think, as follows:

Assume that X is something, which is not already in our world (life), i.e. is something which we do not already possess or which has not already happened or which we have not already done. Would we then want X to become introduced into our world (life), considering also the causal prerequisites of getting (doing) X and the consequences of having got (done) X? Or would we prefer to continue to be without X? In making up our mind we should also have to consider the causal prerequisites and the consequences of *not* having this change in our world (life). It may, for example, be necessary for us to take some in itself unwanted action to prevent X from coming into existence, if we wish to avoid having X, and it may be necessary for us to foresake some other in itself wanted thing Y as a consequence of *not* having had X.

We introduce the symbol '$X+C$' for the complex whole, consisting of X and those other things, which are causally connected with it either as prerequisites or as consequences of its coming into being, i.e. of the change from not-X to X. The symbol 'not-$X+C'$' shall stand for the complex whole, consisting of the absence of X and the presence of those things which are causally connected, either as prerequisites or as consequences, with the continued absence of X.

The question which is presented for consideration in the fictitious preferential choice we are discussing, is whether we should prefer $X+C$ to not-$X+C'$ or whether we should have the reverse preference or whether we should be indifferent (have no preference).

Let the answer to the proposal be that we should rather have than continue to be without X, i.e. prefer $X+C$ to not-$X+C'$. Then we shall say that $X+C$ or the complex whole, consisting of X and the causal prerequisites and consequences of the coming into being of X,

is a *positive constituent* of our good (welfare). Of
the thing X itself we say that it is *good for us* or
beneficial. This we say of X independently of whether
X is wanted or unwanted or indifferent in itself.

Let the answer to the proposal be that we should
rather continue to forego than have X, i.e. prefer
not-$X+C'$ to $X+C$. Then we shall say that $X+C$ is a
negative constituent of our good. Of the thing X
itself we say that it is *bad for us* or *harmful*. This
we say independently of whether X is wanted or unwanted
or indifferent in itself.

The answer can, of course, also be that we should be
indifferent to the alternatives. Then $X+C$ is neither
a positive nor a negative constituent of our good, and
X is neither beneficial nor harmful.

Let us call X the *nucleus* of that complex whole,
which consists of X and the causal prerequisites and
consequences of the coming into existence of X. We
could then say that the things which are beneficial or
harmful, good or bad for a man, are nuclei of those
complex causal wholes, which are positive or negative
constituents of his good (welfare).

We can now state the conditions for answering the
question whether a certain good is worth its 'price'.
When a certain causal whole is a positive constituent
of our good *and* its nucleus is a thing, which is wanted
in itself, then we say that this thing or good *is* worth
its price. When, however, the whole is a negative
constituent of our good, *although* its nucleus is a
thing, which is wanted in itself, then we say that this
thing or good is *not* worth its price.

From our definitions of the beneficial and the harmful it does *not* follow that, if not-X is harmful, then
X is beneficial, and *vice versa*. If, however, not-X
is harmful, then X will be called *needed*. The needed
is that, the lack or loss of which is a bad thing, an
evil. The needed and the harmful are opposed as contradictories, *in the sense* that the contradictory of
the needed is harmful, and *vice versa*. The beneficial and the harmful are opposed as contraries.

To provide a being with that which is beneficial for
it is to *promote* its welfare. To provide it with that
which it needs and to take care that it does not lose
the needed is to *protect* its welfare. Things (acts,
events) which are protective of a being's welfare are
good for the being in the sense of 'good for' which
can also be rendered by 'useful', but not in that sense
of 'good for' which we call 'beneficial'. (Cf. Ch.
III, sect. 1.)

12

The preferential choice, in the terms of which we have defined the notions of the beneficial and the harmful, we have called a 'logical fiction'. That it is a fiction implies two things. First, it implies that we are talking of how a man *would choose*, if he were presented with the choice, and not of what he actually chooses. Secondly, it implies that we assume the causal component involved in the value-judgment to be *completely known* to the subject at the time of the choice. This second assumption entails that there are no imperfections in the subject's knowledge which are such that, if they were detected and corrected, the subject would revise his preferences.

Thus, on our definitions, the answer to the question whether a certain thing is good or bad for a man, is independent of the following two factors: first, it is independent of whether he (or anybody else) *judges* or does not judge of the value of this thing for him. Secondly, it is independent of what he (and everybody else) happens to *know* or not to know about the causal connexions of this thing. Yet, in spite of this independence of judgment and knowledge, the notions of the beneficial and the harmful are in an important sense *subjective*. Their subjectivity consists in their dependence upon the *preferences* (*wants*) of the subject concerned.

Considering what has just been said, it is clear that we must distinguish between that which *is* good or bad for a man and that which *appears*, i.e. is judged or considered or thought (by himself or by others), to be good or bad for him.

Any judgment to the effect that something is good or bad for a man is based on such knowledge of the relevant causal connexions which the judging subject happens to possess. Since this knowledge may be imperfect, the judgment which he actually passes may be different from the judgment which he would pass, if he had perfect knowledge of the causal connexions. When there is this discrepancy between the actual and the potential judgment, we shall say that a man's *apparent* good is being mistaken for his *real* good.

Of certain things it is easier to judge correctly whether they are good or bad for us, than of certain other things. This means: the risks of mistaking our apparent good for our real good are sometimes greater, sometimes less. It is, on the whole, easier to judge correctly in matters relating to a person's health than in matters relating to his future career. For example: the judgment that it will do a man good to take regular exercise is, on the whole, safer than the judgment that it will be better for him to go into business than study medicine. Sometimes the difficulties to judge correctly are so great that it will be altogether idle and useless to try to form a judgment.

Sometimes we know for certain that a choice, which we are facing, is of great *importance* to us in the sense that it will make considerable *difference* to our future life, whether we choose the one or the other of two alternatives. An example could be a choice between getting married or remaining single or between accepting employment in a foreign country or continuing life at home. But certainty that the choice will make a great difference is fully compatible with uncertainty as to whether the difference will be for good or for bad. The feeling that our welfare *may* become radically affected by the choice, can make the choice very agonizing for us.

Also of many things in our past, which we did not deliberately choose, we may know for certain that they have been of great importance to us in the sense that our lives would have been very different, had these things not existed. This could be manifestly true, for example, of the influence which some powerful personality has had on our education or on the formation of our opinions. We may wonder whether it was not bad for us that we should have been so strongly under this influence. Yet, if we know only that our life would have been very different but cannot at all imagine *how* it would have been different, we may also be quite incompetent to form a judgment of the beneficial and harmful nature of this factor in our past history.

It is a deeply impressive fact about the condition of man that it should be difficult, or even humanly impossible, to judge confidently of many things which are known to affect our lives importantly, whether they are good or bad for us. I think that becoming *overwhelmed* by this fact is one of the things which can incline a man towards taking a religious view of life. 'Only God knows what is good or bad for us.' One could say thus - and yet accept that a man's welfare is a subjective notion in the sense that it is determined by what *he* wants and shuns.

13

Are judgments of the beneficial or harmful nature of things objectively true or false? When we try to answer this question, we must again observe the distinction between a first person judgment and a third person judgment. (Cf. Ch. IV, sect. 5 and this chapter, sections 6 and 7.)

When somebody judges of something that it is (was, will be) good or bad for somebody else, the judgment is a third person judgment. It depends for its truth-value on two things. The one is whether certain causal connexions are as the judging subject thinks that they are. The other is whether certain valuations (preferences, wants) of another subject are as the judging subject thinks that they are. Both to judge of causal connexions and to judge of the valuations of other subjects is to judge of empirical matters of fact. The judgment is 'objectively' true or false. It is, properly speaking, not a value-judgment, since the 'axiological' component involved in it is not a valuation but a judgment *about* (the existence or occurrence of) valuations.

The case of the first person judgment is more complicated. Its causal component is a judgment of matters of fact. In this respect the first person judgment is on a level with the third person judgment. Its axiological component, however, is a valuation and not a judgment about valuations. With regard to this component the judgment cannot be true or false. There is no 'room' for mistake concerning its truth-value. In this respect the first person judgment of the beneficial and the harmful is like the first person hedonic or eudaimonic judgment.

Although the first person judgment cannot be false in its axiological component, it can be *insincere*. The problem of sincerity of judgments concerning that which is good or bad for a man is most complicated. It is intimately connected with the problems relating to the notions of *regret* and of *weakness of will*. A few words will be said about them later.

A subject can also make a statement about his own valuations in the past or a conjecture about his valuations in the future. Such a statement or conjecture is, logically, a third person judgment. It is true or false both in its causal and in its axiological component.

Whether a judgment is, *logically,* a first person judgment, cannot be seen from the person and tense of its grammatical form alone. A man says 'This will do me good'. In saying this he could be anticipating certain consequences and *expressing* his valuation of them. But he could also be anticipating certain consequences and *anticipating* his valuation of them. In the first case, the judgment he makes is of the kind which I here call a first person judgment of the beneficial or harmful nature of things. In the second case, the judgment is (logically) a third person judgment. The subject is speaking *about* himself, i.e. about his future valuations.

Sometimes a judgment of the beneficial or the harmful is clearly anticipative both of consequences and of valuations. Sometimes it is clearly anticipative with regard to consequences and expressive with regard to valuations. But very often, it seems, the status of the judgment is not clear even to the judging subject himself. The judgment may contain *both* anticipations *and* expressions of valuations. Perhaps it is true to say that men's judgments of what is good or bad for themselves tend on the whole to be anticipative rather than expressive with regard to valuations.

The distinction between the *apparent* and the *real* good, it should be observed, can be upheld both for third person and for first person judgments of the beneficial and the harmful. In this respect judgments of the beneficial and the harmful differ from hedonic and eudaimonic judgments. (For the two last kinds of judgment the distinction vanishes in the first person case, i.e. in the genuine value-judgments.) Because of the presence of the causal component in the judgment, a subject can always be mistaken concerning the beneficial or the harmful nature of a thing - even when there is no 'room' for mistake with regard to valuation.

14

A man's answer to the question whether a certain good is worth its price or whether a thing is beneficial or harmful, may undergo alterations in the course of time. Such alterations in his judgments can be due either to changes in his knowledge of the relevant causal connexions or to changes in his valuations. For example: a man attains an end, which he considers worth while to have pursued, until years afterwards he comes to realize that he had to pay for it with the ruin of his health. Then he revises his judgment and *regrets*.

There are two types of regret-situation relating to choices of ends and goods in general. Sometimes the choice can, in principle if not in practice, be repeated. To profess regret is then to say that one would not choose the same thing again next time, when there is an opportunity. But sometimes the choice is not repeatable. The reason for this could be that the consequences, of which one is aware and which are the ground for one's regret, continue to operate throughout one's whole life. There is no opportunity of making good one's folly in the past by acting more wisely in the future. Then to express regret is to pass judgment on one's *life*. It is like saying: if I were to live my life over again, I would, when arrived at the fatal station, act differently.

The value-judgments of regret and no-regret, like hedonic judgments and judgments of happiness, are neither true nor false. But they may be sincere or insincere. A person can say that he regrets, when in fact he does not, and he can stubbornly refuse to admit regret which he 'feels'. How is such insincerity unmasked? For example in this way: if a man, after having suffered the consequences, says he regrets his action, but on a new occasion repeats his previous choice, then we may doubt whether his remorse was not pretence only. He was perhaps annoyed at having had to pay so much for the coveted thing and therefore said it was not worth it, but at the bottom of his heart he was pleased at having got it. These are familiar phenomena.

Yet to think that a repetition of the professed folly were a sure sign of insincere regret, would be to ignore the complications of the practical problems relating to the good of man. A good, if strongly desired in itself and near at hand, may be a temptation to which a man succumbs, when the evil consequences are far ahead and the recollection of having suffered them in the past is perhaps already fading. There is no logical absurdity in the idea that a man sincerely regrets something as having been a mistake, a bad choice with a view to his welfare, i.e. with a view to what he 'really' wants for himself, and yet wilfully commits the same mistake over again, whenever there is an opportunity.

When a man succumbs to temptation and chooses a lesser immediate good, i.e. thing wanted in itself, rather than escapes a greater future bad, i.e. thing unwanted in itself, then he is acting wilfully against the interests of his own good. It is in such situations that those features of character which we call *virtues*, are needed to safeguard a man's welfare. We shall talk about them later (in Chapter VII).

That a man can do evil to himself through ignorance of the consequences of his acts or through negligence is obvious. That he can also harm himself through *akrasia* or weakness of will has a certain appearance of paradox. He then, as it were, both wants and does not want, welcomes and shuns, one and the same thing. When viewed in the short perspective, 'prerequisites and consequences apart', he wants it; when viewed in the prolonged perspective of the appropriate causal setting, he shuns it. One could say that, if he lets himself be carried away by the short perspective, then he was not capable of viewing *clearly* his situation in the long perspective. Or one could say that, if a man has an *articulated grasp* of what he wants, he can never harm himself through weakness of will. But saying this must not encourage an undue optimism about man's possibilities of acting in accordance with cool reasoning.

NOTES

1 See, e.g., 'Ethica Nicomachea' (EN), 1094a 18-21, 1095a 14-20, and 1176b 30-1.
2 EN, 1097b 1-2. See also 1172b 20-3.
3 EN, 1097b 2-3.
4 EN, 1097b 1 and again 1097b 5-6.
5 Cf. EN, 1176b 34-5.
6 There is no phrase in Aristotle's ethics which corresponds to our phrase 'the good of man'. 'Eudaimonia' (happiness, well-being) Aristotle also calls the best or the highest good. The notion of a 'summum bonum', however, is not identical with the notion of the good of man as we use it here. But the two notions may be related.
7 Ascetism as an abnegation of worldly desire for the sake of the good of the soul must be distinguished from that which I here call ascetism as an ideal of life. To the first, ascetism is no 'end' or 'value' in itself, but an exercise and preparation for the good life.
8 See 'Ethics', Oxford University Press, 1966, pp. 42-4 and, in particular, Moore's reply to his critics in 'The Philosophy of G.E. Moore', pp. 554-7.

4 Alienation and self-realization

Kai Nielsen

1

Self-realizationist theories are among the classical attempts to develop a comprehensive normative ethical theory. Plato and Aristotle, in giving classical statements of such theories, argue that a man's distinctive happiness, a man's distinctive flourishing, will only be realized when he realizes himself, i.e. when he achieves to the fullest possible degree his distinctive function. And to achieve one's function is to develop to the full those capacities which are distinctive of the human animal. In doing this we are being most truly ourselves and in doing this we are doing what it is our own nature to do. Men who cultivate to the fullest that which men and only men have will be the happiest men and in so acting they will realize themselves most fully; they will achieve their maximum potential or their fullest distinctively human growth. To so realize oneself is the final end of all moral activity. It defines what is to constitute 'the good life' and what is to count as 'a good man'.

A self-realizationist would argue that to find a good x is (i) to discover the function of x and (ii) to find which x's will fulfil this function effectively. And to find the best x is to find the sort of x that most effectively (efficiently) fulfils this function. We will find the end or rationale of all human activity when we clearly apprehend the function of man. The man who realizes himself most fully is the man who develops to the full his distinctive capacities as a man. This is self-realization, this is human growth, and this is the end of all moral endeavour.

More generally, and apart from Plato's and Aristotle's

particular formulations, the ultimate moral ideal should be to attain the fullest degree of self-realization. That is to say, the end of moral activity is to enable us to be most truly ourselves. This, a self-realizationist is contending, should be the underlying rationale and justification of morality. Moral rules, actions, practices, attitudes and institutions are judged good or bad just to the extent that they contribute to self-realization. Rule A or action A is better than rule B or action B if A is more conducive to self-realization than B. The aim of all moral action is to further self-realization to the highest degree. We should always aim to realize our potentialities or capacities - that is, ourselves - as fully as possible.

This comforting formula, as Rashdall calls it, has some very serious ambiguities and difficulties. Taken together they raise a serious challenge to self-realizationist theories of ethics. In fact many philosophers think such accounts are thoroughly discredited - that self-realization is not, and cannot be, the end of moral endeavour or the ultimate standard of moral appraisal. However, in rejecting what has been called - not without point - 'the murky doctrine of self-realization', philosophers have neglected to attend to what may be important insights embedded in the theory. I shall try to show why it will not succeed as an ultimate moral criterion but I do not want to throw the baby out with the bath-water. I think there are insights in such accounts that need to be brought out and that there are problems raised by such a moral theory which need to be faced.

First, we need to ask whether on such an account we are to realize or seek to realize *all* our potentialities as a man or only some. If, in realizing our great Gyntian selves, we are to seek to realize all our potentialities, we are in reality seeking something that cannot be achieved, for we have an indefinitely large number of them, and furthermore, we frequently have conflicting capacities. The plain fact is that they cannot all be realized. We must choose which capacities we ought to realize. But to do this, it would seem that we would need some other criterion than self-realization, for, on the above account, to realize ourselves is simply to realize our capacities to the fullest extent.

It might be replied that where we cannot realize both of two conflicting capacities we should realize that capacity which would tend on the whole to enable us to realize the greater number of our capacities to the fullest extent. Suppose Jones has a considerable potential for, and indeed a liking of, boxing and rapid driving, but he also has a potential for, and extensive liking of, intellectual work. If he develops the latter and inhibits the former he, in turn, is much more likely to develop more potentialities that are distinctive of the human animal. More generally, and in accordance with the above, a self-realizationist might argue that our self-realizationist standard should be: each man should realize as many of his capacities as possible and, where his capacities conflict, he should choose those capacities which will contribute as fully as possible to the actualization of his other potentialities.

To argue in this way is, in effect, to argue that we should become 'good, all round people'. But it seems to me that Rashdall is quite correct in claiming that such an ideal is, in effect, a defence of mediocrity or dilettantism. I can hardly develop my talents, such as they are, as a philosopher, bookie, long-distance runner, preacher, boxer, neuro-surgeon and pianist all at the same time, or without prejudice of one to the other. The analytical powers I develop as a philosopher hardly further my emotional outpourings as a preacher. The time I need to spend at the piano to play it really well, will hardly allow me to become much of a long-distance runner and the punishment to my hands in boxing will hardly serve me well in performing delicate operations or in playing Prokofiev's Second Piano Concerto. I could seek to be an 'all around' fellow and develop all of these capacities a little, but then I will most surely end up doing none of them well, so that in anything I set my hand to I will be a mediocrity. Is such a dilettantish life the best possible life? Would I not do better for myself and for others by developing my philosophic talents to the fullest? That way I indeed do not achieve the harmonious fulfilment of as many of my capacities as possible, but do I not, by doing something else instead - in this case developing my philosophic talents - do something which is more worthwhile and which also serves my own interests more adequately?

If this last question is answered in the affirmative, then self-realization appears at least *not* to be our ultimate moral standard. If answered in the negative, the question immediately springs to mind: what reason is there for claiming that each individual ought always to develop as many of his capacities as possible? Why not argue, alternatively, that each individual should develop those capacities that he *wants* most to develop? Or why not, instead, argue that he should develop those that will make for everyone involved the greatest amount of good all around? It seems to me that in opting for the fullest development of all one's capacities and potentialities, such a self-realizationist theory is offering us an ultimate moral standard that will not survive critical scrutiny.

2

Suppose instead we mean by 'realizing yourself' essentially what Aristotle meant, namely that to realize yourself is to develop those capacities which are distinctive of *homo sapiens*. That is to say, we should develop those capacities which are distinctive of, that is peculiar to, our species alone. This is the quintessence of self-realization and morality. Our injunction should be 'Develop those potentialities which will most fully realize **your distinctive** human function'.

The rub is that man - if he can correctly be said to have any function at all - can be said to have many distinctive functions; that is to say, there are many things which are peculiar to man - that men and only men do. Even *if* being able to reason or more plausibly to carry on rational discourse and act in accordance with what is deliberated upon is distinctive of the human animal, so is having guilt feelings, the capacity for anguish and alienation, the capacity to laugh, to commit atrocities, to drive automobiles, to slaughter one's fellow human beings and other creatures with complicated weapons, etc., etc. There are a multitude of things which are distinctive of man. Why should we pick out reason over such other general distinctive traits or at least putatively distinctive traits as having an opposable thumb and walking upright, having a long period of infant dependency, having permanent sexual drives, having a sense of right and wrong, suffering anguish, or having the ability to laugh? Reason is indeed thought by Plato and Aristotle, and by others as well, to have a special excellence but that is not based on the fact that it is distinctive of human beings, for there are other things which are ignored in a specification of the function of man, which are also distinctive of human beings. This makes it evident that no adequate reason has been given for taking reason - the capacity to reason or the activity of reasoning - as the function of man, as that which makes a man a man.

In defending Aristotle, people may reply to the above argument by saying that to find the function of a thing we not only need to find what is distinctive of it but we also need to find its *essential* characteristics. When this is recognized, it will become evident that having the capacity to laugh is not essential to man while having the ability to reason is.

With respect to this argument, it should be noted that 'essential' in 'essential characteristic' itself functions evaluatively. Thus, in order to specify the function of man or self-realization, one must invoke some unspecified but still more fundamental *normative* criterion to establish what counts as an '*essential* characteristic'. There are many activities which are distinctively and peculiarly human but some are more important than others and thus are more essential. But what is our criterion for importance here? Surely if A is taken to be more important than B, A is something we take to be more valuable, i.e. desirable, as we take the ability to carefully deliberate and reason to be more valuable than the capacity to laugh. But then we still have not decided how we ascertain what is more or less valuable. Certainly we do not do it by appealing to a criterion of self-realization, for we have to know already what counts as a more essential and hence more valuable characteristic in order to know what would count as attaining or approximating self-realization.

It might be replied that we can easily tell that the capacity to reason is more essential to the human animal than the capacity to laugh, for the human animal could survive without laughter or even the ability to laugh but not without the ability to reason. And to the response that this argument presupposes, as a still more fundamental value, the value of survival, it could in turn be answered that it does not presuppose it as a higher value but only as a necessary condition for self-realization. That is to say, trivially speaking, unless man survives, he cannot achieve self-realization or anything else. But this does not mean that the end of life is mere survival without equal attention being given to questions concerning the quality or character of that survival. Moreover, just as there could be some fundamental genetic shift in man such that men no longer laughed, so too there could be a radical change so that men no longer reasoned in the complicated way prized by Aristotle. Both changes are

compatible with the continued existence of man as a
species, though, given such changes, if we (the present
group of people who might read such an essay), unlike
the rest of mankind, continued as we are, we would no
doubt say that such men 'were scarcely human'. But
in saying this, we reveal the *normative* way we are
using 'scarcely human'.

We have many characteristics which are distinctive
of (peculiar to) mankind, but not all of them are regarded as essential characteristics, yet the standard by
which we decide which characteristics are essential and
which are not remains unspecified and whatever the
standard is, it is plainly not derived from a conception
of self-realization, but is actually *presupposed* in the
specification of self-realization and in the specification of the function of man.

We might argue alternatively that by realizing his
highest and *best* capacities man does what is most distinctive of him. And thus in recognizing what these
highest and best capacities are, we find out what the
function of man is, and so come to see what constitutes
self-realization. But here we even more obviously presuppose, as a still more fundamental moral standard
than self-realization, some alien and unexplained
criterion. For how do we ascertain what are our
highest and best capacities? If we knew what they
were, we could know what self-realization is but then
we wouldn't need self-realization as an ultimate standard. But that aside, just how do we ascertain what
our highest and best capacities are? We are not told.
We only have an unexplained and unexplicated reference
to 'highest and best capacities'.

3

There are further difficulties in any self-realizationist account which appeals to a conception of the function
of man. For the very notion of man's having a function
to have even a tolerably clear meaning, it must be the
case that man is conceived on close analogy with an
artifact, a functional part of the body such as the
liver or heart, or with someone such as a policeman or
barber who has a social role. But man *qua* man has no
social role and he is too unlike an artifact or a
functioning part of a body for that analogy to be helpful. We can say quite unequivocally what it would be
like for a corkscrew to be a good one by specifying the
function of a corkscrew and by saying what constitutes

an efficient performance of that function. The concept of the function of a corkscrew is not at all problematic. Similar things hold for our bodily organs even though they are not artifacts made for a purpose. We can find out what it is to have a good heart or good liver by finding out what hearts and livers are for, that is by finding out what role they play in the bodily economy. Similarly, people have different social roles to play in society and we can find out what a good policeman or barber is by finding out what roles policemen or barbers play in society. When we understand what policemen and barbers are for, and what it is to perform that function efficiently, we know what it is for someone to be a good policeman or barber.

The function of a policeman or teacher is not quite as definite as that of many artifacts, but we are still not at a loss for words here, and the notions are by no means utterly indeterminate, though they have their controversial aspects. But the fact still remains that to the extent that we understand what teachers, policemen or barbers are for and what it is to efficiently perform that function, we understand what it is for someone to be a good teacher, policeman or barber. But a man may be a good policeman or barber and still be a bad man; he may be good in several social roles and still be a bad man; conversely he may be a good man and a bad teacher or barber. The fact is that men are not unequivocally *for* anything in the way barbers and policemen are. Being a human being is not the assuming of a social role, though human beings are socialized animals.

Only if we assume some extremely questionable theological framework in which we say that man was made to worship God and fulfil his commands, can we give much sense to the claim that 'human beings are for anything'. But even here we are reluctant to assert quite literally that human beings are for something. And furthermore such a theological claim, particularly if we try to construe it literally, is quite arbitrary. The claim that human beings have a function is quite baseless. There is no unproblematic answer or even sense to the putative question: 'What are human beings for?'

If, to escape these difficulties, we speak instead of a man as realizing himself or fulfilling his own natural tendencies, powers and wants, we should recall our earlier point that man has many different powers, tendencies and wants, and that sometimes they conflict. He cannot do them all, so again it is not clear what he is to do to realize his own nature.

4

However, let us assume that somehow I have been mistaken in what I have asserted above and that man does have a function and that it is what Aristotle says it is. That is to say, let us now assume that man's essential and distinguishing mark is his capacity to reason - this is what distinguishes him from other animals. Now, assuming for the sake of the argument that reason is such an essential characteristic, we still face difficulties. First, we face difficulties concerning exactly what it is that we are claiming. Surely on some readings of 'being able to reason', it is not something unique to men. The way a cat stalks a bird would certainly seem to involve reasoning, i.e. thinking, on the cat's part. We need a characterization here of the ways human beings alone or distinctively act in accordance with or for the sake of reasons. We need a specification of the distinctive ways 'the rational element' is embedded in human nature.

In talking about the function of man, we are talking about what constitutes being a man. As playing the flute is that which constitutes being a flute player, so, Aristotle claims, acting on reasons constitutes being a man. This is presumably the demythologization of Aristotle's remark that 'the function of man is an activity of the soul in conjunction with the rational element'.

What exactly is it on Aristotle's account to act on reasons? One commentator understands it as 'organizing or co-ordinating our desires and emotions, and controlling or checking the immediate impulses to action so as to enable ourselves to secure what we really want'. (1) Human beings presumably can act intentionally in this way and only human beings can so act. (We are assuming now that this is a distinctive and essential human characteristic.) Being able so to act is what constitutes human rationality. This is what makes us distinctively human.

If this is what acting on reasons most essentially comes to, then it may well be the case that two men, acting in quite different and conflicting ways, could on such an account be acting equally rationally and each could equally well be doing what on this account is right. For if they had different and conflicting wants - wants which conflicted, even where they took the most efficient means to satisfy their desires - it would still remain the case (given the above reading of Aristotle) that they were both being equally rational in so acting and were both equally justified in their moral judgments. But if this is so, then ethical relativism, at an extremely important point, would not have been overcome. But it is one of the accounts which claims to overcome relativism and to show how it is that moral beliefs can have an objective basis. This is one of its main attractions; without this promise such an obscure and puzzling account replete with its metaphors would have little attraction. Moreover, what is reasonable to do and what constitutes self-realization would be crucially dependent on such a reading on what *we just happen to want*. We would have no fundamental moral criteria by means of which we could make a critique of wants. Rather what was good and bad on such a theory would be very dependent on what we just happened to want. The kind of subjectivism and relativism that Aristotle's theory was intended to combat would hardly be overcome.

It might be replied, deliberately shifting the grounds of the argument somewhat, that I am neglecting the fact that Aristotle lays great stress on the worth of contemplation. To understand the function of man as that of acting on reasons, we need to understand that contemplation is really the highest form of rationality. In it, according to Aristotle, man's rational nature has its full flourishing. It is in this that man realizes himself and achieves his full humanity.

However, it should immediately be recognized that while the capacity to act on reasons is common to all human beings who are not mentally defective in some way, contemplation is not such a common trait. There are many people who are highly intelligent and indeed are reasonable human beings as well who are not contemplative and do not particularly prize contemplation. Moreover, there are many people who by ordinary criteria at least are fully moral beings and thoroughly reasonable beings, who are not at all given to contemplation. It would appear that in placing such a stress on contemplation, Aristotle is doing little more here than expressing a rationalist prejudice. Contemplation is no doubt unique to man but so is making change. No reason has been given for taking contemplation to be that which is most essential to his human nature or as being that in virtue of which a man realizes himself. It is arbitrary to claim that contemplation is the human activity which is of the highest value. (2)

Suppose we drop the bit about contemplation and continue, in spite of the above arguments, to claim that the function of man is to act on reasons or to reason in his actions and that only by doing this can he attain happiness.

If this is the move, it should be straight away noted that with such an appeal to happiness a new criterion has been introduced. Living in accordance with reason, i.e. acting on reasons or reasoning in one's actions, is not intrinsically good but good because it tends to be conducive to happiness or (more sceptically) if anything like happiness is attainable, it will only be attainable by human beings who generally act on reasons. But then self-realization is not the ultimate standard, happiness is.

Someone might try to avoid this conclusion by arguing that when we consider what Aristotle meant by the concept of happiness, to wit, a virtuous activity of the soul, we will see that happiness and self-realization are not independent concepts independently specifiable. The point being made here is that human happiness is distinctive and can only be understood in terms of understanding man's function, namely his acting on reasons or reasoning in his actions. A man will be happy if and only if he does this well.

However, this surely does not seem to be true of our ordinary and indeed reflective concept of happiness. One might, by acting on reasons intelligently and efficiently, achieve one's aims and attain happiness, but it is also the case that one might be miserable and alienated. And a man who did not think too clearly might be happier than a non-evasive, clear-headed individual who understood his condition very well. This might even be true of an individual who was deceived or even deceived himself. We need Dostoevski as a supplement to Aristotle's rationalism. We need to recognize that self-knowledge is often bitter and disillusioning - one loses certain consolations and an illusory flattering image of oneself. Indeed a clear insight into 'what makes one tick' may be self-destructive rather than something that furthers self-realization. From Plato to Freud we have assumed that self-knowledge, though difficult, is a good thing and ultimately a source of happiness. Both of these rationalist assumptions need challenging.

One thing to be said in reply here is *not* that we will be happy *if and only if* we act on reasons or are reasoning in our actions, but that we will be happy *only* if we act on reasons or are reasoning in our actions. A reasonable creature may be unhappy but he cannot be happy unless he is at least in some measure reasonable.

This is surely far more plausible than claiming one will be happy if one is reasonable. But all the same, it is not a claim that is obviously *universally* true. Yet it seems reasonable at least to believe that it generally holds and incorporates what appears, at least, to be the true claim, indeed the truism, that if a 'man has goals or aims in life it is unlikely that he will achieve his aims if he does not act on reasons'. (3) There is a value to be reasonably placed on rational activity. We need to understand what we are doing and we need to be able to reason in order to get what we want. But this does not entail or even go very far toward establishing that the fullest possible clarity about ourselves and the rationale of our actions carries with it a greater happiness than a life in which one remains confused about some, humanly speaking, very central things. A minimum kind of rationality, where reason is clearly a servant to one's desires and a watchdog concerning desires which are likely to be destructive, is absolutely crucial to anything approximating a human life or a happy life. But a fuller measure of rationality might be counter-productive as far as happiness is concerned.

Perhaps it is an illusion to think that life will ever be substantially freer from human degradation and exploitation than it is at present, but all the same, believing that it could be might enable a man to give sense to his life where otherwise it would be without sense. But a clear knowledge of what was involved here might lead him to despair and suicide. A man with a clear grasp of his condition could be a man in despair and a man with a confused conception of life might be happy. All Aristotle shows about human happiness and rationality is that if a man cannot reason at all well, he is likely to make mistakes which will make him miserable. But people can have an acute rational understanding of their positions and still not flourish and they could be confused and happy and indeed not terribly intellectually acute and still be thoroughly good human beings.

Self-realization can be so construed that it is tied to acting on reasons or for the sake of reasons, in which case it need not be a way to enhance human happiness to the fullest extent. By contrast self-realization may be so construed that it is conceptually tied to happiness, but then self-realization is no longer something which conceptually requires the greatest rationality possible no matter what the circumstances. Rationality and happiness are related but not so tightly that it is the case that human beings *must*, when there are alternative ways of acting, be happiest when they do that action which gives them the clearest - the most rational - understanding of their situation.

In sum it should be stressed here that if what constitutes being a man is acting on reasons, it needs to be pointed out that by so acting it does not necessarily follow that one is discharging a moral obligation or even doing anything beneficial to oneself. No justification has been given for saying that by so acting we realize ourselves or achieve the highest good. If it is responded that, if we act on reasons and consistently reason in our actions, by definition we realize ourselves or achieve the highest good, it should be replied that this definition is arbitrary and stipulative. There is no reason (*pace* Plato) why an unprincipled and immoral man could not act on reasons. An immoralist need not be an irrationalist.

5

In a way that has been too little noticed, self-realizationist theories suffer the same central defect from which so-called ethical egoism suffers. Recall that for 'ethical egoism' the ultimate guiding principle is that each person is to seek what he, on careful regard, takes to be in his own self-interest and he is to consider the interests of others only when doing so will directly or indirectly further his own interests. Similarly for the self-realizationist theories the fundamental moral imperative is for each person to seek to realize himself. But we have moral rules and principles and indeed the institution of morality itself, primarily or at least importantly, to adjudicate in a fair manner conflicts of interest. (4) If that is not its *raison d'être*, it is at least a central function of such discourse. But just as 'ethical egoism' is of no help in adjudicating such conflicts, for on such an account each man is told to seek his own self-interest, including someone asked to arbitrate such disputes, so too the self-realizationist tells men to seek self-realization and this tells everyone, including the arbitrator of a dispute, to look within himself and do that which will most realize him. But this does not tell us what to do when a course of action which will lead to A's self-realization conflicts with a course of action which will lead to B's self-realization and both cannot be done. It does not guide a judge, adviser or arbitrator of such a case in deciding what he is to advise except, unhelpfully, particularly where his own self-realization is not affected, to tell him to seek to realize himself in such situations. But that is not what is needed or wanted in such a situation, and in many cases it is not at all evident what would contribute toward his self-realization. But the crucial thing is that what would contribute to *his* self-realization is not what is at issue in such situations. In fact it very much looks as if self-realizationist theories are in reality *a form* of 'ethical egoism'.

If it is retorted that what a self-realizationist theory should be understood as claiming is that we should work for, advocate, or at least hope for, the greatest amount of self-realization for as many people as possible, this indeed gets the theory out of the difficulties associated with 'ethical egoism' but only by making it into a kind of utilitarianism. We should always seek as our overriding aim to achieve the greatest good for the greatest number. Only here the individual good, which is to be maximized for as many people as possible, is not, as in hedonistic forms of utilitarianism, pleasure, but individual self-realization. This may be a plausible theory, provided that utilitarianism stands up to critical scrutiny and provided that our earlier objections to self-realizationist theories can be overcome. But that, of course, is a big if and it is also the case that the theory in question has been so modified that it is no longer a pure self-realizationist theory, for now it has a utilitarian structure. It only differs from the more standard forms of utilitarianism in that it makes the claim that for each individual what is good for him, when others are not counted in, is self-realization.

6

Given the extensive array of mistakes I have trotted out and shown to be involved in self-realizationist ethical theories, how can I possibly be justified in claiming that in spite of all that, such a theory contains its moral lessons and insights as well? I will argue that, while it does not serve as an ultimate moral standard or principle and indeed cannot be coherently put in this role, it is an important, though tantalizingly vague, element to be utilized in spelling out personal ideals of moral excellence. Furthermore, in any adequate systematic, normative ethic, consideration must be given to these ideals; yet it is just such conceptions which receive scant attention in non-self-realizationist theories.

In this connection, we should not forget that we do not only ask: what am I bound to do or what ought I to do, but what should I become? What should I make of my life and how should I live to live in a non-alienated, non-self-estranged way? What, that is, should my life be like if I am to overcome self-estrangement? But in answering these questions self-realizationist idioms come in quite naturally and indeed perhaps unavoidably. If A can be estranged from himself, he must be able to find himself or perhaps even realize himself. If there can be an alienated self or estranged self, there must be some concept of a true self or an unalienated self.

Suppose that this is resisted and what is claimed instead is that to make sense of your life - to attain your full human flourishing - you should go in an intelligent and single-minded way after pleasure.

However, this in turn should be challenged, for first, one typically does not attain much pleasure by going after it, it is rather something of a concomitant of certain activities - activities that can often be brought off only if one does not think about getting pleasure from what one is doing. (5) Moreover, and second, even if pleasure could be such an end of action, it is hardly the only end of action. A satisfying life indeed has pleasure in it, but it is not constituted by a life in which the rationale of all of one's activities is to maximize pleasure and minimize pain.

When we ask: what sort of things are *worth* having for their own sakes, we will indeed say pleasure and we will also, if we reflect, very likely say, an ability and an opportunity to direct our own lives. But we are also very likely to say a 'fullness of life' and resist the question: 'What do you want a full life for?' as somehow conceptually inappropriate.

Yet how are we to understand 'fullness of life'? What is the literal rendering of this? In trying to get a grip on it we are very likely to invoke notions such as 'a life in which one develops and flourishes', 'a fully human life', 'a life in which there is a measure of self-improvement and growth'. But are not all of these notions, notions which presuppose or imply a conception of self-realization? To grow or develop is to grow or develop into or toward something and is not that something naturally called one's more 'authentic self' or 'true self' or indeed a self which has achieved something in the direction of self-realization?

Note also that we frequently speak of creeds, institutions, forms of life, or practices which compress, stunt, or dwarf us. Are not their opposites those which aid or do not stand in the way of our self-realization? There could be no conception of a dehumanized humanity if we did not at least have some conception of what a humanity that attained or retained its humanity would be like. But to talk of this again is another way of talking of self-realization. The same type of contrast is at work in talk of empty lives, really dead people, zombies and the like. And when we talk of a good life as involving self-expression we imply that there is a 'true self' to be realized.

When Marx spoke of the estrangement of one's self from one's self and from one's own humanity and the humanity of others that we experience under capitalism, he contrasted this with a truly human life and a truly human society wherein man could attain emancipation and where one's labour would not be alienated. But in these very notions we have operating, though expressed by other words, conceptions of self-realization and the non-attainment of self-realization. What exactly this family of notions comes to remains vague - the doctrine of self-realization is indeed a murky one - but it all the same signifies something, we know not clearly what, that we quite unequivocally take as precious. An account of morality and the moral life which ignores these features of morality is plainly thereby impoverished.

NOTES

1 G.C. Field, 'Moral Theory', London, Methuen, 1966, p. 75.
2 This stress on contemplation and this conception of rationality also fits badly, as Bernard Williams observes, with his stress on practical wisdom and the importance of citizenly activities. Bernard Williams, 'Morality: An Introduction to Ethics', New York, Harper & Row, 1972, p. 60.
3 Frederick Siegler, Reason, Happiness and Goodness, in James J. Walsh and Henry J. Shapiro, eds, 'Aristotle's Ethics: Issues and Interpretations', Belmont, California, Wadsworth, 1967, p. 36.

4 Kurt Baier, 'The Moral Point of View', Ithaca, New York, Cornell University Press, 1958 and Kai Nielsen, On Moral Truth, in Nicholas Rescher, ed., 'Studies in Moral Philosophy', Oxford, Basil Blackwell, 1968.
5 Alasdair MacIntyre has importantly criticized such conceptions in his 'Against the Self-Images of the Age', New York, Shocken, 1971, pp. 173-90.

5 Human rights, real and supposed

Maurice Cranston

It is said that when that remarkable American jurist Wesley Newcomb Hohfield tried to make the students at Yale Law School discriminate carefully between different uses of the term 'right' in Anglo-American law, he earned himself considerable unpopularity; his pupils even got up a petition to have him removed from his Chair. (1) If the analysis of positive rights is thus resisted by law students we should not be surprised if the analysis of human rights is ill-regarded by many politicians, publicists, and even political theorists. Some politicians, indeed, have a vested interest in keeping talk about human rights as meaningless as possible. For there are those who do not want to see human rights become positive rights by genuine enactments; hence the more nebulous, unrealistic or absurd the concept of human rights is made out to be, the better such men are pleased.

I shall argue in this paper that a philosophically respectable concept of human rights has been muddied, obscured, and debilitated in recent years by an attempt to incorporate into it specific rights of a different logical category. The traditional human rights are political and civil rights such as the right to life, liberty and a fair trial. What are now being put forward as universal human rights are social and economic rights, such as the right to unemployment insurance, old-age pensions, medical services and holidays with pay. I have both a philosophical and a political objection to this. The philosophical objection is that the new theory of human rights does not make sense. The political objection is that the circulation of a confused notion of human rights hinders the effective protection of what are correctly seen as human rights.

One distinction which seems now well established in

people's minds is that between human rights or the Rights of Man or natural rights (I take these expressions to mean the same thing) and positive rights, a distinction which corresponds to the distinction between natural law (or justice or the moral law) and positive law. The distinction has been made better understood by the critics of natural rights, by men like Edmund Burke who could understand what was meant by the rights of Englishmen but not by the Rights of Man, and Jeremy Bentham who said 'Right is the child of law; from real laws come real rights, but from imaginary law, from "laws of nature", come imaginary rights.... Natural rights is simple nonsense, natural and imprescriptibel rights [an American phrase] rhetorical nonsense, nonsense upon stilts'. (2)

I do not think Bentham's remark is true, but it was worth saying, because it obliges those of us who think natural rights is *not* nonsense to explain what sort of sense it is. For Bentham - and for Burke - the only test of a right was 'Is it actually enjoyed?', 'Is it really enforced?' In other words, 'Is it a positive right?' On this analysis, any right which is not a positive right is not granted the name of a right at all. For Burke the Rights of Man were mere abstractions: the rights of Englishmen were realities - a 'positive recorded hereditary title to all that can be dear to the man and the citizen'. (3) Real rights, again, were positive rights.

Both Burke and Bentham had a political as well as a philosophical interest in this question. Both regarded talk about the Rights of Man as mischievous as well as meaningless. Burke, the conservative, objected to such talk because it stimulated revolutionary sentiments, it injected 'false ideas and vain expectations into men destined to travel the obscure walk of laborious life'. Bentham, the radical, objected to talk about the Rights of Man because it produced declarations and manifestos that had no real significance in positive law, declarations which took the place of effective legislation for the public welfare. Burke disliked the rhetoric that led to public unrest and Bentham disliked the rhetoric that enabled politicians to fob off the public with words instead of deeds. Being thus attacked from Right and Left, it is no wonder that the idea of the Rights of Man, and of Natural Law, became unfashionable in the nineteenth century.

The present century has seen a marked revival of consciousness of what is now generally know as human rights - a term which has the advantage over the older expression 'natural rights' of not committing one too ostentatiously to any traditional doctrine of Natural Law. The reason for this revival is perhaps to be sought in history, first, in the great twentieth-century evils, Nazism, fascism, total war and racialism, which have all presented a fierce challenge to human rights; and secondly, in an increased belief in, or demand for, equality among men. When the United Nations was set up by the victorious powers in the Second World War, one of the first and most important tasks assigned to it was what Winston Churchill called 'the enthronement of human rights'. The efforts that have been made at the United Nations to fulfil this promise have much to teach a political theorist.

At the inaugural meeting of the Economic and Social Council of the UN in May 1946, a Commission on Human Rights was appointed to submit to the General Assembly recommendations and reports regarding an 'International Bill of Rights'. English-speaking delegates on this Commission promptly put forward a draft 'Bill of Rights' in the form of a draft convention or treaty which both named the specific rights to be recognized and provided for the setting up of international institutions to deal with any alleged breach of those rights. The English-speaking delegations not unnaturally interpreted the expression 'Bill of Rights' as meaning an instrument of positive law, and therefore understood the duty of the Commission to be that of finding a formula for making human rights positive rights by making them enforceable. The Russian representative objected to these proposals. He said that it was premature to discuss any measure of a binding or judicial nature; the Soviet Union was willing to support a 'Bill of Rights' only if it was understood as a manifesto or declaration of rights. Some years afterwards the United States followed the Russian example, and announced that it, too, would not commit itself to any legally binding convention for the international protection of human rights.

In the UN Commission on Human Rights a compromise was settled on. The Commission agreed first to produce a manifesto or declaration of human rights, and then afterwards begin to work out 'something more legally binding' which it was decided to call a Covenant. The manifesto did not take long to produce. It was given the name of Universal Declaration of Human Rights and proclaimed by the General Assembly of the United Nations in December 1948 (see Appendix,

p. 143). The 'more legally binding' Covenant of Human Rights, however, is still, after many years, at the stage of discussion.

One of the difficulties of translating the Universal Declaration of Human Rights into any kind of positive law is that the Declaration contains so much. It has no fewer than thirty articles. The first twenty spell out in detail the sort of rights that were named in the various classical statements of the Rights of Man: the rights to life, liberty, property, equality, justice and the pursuit of happiness are articulated as, among other things, the right to freedom of movement; the right to own property alone as well as in association with others; the right to marry; the right to equality before the law and to a fair trial if accused of any crime; the right to privacy; the right to religious freedom; the right to free speech and peaceful assembly; the right to asylum. Among the institutions outlawed are slavery, torture and arbitrary detention.

The Universal Declaration of 1948 did not, however, limit itself to this restatement of the familiar Rights of Man; it includes a further ten articles which name rights of a new and different kind. (4) Article 21 states that everyone has the right to take part in the government of his country, and further articles affirm the right to education; the right to work and to form trade unions; the right to equal pay for equal work; the right of everyone to a standard of living adequate to the health and well-being of himself and his family; the right to security in the event of unemployment, sickness, disability, widowhood, old age or other lack of livelihood; the right to enjoy the arts and to share in scientific advancement and its benefits; and, what is even more novel, the right to rest, leisure and 'periodic holidays with pay'.

The difference between these new rights and the traditional natural rights was not unnoticed by those responsible for drafting the Declaration. In the records of the Commission, the first twenty articles are called 'political and civil rights' and the further rights 'economic and social rights'. These later rights appear to have been included under pressure from the Left; but there are many humanitarian people, apart from those on the Left, who (in my belief, unwisely) agree with their inclusion. (5)

So far as the United Nations is concerned, the Commission on Human Rights soon discovered, when it came to draft the 'more legally binding' Covenant, that

the two kinds of rights did not mix together well; and
the Commission was therefore obliged to draft *two* cove-
nants, one concerning the political and civil rights,
the other the social and economic rights. Neither
draft has so far proved acceptable to the General
Assembly. In the meantime altogether more progress
has been made in the field of human rights by another
international organization, the Council of Europe. In
1950 a European Convention for the Protection of Human
Rights was signed by the member States of the Council
of Europe at Strasbourg. This time the so-called
'social and economic rights' were omitted; the rights
that were named were the traditional 'political and
civil rights'. Moreover, in this case, a European
Commission and a European Court of Human Rights were
set up with full judicial powers to investigate and
remedy any alleged breach of the rights named in the
Convention. Here, clearly, is a tangible attempt to
translate the human rights into positive rights on an
international scale. The only weakness of the European
Convention is that some leading European powers, France,
Italy, Greece, and Turkey, have refused to recognize
the jurisdiction of the European Court or to grant the
right to individual petition to the Commission or the
Court. Nevertheless a dozen other nations *do* recognize these institutions; so that changes in positive
law have helped in those places to make men's 'human
rights' positive rights. (6)

One of the objections to regarding the 'social and
economic' rights as authentic human rights is that it
would be totally impossible to translate them in the
same way into positive rights by analogous political
and legal action. There are other objections: but
the time has now come to consider more carefully what
is meant by a right, and then what kind of right a
human right is. We have already noted the distinction
between human rights and positive rights; I propose
now to rearrange rights into two other categories; the
one I shall call legal rights, the other moral rights.

1 Legal rights may be distinguished as follows:
   (a) General positive rights: the rights that are
enjoyed and fully assured to everyone living under a
given jurisdiction or constitution.
   (b) Traditional rights and liberties: Burke said
that the English people had risen against James II
because he had taken away their traditional rights and
liberties as Englishmen. The Vichy government took

away many of the traditional rights and liberties of Frenchmen. This class of rights includes lost positive rights as well as existing positive rights.

(c) Nominal 'legal' rights: Even the least liberal nations tend to have 'façade' constitutions (7) which 'guarantee' freedom of speech, movement, assembly, and other such rights to their inhabitants. But where these nominal rights are not enforced, they cannot, of course, be classed as positive rights. We nevertheless see the demand in some such places for the nominal 'legal' rights being made positive rights. One example is the demand of certain Polish intellectuals for that freedom of expression which their constitution assures them. An even more publicized example is the demand of the Negroes in the United States for the nominal legal right to vote, enter State schools and so forth, to be translated into positive rights.

(d) Positive rights, liberties, privileges and immunities of a limited class of persons: Under this category we should have to include all rights which are attached to membership of a given category, e.g., the rights of clergymen, of peers, of doctors, of graduates of the University of Oxford and of freemen of the City of London. The twentieth century has become impatient of privileges, and rights which were once enjoyed by a limited class of persons are often now claimed by all the inhabitants of a country. For example, the privileges of citizenship, the rights of ratepayers, as they were known in nineteenth-century England, are now enjoyed by all adult British subjects. A demand for the extension of rights within a political society is often confused with the demand for human rights. But the two are quite distinct.

(e) The positive rights, liberties, privileges and immunities of a single person: Here the examples are few, because the cases are few: the rights of the President of the United States, of the Chairman of the Senate; the rights of the King, or the Lord Chancellor, or of the Archbishop of Canterbury, are examples. Since the decay of the doctrine of the Divine Right of Kings, this class of rights does not present much of a problem.

The foregoing classes cover the category of legal rights. Next in turn is the category of moral rights. In this case it will be convenient to reverse the order of generality.

2 Moral rights

(a) *Moral rights of one person only:* We remember Bradley's famous phrase 'my station and its duties': we can equally speak of 'my station and its rights'. I, and I alone, have a network of rights which arise from the fact that I have done certain deeds, paid certain monies, been elected to certain places, and so forth. Some of these rights are legal rights as well as moral rights. But in considering them as moral rights the question is not 'Does the law uphold them?' but 'Have I just claim to them?' Not all my moral rights may in fact be enjoyed. Often we become most conscious of our moral rights precisely when they are *not* upheld. I am inclined to say 'I have a moral right to be told what is going on in my own house' when I realize I am not being told. So just as the crucial question with legal rights is 'Are they secured and enjoyed?', the crucial question in a moral right is 'Is there a just title?' Is there a sound moral claim? *Justification* is the central question.

(b) *The moral rights of anyone in a particular situation:* This is the class of moral rights which belongs to everyone who comes into a certain specific category, e.g., that of a parent, or a tutor, or an *au pair* girl. So we can say of a person, if he is a member of this class, he is entitled to so and so. Claims to have such moral rights are pressed by proving that one does belong to the appropriate category.

(c) *The moral rights of all people in all situations:* Because these rights are universal we should naturally expect them to be few in number; and we should expect them to be highly generalized in their formulation. It is easier to agree, for example, about the kind of deed which violates the right to life than it is to agree about any philosophical expression of the right to life. Moreover, it is inevitable that such a right as that to liberty will be somewhat differently understood in different societies, where the boundary between liberty and licence will be differently drawn. Again, our understanding of the right to property will differ according to the meaning we give to that richly ambiguous word.

The place which human rights occupy in my classification is readily understood. Human rights are a form of moral right, and they differ from other moral rights in being the rights of all people at all times and in all situations. This characteristic of human rights is recognized in the first paragraph of the preamble to the Universal Declaration of 1948, which says: 'Whereas recognition of the inherent dignity and of the equal and inalienable rights of all members of the human family is the foundation of freedom, justice and peace in the world....'

Part of the difficulty of justifying human rights is their very universality. Moral rights of classes 2 (a) and 2 (b) above are justified by reference to the definite station or situation of the claimants. I claim a right to be told about the health of Nicholas Cranston by showing that I am his father. I do not think anyone else (except his mother) has the same right. But human rights do not depend in any way on the station or the situation of the individual. This is part of what is meant by saying they are 'rights that pertain to a human being merely because he is a human being'. If the validity of a moral right is commonly established by reference to the station or situation of the claimant, it is not altogether easy to see by what tests one could validate the rights which are *not* considered in relation to any definite situation.

Nevertheless there are some tests for the authenticity of a human right or universal moral right. Rights bear a clear relationship to duties. And the first test of both is that of practicability. It is not my duty to do what it is physically impossible for me to do. You cannot reasonably say it was my duty to have jumped into the Thames at Richmond to rescue a drowning child if I was nowhere near Richmond at the time the child was drowning. What is true of duties is equally true of rights. If it is impossible for a thing to be done, it is absurd to claim it as a right. At present it is utterly impossible, and will be for a long time yet, to provide 'holidays with pay' for everybody in the world. For millions of people who live in those parts of Asia, Africa, and South America where industrialization has hardly begun, such claims are vain and idle.

The traditional 'political and civil rights' can (as I have said) be readily secured by legislation; and generally they can be secured by fairly simple legislation. Since those rights are for the most part rights against government interference with a man's activities, a large part of the legislation needed has to do no more than restrain the government's own executive arm. This is no longer the case when we turn to 'the right to work', 'the right to social security' and so forth. For a government to provide

social security it needs to do more than make laws; it
has to have access to great capital wealth, and many
governments in the world today are still poor. The
government of India, for example, simply cannot command
the resources that would guarantee each one of the 480
million inhabitants of India 'a standard of living adequate for the health and well-being of himself and his
family', let alone 'holidays with pay'.

Another test of a human right is that it shall be a
genuinely universal moral right. This the so-called
human right to holidays with pay plainly cannot pass.
For it is a right that is necessarily limited to those
persons who are *paid* in any case, that is to say, to
the *employé* class. Since not everyone belongs to this
class, the right cannot be a universal right, a right
which, in the terminology of the Universal Declaration,
'everyone' has. That the right to a holiday with pay
is for many people a real moral right, I would not for
one moment deny. But it is a right which falls into
section 2 (b) of the classification of rights which I
have set out above; that is, a right which can be
claimed by members of a specific class of persons
because they are members of that class.

A further test of a human right, or universal moral
right, is the test of *paramount importance*. Here the
distinction is less definite, but no less crucial.
And here again there is a parallel between rights and
duties. It is a paramount duty to relieve great distress, as it is not a paramount duty to give pleasure.
It would have been my duty to rescue the drowning child
at Richmond if I had been there at the time; but it is
not, in the same sense, my duty to give Christmas
presents to the children of my neighbours. This
difference is obscured in the crude utilitarian philosophy which analyses moral goodness in terms of the
greatest happiness of the greatest number: but
common-sense does not ignore it. Common-sense knows
that fire engines and ambulances are essential services,
whereas fun fairs and holiday camps are not. Liberality and kindness are reckoned moral virtues; but
they are not moral duties in the sense that the obligation to rescue a drowning child is a moral duty.

It is worth considering the circumstances in which
ordinary people find themselves invoking the language
of human rights. I suggest they are situations like
these:

A black student in South Africa is awarded a scholarship to Oxford, and then refused a passport by the South
African government simply because he is black. We

feel this is clear invasion of the human right to freedom of movement.

Jews are annihilated by the Nazi government, simply because they are Jews. We feel this is a manifest abuse (an atrocious abuse) of the human right to life.

In several countries men are held in prison indefinitely without trial. We feel this is a gross invasion of the human right to liberty and to a fair trial on any criminal charge.

In considering cases of this kind, we are confronted by matters which belong to a totally different moral dimension from questions of social security and holidays with pay. A human right is something of which no one may be deprived without a grave affront to justice. There are certain deeds which should never be done, certain freedoms which should never be invaded, some things which are supremely sacred. If a Declaration of Human Rights is what it purports to be, a declaration of universal moral rights, it should be confined to this sphere of discourse. If rights of another class are introduced, the effect may even be to bring the whole concept of human rights into disrepute. 'It would be a splendid thing', people might say, 'for everyone to have holidays with pay, a splendid thing for everyone to have social security, a splendid thing to have equality before the law, and freedom of speech, and the right to life. One day, perhaps, this beautiful ideal may be realized....'

Thus the effect of a Universal Declaration which is overloaded with affirmations of so-called human rights which are not human rights at all is to push *all* talk of human rights out of the clear realm of the morally compelling into the twilight world of utopian aspiration. In the Universal Declaration of 1948 there indeed occurs the phrase 'a common standard of achievement' which brands that Declaration as an attempt to translate rights into ideals. And however else one might choose to define moral rights, they are plainly *not* ideals or aspirations.

Rights have been variously defined by jurists and philosophers. Some have spoken of them in terms of 'justifiable claims' or 'moral titles'; others have analysed rights in terms of duty ('what we have an overwhelming duty to respect'); others again have preferred to speak of right conduct or obligation or of ought ('a man has a right whenever other men ought not to prevent his doing what he wants or refuse him some service he asks for or needs'). All these words – 'right', 'justice', 'duty', 'ought', 'obligation' – are the key terms of what Kant called the 'categorical imperative'. What ought to be done, what is obligatory, what is right, what is duty, what is just, is not what it would be nice to see done one day; it is what is demanded by the basic norms of morality or justice.

An ideal is something one can aim at, but cannot by definition immediately realize. A right, on the contrary, is something that can, and from the moral point of view *must*, be respected here and now. If this were not so, we should have to agree with Bentham; if the Rights of Man were ideals, to talk of them as rights at all would indeed be rhetorical nonsense. We can give sense to human rights only because we can reasonably claim that men have moral rights, and that among the moral rights which each man has are some that he shares with all other men.

To deny that the 'economic and social rights' are the universal moral rights of all men is not to deny that they may be the moral rights of some men. In the moral criticism of legal rights, it is certainly arguable that the privileges of some members of a certain community ought to be extended to other members (and perhaps all members) of that community. But this matter is correctly seen as a problem of *socialization* or *democratization* - that is, the extension of privileges and immunities - rather than as a problem about the universal rights of all men: and the case for any such specific claims to an extension of legal rights must be argued on other grounds.

NOTES

1 Arthur L. Corbin in his introduction to Hohfield's 'Fundamental Legal Conceptions', Yale University Press, New Haven, 1964.
2 'Anarchical Fallacies'.
3 'The Philosophy of Edmund Burke', ed. Bredvold and Ross, Michigan University Press, Ann Arbor, 1960, p. 205.
4 C.J. Friedrich, in Rights, Liberties, Freedoms: A Reappraisal, 'American Political Science Review', LVII, 4 December 1963, shows that some 'social and economic rights' were known to the Age of Reason. He quotes the 'right to work' being named by Turgot and Robespierre, and gives references to eighteenth-century claims to the right to education.
5 E.g., Professor C.J. Friedrich (cf. previous note). Another champion of the view that social and

economic rights should be interpreted as human rights is the late Pope, John XXIII. I have discussed his views in an article, Pope John XXIII on Peace and the Rights of Man, 'Political Quarterly', October 1963.
6 See A.H. Robertson, 'Human Rights in Europe', Manchester University Press, 1964.
7 See G. Sartori, Constitutionalism, 'American Political Science Review', Vol. LVI December 1962, pp. 853-65.

6 Welfare state and welfare society

R. M. Titmuss

INTRODUCTION

I did not choose this title. It was chosen for me. Despite this assistance, I must say that I am no more enamoured today of the indefinable abstraction 'The Welfare State' than I was some twenty years ago when, with the advent of the National Health, National Insurance and other legislative promissories, the term acquired an international as well as a national popularity.

The consequences have not all been intellectually stimulating. Generalized slogans rarely induce concentration of thought; more often they prevent us from asking significant questions about reality. Morally satisfied and intellectually dulled, we sink back into our presumptive cosy British world of welfare. Meanwhile, outside these islands (as well as inside) there are critics - economic and political critics - who are misled into confusing ends and means, and who are discouraged from undertaking the painful exercise of distinguishing between philosophical tomorrows and the current truths of reality in a complex British power structure of rationed resources, and great inequalities in incomes and wealth, opportunities and freedom of choice.

From what little is known about the reading habits of international bankers and economists, I think it is reasonable to say that they do not include much in the way of studies on welfare and the condition of the poor. How then are their views shaped about the British 'Welfare State'? This we do not know, but at least we can say that if we mislead ourselves, we shall mislead them. But the matter does not end there. Models of public welfare can assume different forms and contain different assumptions about means and ends. Concepts of welfare can imply very different things to different people - as we can see from the Study Group Reports to this Conference.

One particular model is the 'Public Burden Model of Welfare'. In general terms, this sees public welfare expenditure - and particularly expenditure which is redistributive in intent - as a burden; an impediment to growth and economic development. Given this model of the British patient, the diagnosis seems simple. We are spending too much on 'The Welfare State'. Such explanations are, moreover, encouraged by the concept of private economic man embedded in the techniques of national income accounting. An increase in public retirement pensions is seen (as it was seen internationally during the balance of payments crisis in 1964) as an economic burden. (1) A similar increase in spending power among occupational (publicly subsidized private) pensioners is not so seen. Yet both involve additions to consumption demand.

Or take another example: medical care, public and private. It is being argued today that by encouraging the growth of private medical care through a voucher system and by allowing people to contract-out of taxation, the 'burden' of the Health Service would be reduced. The objective it seems is to reduce the assumed 'burden'; thus, those who contract-out diminish the burden. Logically, we should extend to them our gratitude and moral respect for contracting-out of public commitments. But, if Mr Enoch Powell may be accepted as an authority (and I quote from his recent book 'Medicine and Politics', (2) this 'voucher scheme resolves itself merely into a method of increasing state expenditure upon medical care'. In other words, it is a proposal for redistributing more medical resources in favour of private patients. The case for contracting-out must, therefore, be justified on grounds other than the 'welfare burden' argument.

INTERNATIONAL ASPECTS OF WELFARE

If we insist, come what may, on the continued use or misuse and misapplication of the term 'The Welfare State' then we must accept the consequences of international misunderstanding. We cannot assume that observers abroad share, or will share, the social or moral criteria we may apply to welfare; to many of our creditors and currency colleagues in Western Germany,

France and the United States, the 'Welfare State' is equated with national irresponsibility and decadence; an easy way of living off foreign loans. To the political scientist as well as the economist these opinions are relevant facts in the same way as (according to some sociologists) social class is what men think it is. These opinions do not, moreover, differ markedly from those expressed in the published statements on welfare during the past fifteen years by bankers, insurance directors, financiers and others in the City of London. (3)

Many of these monetary experts abroad appear to place a different valuation on countries which depend heavily on 'borrowing' human capital as distinct from those which borrow financial capital. For such transactions, no payment is made to the lending country; there are no interest charges, and there is no intention of repaying the loan.

Since 1949 the United States has absorbed (and to some extent deliberately recruited) the import of 100,000 doctors, scientists and engineers from developed and developing countries. In about eighteen years the United States will have saved some $4,000 million by not having to educate and train, or train fully, this vast quantity of human capital. (4) It has spent more on consumption goods; less on public services. It has taxed itself more lightly while imposing heavier taxation on poorer countries. Estimates have been made that this foreign aid to America is as great or greater than the total of American aid to countries abroad since 1949. Moreover, such estimates leave out of account the social and economic effects in Britain (and much more significantly in the poor countries of the world) of having to train more doctors, scientists and engineers, and of having to pay heavily inflated rewards to prevent American recruitment with all their harmful repercussions on incomes, prices and levels of taxation.

In medicine alone, foreign doctors now account for nearly 20 per cent of the annual additions to the American medical profession. (5) The world now provides as much or more medical aid to the United States in terms of dollars as the total cost of all American medical aid, private and public, to foreign countries. (6) A study I have made recently of the columns of the 'British Medical Journal' and the 'Lancet' from 1951 to 1966 shows that advertisements for British doctors (often accompanied by recruiting campaigns and sometimes actively encouraged by senior

British doctors (7)) rose from a yearly average of 134 in 1951 to over 4,000 in 1966. (8) The total number of newly qualified doctors in Britain in 1966 was around 1,700; each of them cost about £10,000 to train, excluding expenditure on student maintenance. (9)

The United States is not alone in attempting to develop its welfare systems (and Medicare) at the expense of poorer countries through the discovery that, today, it is much cheaper and less of a public burden to import doctors, scientists and other qualified workers than to educate and train them. Britain is also relying heavily on the skills of doctors from poorer countries - due in part to the belief less than five to ten years ago among Ministers and leaders of the medical profession that we were in danger of training too many doctors. (10) And, we may add, the belief among liberal economists and sections of the medical profession that Britain was spending too much on the Health Service which was in danger of bankrupting the nation. Even as late as 1962, there were influential voices in the British Medical Association who were speaking of the profession's recent experience of a 'glut of doctors' and the need to avoid medical unemployment in the late 1960s. (11) Guilty as we have been in our treatment of doctors from overseas, and in our failure in the past to train enough health workers for our own national needs, at least it cannot be said that we are deliberately organizing recruitment campaigns in economically poorer countries.

These introductory reflections on some of the international aspects of welfare point, I believe, to three general conclusions. First, they underline the dangers in the use of the term 'The Welfare State'. Second, they remind us that we can no longer consider welfare systems solely within the limited framework of the nation-state; what we do or fail to do in changing systems of welfare affects other countries besides ourselves. Third, to suggest one criterion for the definition of a 'Welfare Society'; namely, a society which openly accepts a policy responsibility for educating and training its own nationals to meet its own needs for doctors, nurses, social workers, scientists, engineers and others. Just as we have recognized the injustices and the waste in the unrestricted free international movement of goods, material and capital, so we must now recognize the need for the richer countries of the world to take action to protect the poorer countries from being denuded of skilled manpower.

To this end, a number of measures could be taken, some unilaterally, some by international agreement. Among the most important would be for the rich countries to decide to spend less on personal consumption goods and more on training young people for the social service professions; to decide to devote more of their resources for genuine international aid to the poorer countries; to decide to ban the deliberate recruitment overseas of skilled manpower; to decide to revise and broaden their immigration policies so that movement between countries is not restricted to the highly educated and trained; and to take other measures too complex to discuss in this paper.

For the rich countries of the world to take action in such ways would represent a few modest steps towards the notion of 'a Welfare World'. Those countries assuming leadership with policies of this nature might then with some justification regard themselves as 'Welfare Societies'.

This principle of community responsibility for the provision of adequate resources to implement the objectives of national legislation is particularly relevant to the whole field of welfare. The quantity, territorial distribution and quality of any country's social services - education, medical care, mental health, welfare, children's and other personal community services - depends enormously on the quantity and quality of staff; professional, technical, auxiliary and administrative. To enact legislation designed to create or develop services yet not to invest adequately in the training of doctors, nurses, social workers, teachers, and many other categories of skilled manpower and womanpower is a denial of this principle of community responsibility. To rely on the private market and autonomous professional bodies to fulfil these training needs is nothing less than a ridiculous illusion. The private national market has failed lamentably in this country and in the United States to produce enough doctors, teachers, social workers and nurses. To resort to the international market to remedy the deficiency of national social policies can only have tragic consequences for the poorer countries of the world.

In considering the international aspects of these welfare manpower issues there is one further observation I wish to make before turning to other Conference themes. It seems to me the height of collective immorality for the rich countries of the world to

preach to the poorer countries about the economic
benefits of family planning while, at the same time,
making it more difficult for these countries to
develop family planning programmes by drawing away
the skilled manpower they need for the infrastructure
of services required in which to provide birth control
as well as death control services.

Having delivered myself of these thoughts under the
conveniently broad umbrella-theme of this Conference,
I want now to consider certain other questions of
principle in systems of welfare.

UNIVERSALIST AND SELECTIVE SOCIAL SERVICES

In any discussion today of the future of (what is called)
'The Welfare State' much of the argument revolves round
the principles and objectives of universalist social
services and selective social services. Prominence
was given to this issue in Chapters 2 and 4 of the
'Guide to Studies' prepared two years ago for this
Conference. Time does not seem to have eroded the
importance of this issue.

I think it is unnecessary, therefore, to remind you
in detail of the many complex questions of principles,
goals, methods and assumptions involved in this debate.
In regard to some of them - and particularly the
question of freedom of choice - I have set out my views
in a recently published lecture 'Choice and The Welfare
State'.

Briefly, then, I will restate certain of the more
general points emphasized in this 'Guide'. Consider,
first, the nature of the broad principles which helped
to shape substantial sections of British welfare
legislation in the past, and particularly the principle
of universalism embodied in such post-war enactments
as the National Health Service Act, the Education Act
of 1944, the National Insurance Act and the Family
Allowances Act.

One fundamental historical reason for the adoption
of this principle was the aim of making services available
and accessible to the whole population in such
ways as would not involve users in any humiliating
loss of status, dignity or self-respect. There should
be no sense of inferiority, pauperism, shame or stigma
in the use of a publicly provided service; no attribution
that one was being or becoming a 'public burden'.
Hence the emphasis on the social rights of all citizens
to use or not to use as responsible people the services

made available by the community in respect of certain needs which the private market and the family were unable or unwilling to provide universally. If these services were not provided for everybody by everybody they would either not be available at all, or only for those who could afford them, and for others on such terms as would involve the infliction of a sense of inferiority and stigma.

Avoidance of stigma was not, of course, the only reason for the development of the twin-concepts of social rights and universalism. Many other forces, social, political and psychological, during a century and more of turmoil, revolution, war and change, contributed to the clarification and acceptance of these notions. The novel idea of prevention - novel, at least, to many in the nineteenth century - was, for example, another powerful engine, driven by the Webbs and many other advocates of change, which reinforced the concepts of social rights and universalism. The idea of prevention - the prevention and breaking of the vicious descending spiral of poverty, disease, neglect, illiteracy and destitution - spelt to the protagonists (and still does so) the critical importance of early and easy access to and use of preventive, remedial and rehabilitative services. Slowly and painfully the lesson was learnt that if such services were to be utilized in time and were to be effective in action in a highly differentiated, unequal and class-saturated society, they had to be delivered through socially approved channels; that is to say, without loss of self-respect by the users and their families.

Prevention was not simply a child of biological and psychological theorists; at least one of the grandparents was a powerful economist with a strongly developed streak of nationalism. As Professor Bentley Gilbert has shown in his recent book, 'The Evolution of National Insurance: The Origins of the Welfare State', national efficiency and welfare were seen as complementary. (12) The sin unforgivable was the waste of human resources; thus, welfare was summoned to prevent waste. Hence the beginnings of four of our present-day universalist social services: retirement pensions, the Health Service, unemployment insurance and the school meals service.

The insistent drumming of the national efficiency movement in those far-off days before the First World War is now largely forgotten. Let me then remind you that the whole welfare debate was a curious mixture of humanitarianism, egalitarianism, productivity (as we would call it today) and old-fashioned imperialism. The strident note of the latter is now, we may thank our stars, silenced. The Goddess of Growth has replaced the God of National Fitness. But can we say that the quest for the other objectives is no longer necessary?

Before discussing such a rhetorical question, we need to examine further the principle of universalism. The principle itself may sound simple but the practice - and by that I mean the present operational pattern of welfare in Britain today - is immensely complex. We can see something of this complexity if we analyse welfare (defined here as all publicly provided and subsidized services, statutory, occupational and fiscal) from a number of different standpoints.

AN ANALYTICAL FRAMEWORK

Whatever the nature of the service, activity or function, and whether it be a service in kind, a collective amenity, or a transfer payment in cash or by accountancy, we need to consider (and here I itemize in question-form for the sake of brevity) three central issues:
(a) What is the nature of entitlement to use? Is it legal, contractual or contributory, financial, discretionary or professionally determined entitlement?
(b) Who is entitled and on what conditions? Is account taken of individual characteristics, family characteristics, group characteristics, territorial characteristics or social-biological characteristics? What, in fact, are the rules of entitlement? Are they specific and contractual - like a right based on age - or are they variable, arbitrary or discretionary?
(c) What methods, financial and administrative, are employed in the determination of access, utilization, allocation and payment?

Next we have to reflect on the nature of the service or benefit.

What functions do benefits, in cash, amenity or in kind, aim to fulfil? They may, for example, fulfil any of the following sets of functions, singly or in combination:
1 As partial compensation for identified disservices caused by society (for example, unemployment, some categories of industrial injuries benefits, war pensions, etc.). And, we may add, the disservices

caused by international society as exemplified recently by the oil pollution resulting from the Torrey Canyon disaster costing at least £2 million. (13)

2 As partial compensation for unidentifiable disservices caused by society (for example, 'benefits' related to programmes of slum clearance, urban blight, smoke pollution control, hospital cross-infection and many other socially created disservices).

3 As partial compensation for unmerited handicap (for example, language classes for immigrant children, services for the deprived child, children handicapped from birth, etc.).

4 As a form of protection for society (for example, the probation service, some parts of the mental health services, services for the control of infectious diseases, and so on).

5 As an investment for a future personal or collective gain (education - professional, technical and industrial - is an obvious example here; so also are certain categories of tax deductibles for self-improvement and certain types of subsidized occupational benefits).

6 As an immediate and/or deferred increment to personal welfare or, in other words, benefits (utilities) which add to personal command-over-resources either immediately and/or in the future (for example, subsidies to owner-occupiers and council tenants, tax deductibles for interest charges, pensions, supplementary benefits, curative medical care, and so on).

7 As an element in an integrative objective which is an essential characteristic distinguishing social policy from economic policy. As Kenneth Boulding has said, '... social policy is that which is centred in those institutions that create integration and discourage alienation.' (14) It is thus profoundly concerned with questions of personal identity whereas economic policy centres round exchange or bilateral transfer.

This represents little more than an elementary and partial structural map which can assist in the understanding of the welfare complex today. Needless to say, a more sophisticated (inch to the mile) guide is essential for anything approaching a thorough analysis of the actual functioning of welfare benefit systems. I do not, however, propose to refine further this frame of study now, nor can I analyse by these classifications the several hundred distinctive and functionally separate services and benefits actually in operation in Britain today.

Further study would also have to take account of

the pattern and operation of means-tested services. It has been estimated by Mr M.J. Reddin, my research assistant, that in England and Wales today local authorities are responsible for administering at least 3,000 means-tests, of which about 1,500 are different from each other. (15) This estimate applies only to services falling within the responsibilities of education, child care, health, housing and welfare departments. It follows that in these fields alone there exist some 1,500 different definitions of poverty or financial hardship, ability to pay and rules for charges, which affect the individual and the family. There must be substantial numbers of poor families with multiple needs and multiple handicaps whose perception today of the realities of welfare is to see only a means-testing world. Who helps them, I wonder, to fill up all those forms?

I mention these social facts, by way of illustration, because they do form part of the operational complex of welfare in 1967. My main purpose, however, in presenting this analytical framework was twofold. First, to underline the difficulties of conceptualizing and categorizing needs, causes, entitlement or gatekeeper functions, utilization patterns, benefits and compensations. Second, to suggest that those students of welfare who are seeing the main problem today in terms of universalism versus selective services are present a naïve and oversimplified picture of policy choices.

Some of the reasons for this simple and superficial view are, I think, due to the fact that the approach is dominated by the concept or model of welfare as a 'burden'; as a waste of resources in the provision of benefits for those who, it is said, do not need them. The general solution is thus deceptively simple and romantically appealing; abolish all this welfare complexity and concentrate help on those whose needs are greatest.

Quite apart from the theoretical and practical immaturity of this solution, which would restrict the public services to a minority in the population leaving the majority to buy their own education, social security, medical care and other services in a supposedly free market, certain other important questions need to be considered.

As all selective services for this minority would have to apply some test of need - eligibility, on what bases would tests be applied and, even more crucial, where would the lines be drawn for benefits which function as compensation for identified disservices, compensation for unidentifiable disservices, compensation for unmerited handicap, as a form of social protection, as an investment, or as an increment to personal welfare? Can rules of entitlement and access be drawn on purely 'ability to pay' criteria without distinction of cause? And if the causal agents of need cannot be identified or are so diffuse as to defy the wit of law - as they so often are today - then is not the answer 'no compensation and no redress'? In other words, the case for concentrated selective services resolves itself into an argument for allowing the social costs or diswelfares of the economic system to lie where they fall.

The emphasis today on 'welfare' and the 'benefits of welfare' often tends to obscure the fundamental fact that for many consumers the services used are not essentially benefits or increments to welfare at all; they represent partial compensations for disservices, for social costs and social insecurities which are the product of a rapidly changing industrial-urban society. They are part of the price we pay to some people for bearing part of the costs of other people's progress; the obsolescence of skills, redundancies, premature retirements, accidents, many categories of disease and handicap, urban blight and slum clearance, smoke pollution, and a hundred-and-one other socially generated disservices. They are the socially caused diswelfares; the losses involved in aggregate welfare gains.

What is also of major importance today is that modern society is finding it increasingly difficult to identify the causal agent or agencies, and thus to allocate the costs of disservices and charge those who are responsible. It is not just a question of benefit allocation - of whose 'Welfare State' - but also of loss allocation - whose 'Diswelfare State'.

If identification of the agents of diswelfare were possible - if we could legally name and blame the culprits - then, in theory at least, redress could be obtained through the courts by the method of monetary compensation for damages. But multiple causality and the diffusion of disservices - the modern choleras of change - make this solution impossible. We have, therefore, as societies to make other choices; either to provide social services, or to allow the social costs of the system to lie where they fall. The nineteenth century chose the latter - the *laissez faire* solution - because it had neither a germ theory of disease nor a social theory of causality; an answer which can hardly be entertained today by a richer society equipped with more knowledge about the dynamics of change. But knowledge in this context must not, of course, be equated with wisdom.

If this argument can be sustained, we are thus compelled to return to our analytical framework of the functional concepts of benefit and, within this context, to consider the role of universalist and selective social services. Non-discriminating universalist services are in part the consequence of unidentifiable causality. If disservices are wasteful (to use the economists' concept of 'waste') so welfare has to be 'wasteful'.

The next question that presents itself is this: can we and should we, in providing benefits and compensation (which in practice can rarely be differentially provided), distinguish between 'faults' in the individual (moral, psychological or social) and the 'faults of society'? If all services are provided - irrespective of whether they represent benefits, amenity, social protection or compensation - on a discriminatory, means-test basis, do we not foster both the sense of personal failure and the stigma of a public burden? The fundamental objective of all such tests of eligibility is to keep people out; not to let them in. They must, therefore, be treated as applicants or supplicants; not beneficiaries or consumers.

It is a regrettable but human fact that money (and the lack of it) is linked to personal and family self-respect. This is one element in what has been called the 'stigma of the means test'. Another element is the historical evidence we have that separate discriminatory services for poor people have always tended to be poor quality services; read the history of the panel system under National Health Insurance; read Beveridge on workmen's compensation; Newsom on secondary modern schools; Plowden on standards of primary schools in slum areas; Townsend on Part III accommodations in 'The Last Refuge', (16) and so on. (17)

In the past, poor quality selective services for poor people were the product of a society which saw 'welfare' as a residual; as a public burden. The primary purpose of the system and the method of discrimination was, therefore, deterrence (it was also an effective rationing device). To this end, the most effective instrument was to induce among recipients (children as well as adults) a sense of personal fault, of personal failure, even if the benefit was wholly or partially a compensation for disservices inflicted by society.

THE REAL CHALLENGE IN WELFARE

Today, with this heritage, we face the positive challenge of providing selective, high quality services for poor people over a large and complex range of welfare; of positively discriminating on a territorial, group or 'rights' basis in favour of the poor, the handicapped, the deprived, the coloured, the homeless, and the social casualties of our society. Universalism is not, by itself alone, enough: in medical care, in wage-related social security, and in education. This much we have learnt in the past two decades from the facts about inequalities in the distribution of incomes and wealth, and in our failure to close many gaps in differential access to and effective utilization of particular branches of our social services. (18)

If I am right, I think that Britain is beginning to identify the dimensions of this challenge of positive, selective discrimination - in income maintenance, in education, in housing, in medical care and mental health, in child welfare, and in the tolerant integration of immigrants and citizens from overseas; of preventing especially the second generation from becoming (and of seeing themselves as) second-class citizens. We are seeking ways and means, values, methods and techniques, of positive discrimination without the infliction, actual or imagined, of a sense of personal failure and individual fault.

At this point, considering the nature of the search in all its ramifying complexities, I must now state my general conclusion. It is this. The challenge that faces us is not the choice between universalist and selective social services. The real challenge resides in the question: what particular infrastructure of universalist services is needed in order to provide a framework of values and opportunity bases within and around which can be developed socially acceptable selective services aiming to discriminate positively, with the minimum risk of stigma, in favour of those whose needs are greatest.

This, to me, is the fundamental challenge. In different ways and in particular areas it confronts the Supplementary Benefits Commission, the Seebohm Committee, the National Health Service, the Ministry of Housing and Local Government, the National Committee for Commonwealth Immigrants, the policy-making readers of the Newsom Report and the Plowden Report on educational priority areas, the Scottish Report, 'Social Work and the Community', and thousands of social workers and administrators all over the country wrestling with the problems of needs and priorities. In all the main spheres of need, some structure of universalism is an essential pre-requisite to selective positive discrimination; it provides a general system of values and a sense of community; socially approved agencies for clients, patients and consumers, and also for the recruitment, training and deployment of staff at all levels; it sees welfare, not as a burden, but as complementary and as an instrument of change and, finally, it allows positive discriminatory services to be provided as rights for categories of people and for classes of need in terms of priority social areas and other impersonal classifications.

Without this infrastructure of welfare resources and framework of values we should not, I conclude, be able to identify and discuss the next steps in progress towards a 'Welfare Society'.

NOTES

Lecture delivered at the British National Conference on Social Welfare, London, April 1967, and published in the 'Proceedings of the Conference'.

1   See for example, 'The Times', 28 July 1965, and 6 August 1965; article by H. Heymann, Gnomes of Zurich with a London Address, in 'The Times', 8 January 1966, and 'The Times', 4 April 1967 (report by P. Jay, Economics Correspondent), and 'The Economist', editorial Into the Wasteland, 23 July 1966, and editorial note on 'Poverty', 22 April 1967.
2   J. Enoch Powell, 'Medicine and Politics', London, Pitman, 1966, p. 72.
3   See R.M. Titmuss, 'Income Distribution and Social Change', London, Allen & Unwin, 1962.
4   G. Henderson, Institute for Training and Research, 'New York Times', 6 November 1966, p. E 11. See also J.A. Perkins, President of Cornell University and Chairman of the President's Advisory Committee on Foreign Assistance Programmes, 'Foreign Affairs', July 1966; Brinley Thomas, in The New Immigration, 'The Annals of the American Academy of Political

and Social Science', September 1966; G. Sutherland, 'The Political Quarterly', vol. 38, no. 1, January-March 1967; Lord Bowden, House of Lords, 'Hansard', 20 December 1966, cols 1971-80; and H.G. Grubel and A.D. Scott, 'Journal of Political Economy', University of Chicago, 1966, vol. 14, no. 4, p. 231.

5 K.M. West, Foreign Interns and Residents in the United States, 'Journal of Medical Education', December 1965, vol. 40, pp. 1110-29.

6 'The dollar value per year of this "foreign aid" to the United States approximately equals the total cost of all of our medical aid, private and public, to foreign nations'(K.M. West, ibid., p. 1127). About three-fourths of all foreign medical trainees in the USA are from developing countries.

7 T.C. Gibson, British Physicians on Medical School Faculties in North America, 'Brit. Med. J.', 1967, i, 692.

8 Israel, as well as many other countries, is affected by the shortage of doctors in the USA. Of the 265 doctors graduating from Israeli medical schools in 1963-65, nearly 40 per cent left for the USA (statement by Minister of Health quoted in 'Haaretz', 21 March 1967).

9 K.R. Hill, Cost of Undergraduate Medical Education in Britain, 'British Medical Journal', 1964, i, 300-2.

10 Ministry of Health and Department of Health for Scotland, 'Report of the Committee to Consider the Future Numbers of Medical Practitioners and the Appropriate Intake of Medical Students', London, HMSO, 1957. Seven of this eleven-man Committee were eminent members of the medical profession and the Chairman was an ex-Minister of Health, Sir Henry Willink.

11 In May 1962 a special committee set up by the British Medical Association to consider recruitment to the medical profession concluded in its report that in spite of certain obvious indications of a shortage of doctors it was not prepared to commit itself on the need for more medical students ('The Times', 11 May 1962). Dr R.G. Gibson, chairman of this committee (and now Chairman of the Council), said two months later that the profession had recently experienced a 'glut of doctors. At present there seemed to be a shortage, but care must be taken not to create unemployment in the profession a few years from now' ('Brit. Med. J.', Supp., ii, 26, 27 July 1962).

12 B.B. Gilbert, London, Michael Joseph, 1966.
13 'The Torrey Canyon', Cmnd 3246, London, HMSO, 1967.
14 K.E. Boulding, The Boundaries of Social Policy, 'Social Work', vol. 12, no. 1, January 1967, p. 7.
15 This study is to be published by Mr Reddin as an 'Occasional Paper on Social Administration'.
16 P. Townsend, 'The Last Refuge', London, Routledge, 1964.
17 See also R.M. Titmuss, 'Problems of Social Policy', London, HMSO, 1950.
18 See P. Townsend, 'Poverty, Socialism and Labour in Power', Fabian tract, 371, 1967, and R.J. Nicholson, The Distribution of Personal Income, 'Lloyds Bank Review', January 1967, p. 11.

7 Respect for persons and public morality

R. S. Downie and Elizabeth Telfer

1 PUBLIC MORALITY

In our first chapter we tried to elucidate in general terms the view that respect for persons as ends expresses what is fundamental to morality. In this chapter we shall begin the more detailed defence of the view by showing that respect for persons is the ultimate principle presupposed in our ordinary judgments of social morality.

The strategy of the chapter will be to begin by suggesting the partial truth of utilitarianism as a theory of public or social morality, and arguing that this theory hardly makes sense at all unless we presuppose that persons are to be respected. We shall then develop utilitarianism by showing how it can accommodate the existence of moral rules and social institutions. Ordinary moral judgments, however, lay stress on the concept of equality - there is a minimum equality of treatment which ought not to be overridden by any degree of social utility. Hence, we need to qualify our acceptance of the principle of utility by making room for a second principle of equality. Equality, however, also presupposes respect for persons, for the belief that a minimum equality of treatment is morally required depends on the prior notion that each person matters as an individual and so makes some claims which cannot be overridden. Ordinary moral judgments require us also to make room for a principle of liberty, which is roughly to the effect that the restrictions on a person's liberty which are morally permissible ought to be the minimum necessary for the maintenance of social utility and equality. The reason why ordinary moral views lay stress on liberty, we suggest, is that a person must have a certain elbowroom if he is to develop in himself those attributes which make him characteristically a person.

Our contention, then, is that an adequate theory of social morality requires the three principles of utility, equality and liberty, and these, we maintain, all presuppose the principle of respect for persons as their ultimate justification. Alternatively, we may say that they are all the expressions of the attitude of *agape* in the face of the complexities of the organization of a social system.

2 UTILITARIANISM

It is one of the most generally agreed judgments of ordinary morality that unselfishness is to be commended and selfishness condemned. We can therefore say that ordinary moral judgments require us to make the ends of others our own by helping them to get what they want. This will include both a negative aspect - refraining from *interfering* with their pursuit of their aims - and a positive aspect of *co-operation*. It also covers the activity of helping them to avoid what they want to avoid, which can be called by the blanket terms of 'pain', 'distress', 'frustration', 'embarrassment'. Here again, helping people to avoid pain, distress or the like has a positive and a negative aspect: the negative aspect is not *causing* them pain or distress and the positive aspect is the taking of steps to *relieve* their pain or distress. But this gives us no clear guidance for action. For an action may relieve the sufferings of some while causing suffering to others, or we may be faced with a choice between different possibilities of action each of which will bring somebody something he wants. We therefore need a principle of action which would help us to decide what to do in such situations; and the principle which suggests itself at once is some version of the utilitarian greatest happiness principle. There are various ways of stating the principle, but let us make use of the most familiar, that of J.S. Mill: (1) 'Actions are right in proportion as they tend to promote happiness, wrong as they tend to promote the reverse of happiness.'

Now there is surely no point in organizing action to maximize happiness unless we think that happiness matters, and it is unintelligible to suppose that happiness matters without supposing that the people whose happiness is in question matter. But to say that they matter in this way is to say that they are objects of respect. Hence, the principle of utility presupposes that of respect for persons. Indeed, the requirements of ordinary morality which (we have just argued) give rise to the principle of utility are precisely those for which the attitude of sympathy provides a natural motivation (as we saw in Chapter I, p. 24), and sympathy is an integral part of the attitude of respect.

Instead of speaking of 'happiness' Mill could equally well have used the language of wants and their satisfaction, and indeed would have avoided a good many difficulties if he had done so. We may therefore reword Mill's formula to fit what we have said so far about the fulfilment of others' wants, and suggest as a guide to the requirements of the principle of respect for persons the following rule: 'The right action is that which fulfils the most desire' (including in 'desire' both desire to avoid things and desire to have things, and calculating the amount of desire with reference both to the numbers of people whose desire is fulfilled and to the intensity with which they felt it).

The criticisms which might be made of this formula are almost endless, but we shall concentrate mainly on those based on the nature of moral rules (which will enable us to develop our theory of social morality by bringing in the idea of institutional structure), and on the claims of the principles of equality and liberty.

3 MORAL RULES

An objector to utilitarianism might say that although it may be true in some contexts that we call those actions right which make for the best consequences for the majority, in other contexts we seem to call actions right or wrong simply because they are or are not performed in conformity with moral rules. Thus, when we say, 'A promise is a promise', we have not thought that keeping a promise will lead to the best consequences for the majority; we simply issue a reminder that there is a moral rule that one ought to keep one's promise. Again, if a person has borrowed money it is right and obligatory that he should return it simply because there is a moral rule that debts ought to be paid. We do not say or think that a person ought to pay back the money he has borrowed because this will produce the best possible consequences for the majority; we think he ought to pay it back because there is a moral rule that debt-paying is obligatory. Indeed, there may be cases where the consequences of paying a debt will be worse for all than those of not paying it; yet we should still say that debt-paying is right. Suppose, for example, that a person has borrowed £100 and that the lender intends to squander the money in a selfish way when it is returned while the borrower will use it in a worth-while way. The best possible consequences for the majority would seemingly result in this case if the money were not returned, and yet we should still say that there is a rule that debt-paying is obligatory and that therefore the money ought to be returned. The objection, then, is that our ordinary views are not precisely reflected in the utilitarian thesis that actions are right or wrong in so far as they produce the best possible consequences for the majority; some actions may be right for this reason, but we regard others as right simply because they are instances of moral rules.

It is necessary in a reply to the objection to distinguish between two possible ways of interpreting it. The first interpretation takes the objection to be one of fact: that, as a matter of fact, we do not always in everyday life refer to consequences when we are wondering whether acts are right or wrong. The second interpretation takes the objection to be a conceptual one: that there is a conceptual gap between the rightness of (some) actions and consequences, and a conceptual link between the rightness of (some) actions and moral rules. The second interpretation is the one which characterizes the deontologist's position. Let us consider the interpretations in more detail.

The first interpretation is reminding us that we often regard an action as right simply because it is governed by a rule - of truth-telling, promise-keeping, or the like - but it leaves open the question of the connexion between rightness and consequences. Now if the utilitarian can provide a justification for the existence of rules it might seem that he can consistently meet the objection so interpreted.

In his attempt to provide such a justification the utilitarian can point out that we do not as individuals have the necessary capacities to work out the consequences of all our actions. Our experience is limited and our knowledge and understanding are limited and we therefore cannot always work out the calculus of consequences for ourselves, let alone for society as a whole. Moreover, supposing we could calculate the effects of our actions, we do not always

have time to do so before acting; we are often obliged
to make up our minds quickly on what is right or wrong,
whereas it would take time to go into the probable
consequences of our actions. Hence, the argument runs,
moral rules have grown up which express the accumulated
wisdom of mankind on the consequences of action.
Mill compares this function of moral rules to that of
signposts or the 'Nautical Almanack': we have signposts to guide us across country which may be unknown
to us. (2) Again, the sailor does not need to make
his calculations at sea but goes to sea with his calculations already made for him in the 'Nautical Almanack',
and similarly, we go across the sea of life with the
consequences of our actions already calculated for us
in moral rules. Thus, the utilitarian sees moral
rules as being rules of thumb or ready reckoners which
compensate for the deficiencies in the experience, knowledge, understanding and time of the individual person.

   A utilitarian can also stress another function performed by moral rules. The nature of this function
emerges if it is pointed out that in addition to the
deficiencies for which 'lightning calculators' can
compensate, human beings are also deficient in altruism
and therefore require the threat of coercion to
encourage them to seek majority interests rather than
their own. The advantage of rules is that not only
do they prescribe the types of action which are conducive to majority interest, their very existence
helps to secure the compliance of most people. The
reasons for this are, first, that habits of obedience
and the desire to conform to established custom are
deeply engrained in most forms of society, so that
people will conform to a rule simply because it is a
rule. Second, where the rules are basic to the continued stability of a society they may be incorpora-
ted in a legal system and supported by the threat of
legal sanction, and also by the sanction of social
approval and disapproval. Here then is another main
function of moral rules - by their very existence, and
by the legal and social sanctions which can be attached
to them, they can reinforce behaviour patterns of
proven utility. It may therefore seem that far from
being an objection to a utilitarian view of the criterion of right action, such an interpretation of moral
rules enriches the theory and makes it more accurately
reflect our ordinary views.

   But moral rules can be assimilated by the utilitarian
theory only in so far as they are regarded merely as
guides, as administrative rules to ensure that in view

of human weakness the best possible consequences for the majority are in fact brought about. It is possible to argue, however, (and this is the second, the deontological, interpretation) that such a view of moral rules does not adequately reflect our ordinary views about them. (3) According to the utilitarian interpretation, moral rules are guides - signposts or almanacks - to help us calculate the consequences of our actions. But if we are ourselves lightning calculators it would seem on this interpretation of them that we are entitled to ignore rules, whereas our ordinary view is that we are not entitled to be cavalier about rules. Again, if for some reason of flood or landslide a signpost no longer points to the right route, we are entitled to pick our own route; and so it would seem that if for some reason keeping to a moral rule will no longer bring about the best possible consequences then we may, or perhaps should, ignore a rule such as that debts ought to be paid. But this, it may be argued, is precisely not our ordinary view, which is rather that debts ought to be paid regardless of the consequences. We may sum up the points of difference by saying that on the utilitarian interpretation the rightness of actions is necessarily connected with the production of the best possible consequences, and only contingently connected with moral rules, whereas on the rival deontological interpretation the rightness of some actions at least is necessarily connected with rules and only contingently, if at all, connected with good consequences. The objection of the deontologist - and it seems a valid one - is that, if the existence of moral rules admits of no justification other than the utilitarian one so far provided, we ought to have no hesitation at all about ignoring a rule if we think we can thereby bring about the best possible consequences; but this is simply not our ordinary attitude towards moral rules.

In reply, the utilitarian can point to the consequences of the conceptual gap between rightness and the production of the best possible consequences. If the deontologist is correct, it is theoretically possible that the performance of a duty could on a given occasion make the world a worse place than it would have been if the duty had not been performed. It might be argued that the very fact that a duty has been performed must mean that some good consequences will be brought about. But even if we grant that the mere fact of duty-performance is itself good, it still may be the case that the total state of the world after the duty-performance is worse than it would have been if the duty had not been performed. And if this is a consequence of the deontologist's interpretation of moral rules his interpretation must be rejected as a bad case of rule-worship. There are other objections to deontology, but this is the strongest, and the one which arises most directly from the utilitarian position. But, even if we grant that this utilitarian criticism of deontology is valid as far as it goes, the question still arises as to whether the utilitarian can answer the criticism made by the deontologist.

It may be said that he can, by distinguishing two different kinds of rules. (4) Some rules, he may contend, are, when all is said and done, only empirical generalizations about the results of types of action. Actions are not made right or wrong because of the existence of these empirical generalizations forbidding or enjoining them; rather we have the empirical generalizations because we have learned by experience that certain types of action are liable to have consequences which are morally bad or good. For example, 'One ought not to pass on malicious gossip' is a rule based on the fact that the transmission of malicious gossip can be misleading, hurtful or injurious to a person's reputation. It is not that any one case of malicious gossip is wrong *because of* the rule, for in judging the action as wrong in a given case one need not refer to the rule at all; it is simply that the rule provides safe moral guidance if one is in doubt. Again, it is often tiresome, irritating or hurtful to make a joke to someone about his appearance, and consequently one may make it a rule to avoid this line of witticism. But such a rule merely expresses what experience teaches; the wrongness of hurting a person's feelings in this way does not depend on the existence of the rule. The utilitarian can therefore recognize the existence of rules in the form of 'wise saws and modern instances', but the rightness or wrongness of the actions is established independently of the rules. Moreover, since rules of this type are only generalizations, they readily admit of exceptions - cases where an action of a kind which normally has bad consequences will have good consequences, and *vice versa*. When exceptions do occur we may abandon the rule without a qualm, since the rightness or wrongness of the action does not depend on it. The utilitarian may however add that we should be very cautious about assuming that any particular case is an exception, and perhaps leave a margin for error, as it were.

Other rules, however, have a different logical status. They are not empirical generalizations about the consequences of actions; rather they lay down the obligations inherent in some institution which is artificial in the sense that it owes its existence to rules. This is the case, for example, with rules that one should keep promises and with rules concerning property, such as 'Do not steal' and 'Pay your debts'; there would be no such things as promises, stealing or debts if there were not rules of conduct defining them. The rightness of promise-keeping or debt-paying and the wrongness of stealing can therefore be said to depend essentially on the existence of rules, and thus to be artificial, in that it owes its existence to the institution which defines the practice. Because of this, one can say that 'Promise-keeping is right' or 'Debt-paying is right' or 'Stealing is wrong' can all be in a sense analytic propositions: one could not explain the notion of promising, for example, without reference to the rule laying down the obligation to keep promises. But it should be noted that it is only *within* the institution (as it were) that 'Promise-keeping is right' etc. are analytic; there is presupposed a logically prior *synthetic* moral judgment that it is right that the given institution should operate. The utilitarian argument is that the operation of such institutions as a whole may be in the general interest even although individual instances of promise-keeping and debt-paying (say) may seem to be against it. We undermine the institution if we raise the question of interest in every case; the rules of the institution must be applied to preserve the institution. In this way the rules of institutions differ from empirical generalizations about the consequences of individual actions.

Now to say that the rules of institutions must be applied because they are rules sounds like an appeal to a new moral value of impartiality - 'If you keep your promise to A, you must also keep it to B'. But in fact it is only a reminder that since we all benefit from the operation of the institution as a whole we are not justified in making exceptions to its rules simply because some bad consequences may result from keeping to them in a given instance. Rather, since the utility of the institution depends on continued trust in its operation, *any* departure from its rules is *prima facie* wrong and to be regretted. Here there is a contrast with empirical generalizations about consequences, which can be ignored without a qualm if a person can calculate the consequences more accurately for himself. To say that any departure from an institutional rule is *prima facie* wrong is not to say that exceptions are never permissible; but it is to say that an essential element in any calculation of the consequences of the projected exception must be the effect that making an exception will have on the status of the institution itself. In other words, where the rule is that of an institution from which we all benefit, the consideration 'What would happen if everyone did it?' is morally relevant when an exception is mooted. No new moral value of impartiality is introduced simply by this consideration. And, in fact, as far as *moral* substance goes, rules such as 'Keep promises' actually incorporate a certain partiality or inequality. The promisee or the creditor is in a privileged position, and his claim overrides that of others concerned. We may say here that a man's position as promisee or as creditor gives him special *rights* which must be considered in preference to the majority interest; but that this inequality is justified in the majority interest.

The institutions of property and promise-making, with the rights and correlative duties bound up with these, are institutions in a rather vague and weak sense; the rules are not necessarily written down but are agreed upon by a kind of tacit consent. In any society, however, there will be many other institutions, some of a far more formal character. Indeed, viewed as a system, society consists not of an aggregate of individual persons but of a complex of institutions, such as businesses, factories, trade unions, schools, churches, military organizations, political and legal institutions, welfare organizations, banks and so on. An institution, in this sense, is a cluster of rights and duties with some social function, although, of course, it does not operate on its own but is operated by individual persons, who are vested with the rights and duties of the institution in which they operate. As before, the exercise of specific institutional rights or the performance of specific institutional duties will not be directly connected with the general welfare but obliquely so, *via* the operation of the institution as a whole. Thus, while it is not always apt to ask whether a specific institutional duty promotes the general welfare it is always apt to ask whether an entire institution, or the current form of it, does so.

These facts about institutions explain many judgments

we make which at first sight go against the principle of utility. For example, we do not feel that a man is doing wrong in confining the area of his service to others to a small circle such as his immediate family and friends, although it might seem that the general interest would be better served if he did not merely consider a privileged group. The reason why we do not think it wrong is now clear; a man should consider his family in preference to others because he has special duties to his family and they have special rights against him; a man is justified in 'taking on' these special duties because the institution of the family is (we may suppose) more conducive to the general interest than any viable alternative. A great many of the ordinary person's duties are institutional duties of this kind; the scope left to him for direct consideration of the general welfare (such as by charitable contribution of money or service) will be small. To say this (it must be repeated) is not to say that institutional duties *never* admit of exceptions; such a position would not be utilitarian and would smack rather of the rule-worship of which we accused the deontologist. It is to say that exceptions to institutional duties will be very infrequent indeed, since the connexion between the rightness of such a duty and the best possible consequences is oblique; the good consequences stem from the continued operation of the system as a whole.

We can now sum up our discussion by saying that it is possible to state utilitarianism in a way which does justice to our ordinary views on moral rules, provided we distinguish between empirical generalizations about the consequences of actions and institutional rules. Such a distinction enables us to incorporate the valid insights of deontology without committing us to the conceptual gap between rightness and good consequences which was the weak point of the theory. No crucial objection to utilitarianism can therefore be based on a consideration of the place of moral rules in our moral outlook. But a crucial objection can be based on an analysis of the concept of equality.

4 EQUALITY

So far we have suggested that rights are claims of privilege, asserting an inequality which, if justifiable at all, is justifiable in terms of majority interest. But is extreme inequality morally justified if it promotes the general welfare? If this were so, it would justify building the happiness of the majority on the sufferings of the minority.

An example of this would be a society where there are a few slaves in proportion to the free community, and it seems that the majority of society will be more prosperous under this arrangement than if the slaves are freed. We would, however, be likely to criticize this society, on the grounds that it is *unjust* or inequitable; it therefore seems that we judge such situations not only in terms of the amount of benefit but also in terms of the way the benefit is distributed, and may prefer a situation where it is reasonably equally distributed to one where the total of benefit is higher but the disparities between the best off and the worst off are great.

Utilitarians have often quite cheerfully admitted the need for the principle of equality, but have not seen that this means abandoning the claim that the principle of utility on its own can account for our views on the rightness of actions. Mill, for example, in his chapter on Justice in 'Utilitarianism' (5) says that the dictum - 'everybody to count for one, nobody for more than one' - expresses the principle of equality, and that it might be written under the principle of utility as an explanatory commentary. In a footnote he goes on: 'This implication, in the first principle of the utilitarian scheme, of perfect impartiality between persons, is regarded by Mr Herbert Spencer (in his 'Social Statics') as a disproof of utility to be a sufficient guide to right; since (he says) the principle of utility presupposes the anterior principle, that everybody has an equal right to happiness.' Mill, however, denies that the impartiality to which Spencer refers involves a second principle alongside that of utility. Impartiality, he says, 'is not a *pre*-supposition; not a premise needful to support the principle of utility, but the very principle itself.... If there is any anterior principle implied, it can be no more than this, that the truths of arithmetic are applicable to the valuation of happiness, as of all other measurable quantities.' In the passage quoted Mill seems to have missed the point Spencer was making. Thus he says that Spencer's account of the anterior principle to the principle of utility, that everyone has an equal right to happiness, 'may be more correctly described as supposing that equal amounts of happiness are equally desirable, whether felt by the same or different persons.' But this latter thesis, so far from being a mere re-wording of Spencer's, is surely incompatible with it. Mill's version allows the grossest inequalities in the way the happiness is *distributed,* whereas Spencer's does not. Bentham's dictum in itself seems to be ambiguous as between the two possibilities; but his general account of the felicific calculus is clearly compatible with inequality in distribution, and thus we may assume that his account does not incorporate equality any more than does Mill's thesis.

We have raised the question of equal distribution of benefit in connexion with an institution or system of rights and duties, but the same question can arise in connexion with the consequences of an individual action; it sometimes seems that the best consequences overall can be secured only at the price of the suffering of a few. Again, it seems that in judging such situations we take account not only of the total of benefit but also of the way in which it is distributed. In short, we judge consequences not only by a principle of utility but also by a principle of equality.

The principle of equality demands that any inequality in treatment must be justifiable in some way; the presupposition is that equal treatment is appropriate, and the onus is on him who discriminates to justify his procedure by pointing to some difference between the parties which affords a reasonable ground for discrimination. The concept of 'relevant differences' between people (differences which do in fact justify the discrimination being made) is thus an important one in connexion with equality.

It is in this context that the idea of universalizability can be introduced. There are really two distinct notions covered by the term 'universalizability', the logical and the moral, and these notions are employed in two distinct principles of universalizability. The logical principle concerns rules and reasons, and states that if a rule of action or reason for action applies to one case, it must apply to all similar cases. In other words, if one is applying a rule or acting for a reason no distinction of treatment may be made which is not based on some criterion of difference. This principle simply follows from the fact that rules and reasons are (at least by implication) *general* in scope. But it is of the greatest importance in connexion with the rule-following nature of persons. For human beings often justify their conduct in terms of rules and reasons; and in so doing they are logically bound to see those rules and reasons as justifying similar conduct by others in similar situations. (This indeed is part of what Kant meant when he spoke of men as legislating for others.) This is not, of course, to say that rules apply without exceptions, but only that differences in application logically must be on *principle* - that is to say, they must really constitute qualifications in the original rule, rather than arbitrary departures from it.

As an example of the logical principle of universalizability, consider a rule like 'All young men must serve in the Army for two years'. This rule as it stands applies to all young men. I cannot logically hold this rule and then say that it does not apply to some particular young man - unless I am prepared to explain what is different about him which exempts him (for example, poor eyesight) and thus in effect add a qualifying clause to the rule which could exempt others also. In other words, the rule becomes: 'All young men except those with poor eyesight must serve in the Army for two years'. This example shows how reasons are universalizable too; if I say 'This young man ought not to serve because he has poor eyesight' I am giving a reason which would apply to all other young men in the same situation.

The *moral* principle of universalizability is really a statement of the presupposition that equal treatment is appropriate. It may be expressed as follows: 'No distinction of treatment may be made which is not based on some *morally relevant* criterion of difference'. It thus requires that differences of treatment be not merely explained (as the logical principle demands) but morally justified. For example, I would satisfy the logical principle of universalizability if I gave as grounds for exempting certain people from the Army the fact that they all had blue eyes. But this fact is of no moral relevance. If on the other hand the criterion is something like 'being married' we can see why such a factor might be held to *justify* discrimination, not merely explain it.

Often the kinds of difference which are held to be morally relevant derive from the gap between equal treatment and equal satisfaction; if people differ sufficiently in need or capacity or situation they will not get equal satisfaction from equal treatment. For example, the married soldier's difference in situation means that treating him similarly to the unmarried soldier will not produce similar results in terms of happiness. But morally relevant differences may stem also from demands separate from equality altogether. Thus utilitarian grounds may justify a difference in treatment between some people and others, and so may grounds drawn from the principle of liberty. We shall shortly see how this happens when we discuss education as an example of the working of the principle of equality.

Difference in treatment is held by some to be justified also by difference in *desert*. (6) The notion of desert is the notion that how a man should be treated depends on his merits and demerits. These may be either moral or non-moral. Thus Aristotle, assuming that just distribution must be according to merit, suggests as possible candidates for merit free birth, noble birth, or wealth. (7)

Now opinions differ as to how far desert really creates a moral demand separate from those of utility and equality. (8) An extreme view would be that it is desert which is the primary value and that equality is not a separate value at all but is simply a corollary of a principle of desert. For if we have a principle that each should be treated according to his deserts, this implies that those of equal desert should be treated equally and those of unequal desert should be treated unequally, but it does not set up equality as an independent value. This seems indeed to be Aristotle's view.

But our current moral views seem rather to assign a comparatively small part in justifying inequalities to the notion of desert. This is especially so in the case of merits or demerits for which the possessor is not responsible, where we are apt to think that equality demands the rectifying of the imbalance rather than 'giving to him that hath'. Exceptions to this, such as 'He's a bright boy and deserves to succeed' are often to be seen as expressions of the principle of liberty rather than of desert. (9)

The principle of equality, then, is not absolute. We do not hold that all people must be treated equally in all respects, but rather that the claim of equality must be balanced against other claims. But at the same time we hold that there is a minimum claim of equality which *is* absolute. There are inequalities so extreme that they cannot be justified by appeal to the general utility or to any other value. This can be put another way by saying that each individual has rights to certain basic benefits (or at least to

freedom from certain basic evils) which must not be
infringed however far others would benefit thereby.
The degree of inequality allowable will depend partly
on whether those who come out of it badly choose or
consent to it in some sense, and also partly on
whether they (as well as the more privileged party)
will be better off than they would have been under a
more egalitarian arrangement (as may be the case for
example with the paying of high wages as an incentive
to acquire skills).

We can now see that even the moral principle of
universalizability ('No distinction of treatment may
be made which is not based on some morally relevant
criterion of difference') expresses only one aspect of
the principle of equality. To do justice to the
demands of equality we must add another principle to
that of moral universalizability, viz 'Extreme inequalities are not permissible on any grounds'.

We shall now discuss briefly some concrete examples
of the interplay of the principles of utility and
equality. Take first participation in government,
which for most people is equivalent to voting.

We would normally say that everyone has an equal
right to vote, and that differences such as the colour
of a man's skin could not be relevant grounds for
excluding him. The only criterion for relevance here
is whether any fact about a man disables him from
benefiting by the exercise of the right. This sounds
at first sight as though we could exclude people from
voting if they were sufficiently ignorant or unintel-
ligent, on the grounds that such people cannot know
what is in their interest and so the vote is of no use
to them. But this would be a mistake. Voting is
valuable not only for the benefits which the voter can
win for himself by exercising his vote wisely. To
be able to vote is a benefit in itself; the right to
a say (however misguided) in matters which concern a
man is demanded by respect for persons as self-deter-
mining creatures. One can indeed speak of a right to
make one's own mistakes, and this is one instance of
it. (10)

Education is another commodity which is good both
in itself and in the further benefits which it brings.
Here again the basic presumption is that everyone has
an equal right to education. But educational resources, such as money, equipment and manpower, are
in practice concentrated on two groups: those who are
especially handicapped mentally or physically (and, if
the Plowden recommendations are adopted, by their

environment), and those who are especially gifted. These two types of 'positive discrimination' (to use Lady Plowden's expression) (11) can both be justified by the principle of respect for persons, but in entirely different ways. Thus discrimination in favour of the underprivileged is in reality an equalizing measure to reduce their handicap. Unequal *treatment* is needed to produce *results* which are not too unequal. On the other hand, discrimination in favour of the gifted is justified partly by the fact that they are especially capable of benefiting by extended education and partly by utilitarian considerations. The utilitarian justification is obvious; this is an example of a situation where everyone, not merely the privileged group, benefits from inequality. The justification in terms of difference of capacity is a more complex one and depends on an understanding of what kind of benefit education is. It seems to be valuable because it contributes to a particular kind of self-development - some would say the most important kind. (For a discussion of self-development see Chapter III.) Now one cannot speak of a right to equal self-development through education, since this type of self-development is not something of which everyone is equally capable. What we can say however is that everyone has a right to benefit as far as he is able from education, that equal capacities should be treated equally.

We can now see why the public school system is thought by some to be unjust - it gives educational privilege to those who differ neither in need nor in ability to benefit. But if we consider the chief arguments against abolishing it, we shall see the workings of another principle which is a very important part of respect for persons, that of liberty, or the right to do as one wishes unless it causes harm to others. This principle is important enough to need separate discussion and we shall turn to it when we have touched on the right to a minimum standard of living as a final example of the principle of equality.

Equality demands, not an equal standard of living for all, but a minimum redistribution of resources which ensures that everyone reaches a minimum standard of living. Greater equalization than this is ruled out partly by utility, partly by what appears to be an appeal to desert. Thus we think that giving everyone much the same standard of living whatever he does removes all incentives to work, and also constitutes an injustice to the industrious who 'deserve to succeed' while the lazy man 'deserves to fail'. Now in saying that the lazy man deserves to fail we are not necessarily condemning him morally. Rather we think that the lazy man may be deemed to have *chosen* a lower standard of living for the sake of a quiet life, and that if this seems to him the greater benefit we should not introduce what is in effect an *inequality* by allowing him to have it both ways. But not everyone would rather be poor than hard-working. Of course, people can also be poor through no 'fault' of their own but simply because they possess no talent of high market value; many a dustman would be a doctor or a dancer if he could. We still think, however, that it is justifiable that dancers and doctors should get more than dustmen, partly as an incentive to them to develop their talents, for which industry is needed, and partly because it seems right that by and large a man should be allowed to make what profit he can out of his talents. The first of these considerations appeals to utility, the second to the principle of liberty (which we shall discuss in the next section).

Before we sum up our argument so far let us consider two terms which often cause confusion in this context, namely, 'equity' and 'justice'. 'Equity' means roughly 'treating people equally when they should be treated equally, and differently when they should be treated differently'. Thus, equity is not the same as equality, and is quite consistent both with the view that equality has no independent claim, and with the view that there is a minimum independent claim of equality. Accordingly, it is not very informative to say that something is equitable; it does at least suggest however that due regard has been paid to the desert and the claim to equality of the *individual*, and that the issue has not been settled exclusively by an appeal to the expedient, which is of merely utilitarian value.

'Justice' can be used in two ways. It may refer to a man's rights under the specific institutions of a society, his institutional rights as we have called them. Or it may refer to deeper and more important principles in the light of which both instutional rights and the dictates of utility may be judged. These rights are those of equality and of liberty (which we shall discuss later). Justice, if it is conceived of in this more basic sense, is that which asserts the claims of the individual against the utilitarian claims of society. Because of this it is easy to think of justice as embodying respect for persons and of utility as hostile to it. But to think thus is to forget that the majority is made up of individuals. As Raphael says: 'By contrasting the claim of justice, as looking to the interests of the individual, with the claim of utility as looking to the interests of society at large, I do not imply that society is anything other than its members. In our practical deliberations, however, we often find it convenient to think of "the interests of society" as an abstracted entity, since we may know from experience that a course of action is likely to benefit or harm a number of members of our society, while not knowing which particular members will be affected on this occasion. The dangers of the abstraction are countered by the concept of justice, which emphasizes the claims of the individual as such.' (12)

We are now in a position to recapitulate the argument so far. Our burden has been that the principle of utility, in terms of the maximization of the satisfaction of desires, is related to ordinary moral rules in two distinct ways: rules can either be empirical generalizations about the best way to implement the principle, admitting of exceptions like other generalizations, or they can lay down men's duties and rights under some institution which can be justified as a whole in utilitarian terms. We compared this second type of rule to the duties and rights of various roles in the social system, and saw how in both cases rights were privileges giving their possessor a claim prior to that of utility. We then suggested another kind of claim which competes with and perhaps takes precedence over what one might call institutional claims, and modifies the claim of utility - namely, the claim of equality. This too can be expressed in the language of rights; it asserts the right of every man to some basic necessities, however much society at large might benefit by depriving him of them, and it further asserts the right of everyone to equal treatment in all respects unless the inequality can be justified by relevant differences. This demand for a minimum degree of equality in a system of social organization embodies the idea that each individual matters *in himself* as a person quite apart from any special features which may distinguish him. Hence, equality, no less than utility, presupposes the principle of respect for persons.

5 LIBERTY

We have so far suggested by argument and example that the principle of utility must be modified by one of equality if we are to have an account of public morality which reflects our ordinary moral attitudes, and that both these principles presuppose that of respect for persons. We shall now suggest that ordinary moral attitudes require us to modify the requirements of utility yet further by making room for another principle - that of liberty.

The principle of liberty states that it is wrong to curb people's desires unnecessarily, to interfere without justification in people's pursuit of objectives which are of interest to them. This principle seems especially germane to the principle of respect for persons, as the word 'respect' is often used in just this sense of 'tolerate' or 'refrain from interfering with'. The force of 'respect' in this sense is brought out by the example given by the Shorter Oxford Dictionary - that Louis respected the interests of his Protestant subjects. Again, in a characteristic passage, Hare tells us that what 'distinguishes the liberal is that he *respects* the ideals of others as he does his own. This does not mean that he agrees with them - that would be logically impossible, if they are different from his own.... In saying that the liberal respects the ideals of others we mean that he thinks it wrong to interfere with other people's pursuit of their ideals just because they are different from his own; and that he also thinks it wrong to interfere with their interests merely because his own ideal forbids their pursuit, if *their* ideals permit the pursuit of these interests.' (13) It is clear that the concept of respect as non-interference is being used here, and it would be possible to quote from other influential moral philosophers to make the same point.

This notion of respect, in the sense of refraining from interference or regard for liberty, is the central theme of Mill's 'On Liberty', and his main principle expresses it as follows: 'the sole end for which mankind are warranted, individually or collectively, in interfering with the liberty of action of any of their number is self-protection. His own good, either physical or moral, is not a sufficient warrant.' (14) Now what does Mill mean by 'self-protection' here? To answer this, we must consider what was meant above by 'unnecessary' when we said that *unnecessary* interference with the liberty of persons is wrong, and in the course of this discussion we can show how liberty is related to equality and utility.

We have said that the principle of liberty declares that we ought to be free to pursue objects of interest. But since human beings tend to clash in their pursuit of objects of interest it is obvious that complete liberty is self-defeating. The principle of liberty must therefore be combined with the principle of equality, to produce the conclusion that each person has an equal right to pursue objects of interest; in other words, he may act at liberty to the extent that every other person may do likewise. Thus, when Mill speaks of 'self-protection' he means that it is legitimate to forbid a person to perform certain actions only if it can be shown that his performance of them will interfere with the liberty of others.

How does the principle of liberty relate to that of utility? At first sight the answer seems to be that liberty as governed by equality is the same thing as the *negative* side of utility when governed by equality. (The negative side of utility, as was explained at the beginning of the chapter, consists in refraining from interference in men's pursuit of their aims and in not causing them pain or distress.) It may therefore seem that the principle of liberty is not an *independent* principle but simply an expression of one aspect of the principle of utility.

It can be shown, however, that the principle of liberty may conflict with the *positive* aspects of utility as governed by equality. These positive aspects stress the importance of achieving the maximum satisfaction of interests, and for this to be possible some degree of social co-operation is necessary. For instance, with a system of rules based solely on social harmony a person could be at liberty to seek medical help when he was ill; but it is only in a society with rules of co-operation that his seeking of medical help is likely to be materially effective. In other words, to have medical benefits it is necessary to have rules governing, say, taxation, and these cannot wholly be justified by the conception of social harmony but require also the concept of social co-operation to render their existence legitimate. Now such rules of social co-operation infringe people's liberty to do as they want, and we do in fact regard it as at least debatable how far individual liberty ought to be restricted in order to develop a system of co-operation in the interests of all. It is clear that there should be rules enforcing co-operation on matters such as health and hygiene, but how far beyond these matters a government or official body is justified in imposing further restrictions is a question which raises the issue of socialism versus *laissez-faire* individualism. It can be argued, for example, that the formal freedom to enter a university or to be employed is of no value. Freedom is worth having only if it is material, and it becomes a material freedom only when it is guaranteed by the state. The costs of this guarantee, however, are the restrictions with which anyone living in a socialist state is familiar. The price may be worth paying, but the point is arguable.

But what does 'worth paying' mean here? If the principle of liberty is simply one aspect of utilitarianism, the issue between (say) socialism and *laissez-faire* individualism amounts to no more than the question whether the greatest happiness is in fact achieved by not interfering with others and thus losing the benefits of co-operation, or by co-operating with others and thus losing the benefits of liberty. Now it is sometimes held that interest is maximized by a *laissez-faire* policy (though if we consider the need to meet the demands of equality this is perhaps an implausible view). But very often the point at issue is not how interest can be maximized. Most people would hold that it is worth *sacrificing* some measure of the general interest for the sake of a high degree of individual liberty. Thus the problem usually concerns the *degree* to which this should be done.

We can now see why the principle of liberty cannot in the end be identified with the negative aspect of the principle of utility. If it is admitted that the claims of liberty sometimes prevail over those of utility, then liberty, like equality, must be an independent value - one which cannot be accounted for solely in utilitarian terms. It remains to consider why we put this high value on liberty for its own sake.

We have said that to stress the importance of liberty is to stress that the area of his life in which a person is free of the restrictions of rules must be as large as is compatible with the existence of a similar freedom in the lives of others. The most plausible explanation of this stress is that we all recognize that freedom from external compulsion is necessary over a certain area of a person's life if he is to develop those attributes which make him characteristically a person. If a certain minimum freedom of action is violated by external compulsion then the individual will fail to achieve the level of self-realization which makes him a person: at first failing to express himself in characteristically human actions he will in the end fail even to envisage these actions as possibilities in his imagination. The principle of liberty is therefore the principle of respect for persons expressed in a context where the importance of self-realization is being weighed against that of achieving an harmonious and co-operative society.

It may be objected that the principle of liberty cannot be connected with that of respect for persons by insisting on the need for the human person to grow, because there is much evidence that this growth takes place in communities lacking in liberty. For example, in Scotland at the height of Calvinism there was little room for the expression of inclinations and ideals in the tight system of rules and regulations imposed by the Calvinists. Yet during this period, it may be argued, there was no sign of the human personality wilting away: on the contrary, it was a period of fierce individualism and independence in Scottish history. Hence, it may be said that liberty is not essential to the development of the human person, and consequently that the principles of liberty and respect for persons are only contingently connected.

In reply it can be argued, to begin with, that the restraints of Calvinism were self-imposed by the Calvinists. They were not the restraints of a secular state imposed from the outside, but were rather voluntarily adopted, and do not therefore offend against the principle of liberty. It was by means of the discipline of their restraints that Calvinists believed they were realizing what made them truly persons. Indeed, the importance of the principle of liberty to Calvinists is brought out if we consider how much they resented any interference with their liberty to be Calvinists. It is true that Calvin tended to impose suffocating regulations even on those who did not accept his beliefs, and that Calvinism stultified the artistic and cultural life of Scotland for hundreds of years. But this merely supports the point that enforced rules not connected with the maintenance of social harmony and co-operation kill human personality. Where Calvinism did lead to the growth of the human person its restrictions were freely accepted, and so were not felt as restrictions: but where they were externally imposed, and felt as restrictions, they did not lead to the development of the human person.

A fuller discussion of what is meant by self-development must be postponed till Chapter III. There, it will be noted, it is presented chiefly in terms of the way in which a man should respect humanity in his own person. This is indeed its chief importance. But we do have some duties to respect others' need for self-development and others' self-respect. Now these duties are mainly duties to respect another's liberty, as we have seen. To try to contribute to a man's self-development in some more positive way, by preventing him from indulging in the lower pleasures and forcing him to indulge in the higher ones, is a self-contradictory activity, as his own processes of choice are an important aspect of his self-development.

Two qualifications should, however, be added to this. When we are dealing with children we consider it legitimate to apply a certain amount of pressure on them to follow self-developing pursuits; for example, we think it right to compel them to be educated. We make an exception of children because we think they have not got the knowledge and experience to make any choice worthy of the name, and also because there are some talents which have to be cultivated young if at all, so that the adult's ability to make a valid choice (one with plenty of possibilities) itself depends on early restriction of liberty.

It might here be objected that if the restriction of a child's liberty is permissible in this way, we cannot speak of the *self-contradictoriness* of making a man indulge in higher activities for the sake of his self-development, as we did in the previous paragraph. But we may restrict the child's liberty only if this is in the interests of his own freedom later in his life. Thus we must not seek to indoctrinate him in such a way that he cannot later genuinely choose between one activity and another. It might also seem that what we have said about children would justify an over-paternalistic attitude towards childlike adults (primitive peoples for example) or even towards the less well educated who 'don't know what's good for them'. But the cases of the child and of the childlike adult are not similar. In the child we are endeavouring to develop the potentiality for choice in such a way that he can eventually take over. In the case of the childlike adult, however, we are not envisaging a time when he can take over, but are managing his life for him. And it is the span of the *individual's* life which counts - we cannot speak in terms of the childhood of a race and use this metaphor to justify treating its adults as children.

The second qualification is that we think that a

government ought to subsidize the arts where there is not enough private patronage for them to be self-supporting. This involves using the money of those who are indifferent to the arts, and to that extent may seem to be an imposition of standards of worth-whileness on others. But there is a difference between imposing worthwhileness and making it possible. Money spent on the arts by the government makes worth-whileness possible for the few who desire it, and in so doing increases the range of possibilities for all, including those who are not interested. But the sums of money involved are too small to constitute an interference in the pursuit of whatever the individual chooses for himself. The Philistine would have a case against art subsidies only if he could plausibly maintain that his contribution restricted his area of choice rather than enlarged it.

We have said that liberty is to be valued not only for the sake of its possessor's interests, but also with a view to his self-development and self-respect. In discussing this we have partly answered a question which might be raised: how far making another's ends my own involves treating all his ends on a par. The answer seems to be that it is not for us to prevent him from pursuing ends just because we think them unworthy. But it may be legitimate to encourage some ends more than others. This does not, however, deal with the special case of a man's moral ends. Ought we not to regard these with special deference?

This is a very complex issue which we do not propose to investigate in detail here. (15) It arises most sharply when a man's moral convictions prevent us from carrying out some policy which we feel to be demanded on moral grounds. Are we justified in trying to get him to do what he believes to be wrong, by threats or bribes, for example - in other words, trying to corrupt him? Notice that this is not simply a question of taking his ends into consideration; rather the question is which of his ends should be regarded as paramount. And the question is not answered by declaring that a man would *rather* be bribed than overcome by force in some way. For even if in a given case this were his choice we can still ask whether such a preference is the right one, and thus again raise the question of the relative value of different types of end.

The conclusion of this discussion of liberty, then, is that ordinary moral views require us to modify the public morality of utility to make room not only for a principle of equality but also for one of liberty, and that the importance we attach to these principles in each case can be explained only if we assume that they are expressions of the basic principle of respect for persons.

6 FRATERNITY

We have discussed liberty and equality at some length. What (it may be asked) of fraternity, which is so often linked with liberty and equality? Is there such a thing as a separate principle of fraternity? The answer seems to be that there is no one thing to which the term 'fraternity' unambiguously applies. (16) The best we can do is to try to distinguish various possible meanings of the word and show how they relate to what we have so far said.

First of all, then, the term 'fraternity' may be applied to the policy of co-operation in the interests of all which, as we mentioned earlier, is apt to conflict with individual liberty. Thus we may say that in a communist state the principle of fraternity is exalted at the expense of that of liberty. Coupled with this may be a tendency to regard the community as an entity over and above the individuals which compose it, so that fraternity is held to demand the sacrifice of the individual to some abstraction such as 'the State'. (17)

Now this notion as it stands may be illogical, but at the same time it reflects a real deficiency in classical utilitarianism with its exclusive concentration on the individual. Thus writers like Mill do not make clear that a community is not merely an aggregate of individuals but has an institutional structure. How far this omission matters depends on whether Mill is thinking simply in terms of the whole of humanity from now to eternity as the field of reference from which the majority is drawn, or whether he is thinking rather in terms of present and future members of a particular community (the British nation?) which needs institutional definition to explain its continuity. If (as is likely) he is thinking of a particular community then his account is deficient in not explaining what constitutes a community such as a state. Those who think of the state as a self-subsistent entity have merely erred in the opposite direction.

The word 'fraternity' is also used sometimes to

suggest something different in kind from a principle of social co-operation. It may stand for something more like the *spirit* in which rules should be applied. The force of this comes out when we consider what happens when the letter of the law is put into practice without its spirit and we have 'working to rule' with all that that implies. Even granting that 'working to rule' often means doing somewhat less than the rule indicates, we can still appreciate that for efficient operation of rules a certain 'spirit' is required which is something more than an administrative matter, even if it is less than an ideal of creative service. This spirit obviously involves a certain intelligence in the operation of rules, but more significantly it involves also a certain humanity.

The principle of fraternity so understood has to do with the need in society for a recognition of human fallibility in the pursuit of common social objectives. It does not refer to a set of rules but rather to a willingness to be of service where there are no rules and to a manner of enacting rules which speaks of the consciousness of a common human predicament. Such a spirit may be called one of 'co-operation', but co-operation in this context must be distinguished from the social co-operation which was equivalent to 'fraternity' in the first sense. 'Co-operation' or 'fraternity' in this second sense covers a host of detailed concepts concerned with our response to contingencies, with the quality of our enactment of social roles and with the manner of our adherence to and application of rules. For instance, fraternity in this second sense would cover concepts such as 'neighbourliness', 'tact', 'courtesy', 'discretion', 'give and take'. If we use the metaphor of social machinery we may say that fraternity in the second sense draws our attention to the need for oil.

So far, then, we have discussed fraternity as the *principle* of co-operation and as the *spirit* of give-and-take. A third meaning of 'fraternity' is again different in category. 'Fraternity' suggests above all a *motive* for action, a devotion of a kind resembling that felt to brothers but extended to the members of some community to which one belongs. In so far as people in a community really are imbued with a feeling of fraternity, they will not see restraints on liberty in the general interest as restraints - in fact they will not *be* such, but rather ways of bringing about what the individual wants most. This is the feeling which communism hopes to foster in its members. From motives such as these, people in a democracy choose to spend time in the service of others; and whereas it would be an infringement of liberty to *make* them do so, it is an exercise of liberty if they choose to do so.

It may be asked whether 'fraternity' is the same as 'respect' or '*agape*'. The answer to this question depends on the sense of 'fraternity' involved. Where fraternity is to be interpreted as a principle of social co-operation (our first sense) it simply amounts to another way of regarding one aspect of the principle of utility. As such it cannot wholly be explained in terms of *agape* for, as we have seen, the principle of utility is at best an imperfect crystallization of the attitude of *agape*. Fraternity in the second sense is similar to *agape* in that both concepts refer to a quality of response to people and situations which cannot be pinned down in precise rules. But *agape* is, of course, a wider conception than fraternity. Fraternity in the third sense - a motive for action within a community - may or may not be explicable in terms of *agape*. If kinship is acknowledged only within some restricted group (of fellow-workers or the like) it is not the same as *agape*. But where fraternity can be expressed by a saying like 'The whole world is my kith and kin' it does seem to be the same as *agape*, where *agape* is regarded as a motive for action.

7 CONCLUSION

In our first chapter we investigated the attitude of respect for persons and suggested that it would give rise to the fundamental principles of morality, and in this chapter we have tried to show how this works out in detail for public or social morality. The theory of utilitarianism seemed at first to reflect our ordinary moral views since it suggested a detailed programme for 'making the ends of others one's own' in the life of a large and complex society. It turned out, however, that utilitarianism on its own provided only a distorted image of ordinary views and we had therefore to amend it to take into account the demands of the principles of equality and liberty. But the importance attached to the three principles of utility, equality and liberty can be explained only if we say that the principle of respect for persons is assumed. Our contention that respect for persons is the ultimate principle of morality is therefore justified to the extent that the ordinary judgments of social morality presuppose it. Fraternity turned out to be not an independent principle but (depending on its interpretation) a principle analysable in terms of utility or of *agape*.

NOTES

1. J.S. Mill, 'Utilitarianism', London, Collins, Fontana Library, ed. Mary Warnock, 1962, ch. 2, p. 257.
2. Ibid., ch. 2, p. 276.
3. For a discussion of Deontology, see D. Daiches Raphael, 'Moral Judgement', London, Allen & Unwin, 1955, ch. 3.
4. See J. Rawls, Two Concepts of Rules, 'Philosophical Review', 1955.
5. Mill, op. cit., ch. 5, pp. 318-20.
6. For a discussion of the concept of desert, see D. Daiches Raphael, op. cit., pp. 67-79. Our whole discussion owes a great deal to the chapter on Justice in Raphael's book (pp. 62-94).
7. Aristotle, 'Nicomachean Ethics', Book V, ch. 3.
8. Raphael, op. cit., pp. 65-6.
9. Ibid., pp. 77-9.
10. See R.S. Peters, 'Ethics and Education', London, Allen & Unwin, 1966, p. 128.
11. 'Children and Their Primary Schools' (The Plowden Report), London, HMSO, 1967, ch. 5, esp. p. 57.
12. Raphael, op. cit., pp. 73-4.
13. R.M. Hare, 'Freedom and Reason', Oxford University Press, 1963, p. 178.
14. J.S. Mill, 'On Liberty', London, Collins, Fontana Library, ed. Mary Warnock, 1962, ch. 1, p. 135.
15. For a discussion of this question, see W.G. Maclagan, How Important is Moral Goodness?, 'Mind', 1955.
16. For a discussion of the concept of fraternity, see R.S. Peters, op. cit., pp. 215-27.
17. Ibid., p. 216. Compare also the passage quoted earlier (p. 54) on justice and utility from Raphael, op. cit.

8 Liberty, equality and fraternity

David Donnison

Governments of this country are being compelled to formulate increasingly explicit policies about prices and incomes, about the structure and growth of our towns, and therefore about the distribution of this world's goods among our people. To do so they must decide where they stand on some very old questions. These questions - about liberty, equality and fraternity - were much discussed by our forbears, but are now obscured beneath the dust of a decaying liberal faith. I shall try to shake the dust off some of these ideas and show how they can be brought to bear on today's problems. This discussion will not conjure our confusions into miraculous consensus, but it may help us to disagree more fruitfully.

POLICIES NEEDED

The British pride themselves on going about their politics in a practical, unemotional way: 'unflappable' was the word they coined to honour their most successful politician of recent years - the pipe and the umbrella their leaders' chosen symbols. Ask them about their fundamental social and political beliefs and they grow embarrassed, rather as their Victorian forbears would have been if questioned about their sexual mores: gentlemen don't discuss such things. But we shall have to discuss them.

The basic, if unspoken, social and political agreements which make urban, industrial society governable may be breaking up. Workers in every trade and profession are growing more militant than ever before, and Governments, it is clear, can only restore order to the economy by formulating policies about incomes and

prices which command some support. They must help us
work out the rules which determine who gets the gravy.
Otherwise there will be no gravy, for to decline this
responsibility and 'leave it to the market' will con-
sign us to galloping inflation or to unemployment.

Debates about poverty, urban squalor, race relations
and the deprivations which afflict economically back-
ward regions pose the same distributional questions in
spatial form. *Where* is the gravy to go - the regional
premiums and investment allowances, the new motorways,
factories and houses? Nationalists at regional level,
squatters and demonstrators at street level, are
teaching the nation that militancy pays. The voters
have learnt that, on some occasions at least, Government can determine people's incomes (farmers', for
example), can regulate prices (house rents, for
example) and can decide where jobs are to go (in alumi-
nium smelters, for example). Thus, paradoxically,
Governments' only hope of avoiding daily intervention
in such matters is to formulate more explicit principles
about the distribution of income, wealth and opportunities, and to seek public support for these principles.
To have no incomes policy will mean more strikes and
more inflation; to have no planning policies will
mean more protests, less action and less development.

If we shirk these tasks we should not assume that
we shall muddle through. The people of this country
have shown they are as capable of racial conflict and
religious hysteria as their neighbours. Their tolerant
political traditions may be the lucky and temporary
result of a conservative and reasonably prosperous
society, not its statesmanlike cause.

THE CONVENTIONAL WISDOM

Our Victorian forbears delighted in debating great
moral issues but we are ill-equipped for the task, as
the 1970 election - possibly the dullest in our
history - only too clearly showed. Since inequalities
persist in every corner of our society most of us
must approve, or at least tolerate, inequality. But
it would no longer be polite to say so. Even the
most resolute defenders of hierarchy feel compelled to
assume an egalitarian guise: they argue, for example,
that the direct grant grammar schools should be pre-
served because they 'offer a valuable opportunity to
clever boys and girls from poor or culturally deprived
homes' (1) - despite the fact that the same publication

clearly shows that poor children are almost wholly excluded from these schools. This prudery - for that is what it amounts to - does their opponents no good, for it allows advocates of equality to shirk the clarification of their own point of view.

When rational argument is lacking, people rely on cliques to determine their loyalties and on stereotypes to express their views. Since they are largely unspoken, our attitudes and assumptions about equality are difficult to pin down clearly, but I believe two contrasting standpoints can be identified. To summarise is inevitably to caricature them: no one, perhaps, would wholly assent to every proposition in either of the sets that follow. The first, which might be called the standpoint of the tough-minded, economically oriented Right, goes something like this:

1 When policies are decided for this country, top priority should normally be given to economic growth.
2 Economic growth means growth in the goods and services produced by private enterprise.
3 The fruits of growth should reach people in the form of money incomes, because it is healthier, both for the individual and for the country, if people buy what they want with their own money rather than getting things free through the social services.
4 To succour the casualties growth leaves in its wake there must be some redistribution of incomes. This is brought about through the social services which confer most of their benefits on poorer people, at the cost of taxes levied mainly on richer people.
5 So far as the poor are concerned, our aim must be to raise their living standards to an adequate minimum from which they should be encouraged to make further advances by their own efforts.
6 The growth of the social services must wait on the growth of the private sector of the economy, for it is only from the surplus generated in this sector that the resources for their expansion can be found.
7 Greater equality of incomes may be morally desirable, but it tends to be economically self-defeating because it is apt to be inflationary (the poor having low marginal propensities to save) and because it penalises the most productive, rewards the idle and thus frustrates growth itself.
8 The success or failure of individuals is largely

due to their psychological inheritance, cultivated by will and character. It is thus impossible to create a much more equal society than the one we now have.

The standpoint of the tender-minded, socially oriented Left goes somewhat as follows:

1 When policies are decided for this country, top priority should normally be given to the equalisation of incomes and living standards. That should be achieved by raising the standards of the poorest.
2 Equality is valued for essentially moral reasons: the more equal we become, the more civilised and compassionate will be our relationships with our fellow citizens.
3 Poverty does not mean failure to attain a fixed minimum, but exclusion from the continually rising standards of the country's middle income groups. Thus the problem of poverty can only be resolved by movement towards equalisation of rewards.
4 The main instruments for redistribution are the social services (here the tender-minded broadly agree with the fourth point in the tough-minded set of propositions).
5 Economic growth, which is valuable if it enables the country to move towards greater equality, consists partly of the growth of the social services.
6 It is healthier, both for the individual and for the country, to distribute many of the basic essentials of life according to need and preferably without payment, rather than through the market.
7 The success or failure of individuals is largely due to environmental influences, many of which society is capable of modifying.

In real life, people do not divide as neatly as these formulae suggest. At least three different dimensions of attitude are involved - from tough- to tender-minded, from economically to socially oriented, and from Right to Left. A man may talk about one problem like a tough-minded, economically oriented Leftist, and about another like a tender-minded, socially oriented Rightist; and how he acts on either may be yet another matter. Nevertheless patterns of belief much like these go far to shape British discussion of distributional questions. And that is alarming because most of the factual assertions in both sets of propositions are false.

The social services do *not* confer most of their benefits on poorer people: indeed, some of the most expensive of them - the education and health services

for instance - were never intended to. The taxes
which finance them are *not* levied mainly on richer
people. (2) The social services are *not* merely
parasitic upon the private sector of the economy:
some of them furnish an important part of the national
income, some instigate growth in the private sector,
and some are an essential part of the social infrastructure required for a thriving economy. A more
equal distribution of income and wealth does *not*
necessarily frustrate economic growth: it is in the
wealthiest and most highly industrialised countries
that the pre-tax distributions of earnings tend to be
most equal. The same countries also tend to spend the
largest proportions of their national incomes on social
services. (3) Greater equality does *not* necessarily
make a society more compassionate and less conflict-
ridden: it sometimes has the opposite effects. (4)

Many of our factual assumptions about Britain's
central social problems are mistaken or ludicrously
obsolete (some were truer when the Poor Law, financed
by taxes on property owners, was this country's largest
social service - but that was before 1870). The
moral judgments which underpin arguments about these
problems are equally shaky. Take the central question
of equality, for example. Since most people seem to
agree that greater equality would be a good thing
(even if unattainable in practice) they should have
no difficulty in explaining why they want more
equality.

FRATERNITY, THEREFORE EQUALITY

It is to social philosophers of the Left that we must
look for an answer to this question - and first to the
pervasive influence of Richard Tawney. One of the
latest American books on poverty still relies wholly
upon him; 'In this book we do not argue the reasons
why inequality should be reduced. For one, it is
difficult to be more eloquent and moving than R.H.
Tawney'. (5) That great and Christian teacher based
his case for equality upon man's need for fellowship.
'What a community requires, as the word itself
suggests, is a common culture, because, without it, it
is not a community at all.... But a common culture
cannot be created merely by desiring it. It rests
upon economic foundations.... It involves, in short,
a large measure of economic equality....' (6) Twenty-
five years later Anthony Crosland went further, saying

'if we want more equality, the case for it must rest on statements largely, if not entirely, unrelated to economic welfare'. (7)   Although economic arguments - about wasted talent, for example - do appear in it, most of his chapter on 'The Case for Social Equality' is devoted to sociological, psychological and moral argument about industrial conflict, personal envy and social justice.   The very latest statement from this quarter concludes on a similar note.   Lord Balogh advocates equality because 'without greater equality in consumption, that consensus of opinion will never be reached which is needed to safeguard the steady progress of this country'. (8)

Tawney was not the first to use these arguments. They appear much earlier in discussion of another type of equality: the equality of relationships between people who live and work alongside each other in a non-deferential society.   Ebenezer Howard echoed the utopian writers of a century and more when he condemned, in 1898, 'the large cities of today' because they were not 'adapted for the expression of the fraternal spirit', and called for 'garden cities of tomorrow' which would 'silence the harsh voice of anger, and ... awaken the soft notes of brotherliness and goodwill'. (9)

No civilised person could deride human aspirations for fellowship.   Without the good Samaritan's capacity to perceive strangers as sentient, suffering human beings, we have no way of making judgments about social policies: we literally do not know what we are talking about.   Brian Abel-Smith put the matter very clearly:

> If we abandon the market-choice criterion, how do we decide what to spend on welfare?   All I can suggest is a very homely way.   Take a cross-section of population, show them the standards in the Welfare State and then ask them the following questions. Would you let your mother go into this home?   If your husband had a nervous breakdown, would you like him to live in this mental hospital?   Would you let a child of yours go into this institution ...? And finally, if you don't like the look of the Welfare State, now you have seen it, would you be prepared to pay ... more ... to have it put right? (10)

These are the accents of Tawney who taught a whole generation that their fellow citizens were also their neighbours, and thereby laid the foundations on which the great social reforms of the 1940s were built. But it is an altogether different matter, and a dangerous error, to rest the case for equality on man's need for fraternity in Tawney's sense of 'a common culture', or to say with Crosland that 'the first argument for greater equality is that it will increase social contentment and diminish social resentment'. (11) Societies that grow more equal may prove to be not more, but much less, fraternal - at least for a time. (Something like this appears to have happened in Ulster.) Liberals who lose their nerve at this discovery are apt to turn against equality, and liberty too.

Many brands of fraternity are much less attractive than Tawney's. There is a cosy, conservative brand, which seeks protection from new ideas, disturbing people and competition of all kinds; and there is a harsh, authoritarian brand: *Ein Reich! Ein Volk! Ein Führer!* was a call for fraternity of a sort. A free world will be full of conflict: it cannot be a fellowship of friends, ruled by love, because the search for friends soon degenerates into the exclusion of enemies, the suppression of conflict and, ultimately, rule by hate.

LIBERTY, THEREFORE EQUALITY

When the arguments for them are so unconvincing it is difficult to see how egalitarian ideals came to be so widely accepted - but much easier to understand why so little is done about them. Where did they begin?

Some have traced the origins of British egalitarian thinking to the Levellers of Cromwellian times. But the Levellers' plea was for political rights, not for economic and social rights - 'the poorest that lives, hath as true a right to give a vote, as well as the richest and greatest' - and they would have excluded from the franchise all 'servants' (or employees as we would now say) 'because they depend upon the will of other men and should be afraid to displease'. (12) That would have left more than half the men in Britain without a vote. Serious advocacy of something we would recognise as an equal society begins much later - with the Utilitarians.

In essays published in 1859 and 1861 John Stuart Mill gave us the clearest and most comprehensive statement of the Utilitarian point of view. By then the doctrine was already in decline, encrusted with the qualifications that ultimately bereft liberalism of its cutting edge. But the vigour of the original faith still shines through his exposition. Shorn of the encrustations, this is what it amounted to:

1. A government which must decade what to do should not look for guidance to history, religion, the ruling classes, or some mythical social contract. It should consider the consequences of the different courses of action open to it, and the essential consequences to ask about are those that affect people.
2. People should, so far as possible, be enabled to attain their own ends, for each of us 'is the person most interested in his own well-being ...' and 'with respect to his own feelings and circumstances, the most ordinary man or woman has means of knowledge immeasurably surpassing those that can be possessed by anyone else'. (13)
3. It is not enough to abolish monopolies and arbitrary powers, and to extend political rights and religious toleration. We must also protect individuals from 'the tyranny of the majority' which may be exercised not only 'through the acts of the public authorities' but also through 'a social tyranny more formidable than many kinds of political oppression, since ... it leaves fewer means of escape, penetrating much more deeply into the details of life, and enslaving the soul itself'. (14)
4. When the interests of different people conflict, as they often will, we should try to follow 'Bentham's dictum, "everybody to count for one, nobody for more than one"', for Utilitarianism 'is a mere form of words without rational signification, unless one person's happiness ... is counted for exactly as much as another's'. (15)
5. This 'equal claim of everybody to happiness ... involves an equal claim to all the *means* of happiness ...' (16)
6. Restrictions on liberty can only be justified if they are necessary to protect other people's liberties.

This philosophy is regularly shot full of logical holes in lectures to first-year students (which seldom offer anything half so interesting in its place). My concern is not with its moral logic, but with the mix of ideas it presents. Utilitarians sought liberty, and *therefore* equality. Bentham, their founding father, was confident that the trinity of liberty, equality and industrial progress went naturally together: 'if the laws do not oppose [equality], if they do not maintain monopolies, if they do not restrain trade and its exchanges, if they do not permit entails, large properties will be seen without effort, without revolutions, without shock, to subdivide themselves by little and little'. (17)

In its day this philosophy moved men to poetry and to heroism. In his poem on 'London' William Blake gave us the most searing indictment of the inseparable evils of oppression, inequality and human degradation to be found in the English language. Shelley was more gaily savage about the capital 'Hell is a city much like London' (18) - but as grimly aware of the injustices suffered by 'The Men of England'. And when, in 'Prometheus Unbound', his 'Spirit of the Hour' proclaims man's release from these injustices it is to a paradise of liberty, and *therefore* equality, that he is admitted.

... thrones were kingless ...
None fawned, none trampled ...

... the man remains
Sceptreless, free, uncircumscribed, but man
Equal, unclassed, tribeless and nationless,
Exempt from awe, worship, degree, the king
Over himself ... (19)

The poets of revolutionary liberalism and the capitalist creators of the industrial revolution were not 'really on the same side': had they been, the poets would not so often have died young, poor and exiled. But they were inspired by a common intellectual and spiritual tradition - a tradition more robust than our own.

We set out from a world in which educated, liberal people believed that economic and social progress could both be achieved, and could only be achieved, in a society that was both freer and more equal. We have arrived in a world where guardians of the conventional wisdom assert that there are inherent and possibly insoluble conflicts between social justice and economic growth, and between equality and freedom. How did it happen? It would take two centuries of history to answer that question, and I can only offer a few glimpses of the story.

THE DECAY OF LIBERALISM

Britain's industrial revolution took shape at a time when Governments were, not occasionally but *usually*, oppressive, incompetent and corrupt. Thus liberals who cared about freedom, dissenters who sought religious toleration, and capitalists who needed peace, prosperity and legally enforceable contracts, could all make common cause in demanding freedom, constitutional government and an end to arbitrary power. As dissenters and capitalists gained rights and riches they shed the libertarian language in which they had clothed their demands, like other revolutionaries before and since. And when, from the Left, there eventually emerged the countervailing drive to control the excesses and rescue the casualties of ungoverned industrialism, this drive had to take the form of a reassertion of the rights of government over unbridled, profit-motivated, private enterprise. These demands were voiced by Marxists, who did not greatly care about freedom, and by social democrats for whom the twin objectives of equity and public ownership became inextricably linked. As its membership cards still testify, the Labour Party's aims are: 'To secure for the workers by hand or by brain the full fruits of their industry and the most equitable distribution thereof that may be possible, upon the basis of the common ownership of the means of production, distribution and exchange....' In countries where industrial revolutions came after the political and administrative revolutions which made government constitutional, efficient and reasonably democratic, demands for social justice and equality were never so completely identified with the extension of public ownership and the social services, or so divorced from policies for economic growth.

By the time of John Stuart Mill, liberals were already losing their nerve. He foresaw and dreaded the descent into democracy which lay ahead, like Niagara, down the stream of history. Such fears could only be dismissed today by those who forget the terrible things that were to happen in Germany and Russia, and all that is still happening in many countries which are struggling to make the transition to parliamentary democracy. But these fears, understandable though they were, repeatedly blunted the cutting edge of liberal thought. Mill's own proposals for the franchise - a shameless attempt to rig the poll in favour of high-minded, professional people like himself - were a classic example of their debilitating effects.

Our brand of parliamentary democracy has meant that major steps towards greater equality have only been taken with the blessing of that middle-of-the-road opinion on which all our Governments depend; and that means during or immediately after major wars. These wartime associations may explain why egalitarians generally tend to carry with them a slight whiff of rationing, puritanism and worse - all the things Orwell so brilliantly evoked in '1984'. Thus the pursuit of equality - once heralded by a trumpet blast from the Spirit of the Hour - has been degraded into a dreary matter of butter rationing, utility furniture and municipal restaurants.

All sorts of less subtle corruptions have followed. People calling themselves 'social-liberals' say they 'would resolutely oppose all social levelling and uniformity' (20) - thereby implying that equality and uniformity are the same thing. Others have said there must inevitably be a conflict between equality and freedom. There are indeed cases - typically rather trivial ones - where equality does amount to uniformity and does eliminate freedom. If all schoolboys are to be 'equally' dressed they must wear the prescribed uniform and no other. In more important cases a self-respecting independence, born of equality in human relationships, is the essential basis both for freedom and for variety. It is the social pressures imposed by the hierarchies of an unequal society that restrict freedom and variety, fastening William Blake's 'mind-forg'd manacles' upon us.

For many purposes, the aim of 'equality of opportunity' has been substituted for equality. Most people can spot inequalities readily enough when they see them; but it is far harder to be sure whether we have equality of opportunity - and if we do have it, the comforting conclusion can be drawn that all remaining inequalities must be the fault of those who fail to seize their opportunities.

The old-fashioned demand for greater equality *of* incomes, education, housing conditions and the like has in many quarters given way to demands for greater equality *for* negroes, women, Catholics and other deprived groups. The new version often sounds fiercer, but its implications are nowhere near so radical. It suggests that negroes, women and Catholics should be satisfied (as indeed some of their leaders will be) when they secure their fair share of positions among the bosses. We may applaud or join such campaigns, but we should not delude ourselves into thinking they are egalitarian. The rich and powerful may eventually be recruited from slightly different sources, but if the sources are good they may be all the better equipped to maintain their privileges thereafter. (21)

A REFORMULATION

The philosophical and practical difficulties of distributing policies have baffled scholars and statesmen for a very long time. Properly speaking, they are not problems (to which solutions can be found), they are dilemmas (to which a more or less creative response can be made). But we would avoid the sillier muddles if the egalitarian ideal could be extricated from the debris of decayed liberalism and reconnected to the ideas from which it originally sprang.

To formulate a new social philosophy, or rather to reformulate an old one, calls for thorough analysis of the economic and social systems to which it must be applied, and the political institutions through which it must be put into practice. That is not a task to be tackled from the armchair, or completed in a few pages. But after writing so unkindly about other versions I should try to outline a better ideology than those with which this essay began, and suggest directions in which it may lead us.

1 When policies are decided for this country, top priority should normally be given to the extension of liberty, particularly among the underdogs - those whose lives are most severely stunted by economic, social and political constraints.

This starting point commits us heavily to trusting in people's capacity to choose better for themselves than anyone else could choose for them (a faith that will naturally be bitterly disappointed from time to time). It precludes the construction of utopias because the future character of society cannot be precisely forecast or planned: people will use their freedom in unpredictable ways. It is based on confidence that we can solve the practical problems which arise when freedom produces chaos (such as the congestion and pollution caused by the unforeseen growth of motor transport) as it sometimes will.

2 To be freer, a society must be less deferential and less constrained by social hierarchies. That means its distributions of status, living standards and command over resources must become more equal.

An English-speaking country which may enter the Common Market offers its people exceptional and growing opportunities for migration. Until we have international policies for incomes, our scope for modifying the distribution of earnings will therefore be limited. The scope for change will be greatest among groups suffering (or gaining) from discrimination that owes little to market forces - among some groups of women and some racial minorities, for example. But there is greater scope for redistribution of wealth through the fiscal system, and for redistribution of income through family allowances and other social security payments which could be much more effective instruments for this purpose than they have yet become. No one can say such policies must fail, for they have not yet been tried. Until now, as a United Nations study shows, 'incomes policies have been seen as one among several possible instruments for countering the forces of inflation, rather than as policies directly concerned with improving the distribution of income'. (22)

We must take more trouble to ensure that social services offered in kind reach everyone in a form that really enables the deprived to seize the opportunities they purport to offer. Otherwise they will reinforce the economic and social handicaps from which the underdogs already suffer - as has happened in education. Recent research strongly suggests that early selection and specialisation in our schools handicap the deprived without benefiting the privileged. (23) Other social services may have similar tendencies to exclude those who most need their help. (24) But we must learn far more about our society and the way it works before the social services can be made into the liberating and opportunity-extending instruments they could become. (25)

3 We should ensure, wherever possible, that our towns grow in ways that make it easier, not harder, for people to seize new opportunities, and to encounter others of different ages, races, classes and incomes.

We should not assume, with Ebenezer Howard, that this will 'awaken the soft notes of brotherliness and goodwill', or be discouraged if it does not. Fraternity is desirable, but liberty is more important still. And where do people feel most free to experiment, to try new ways of doing things, and to be themselves: where are children most likely to take their education further than their parents did: to take jobs their parents would never have contemplated, to work and save to buy better homes, and help their own children get an even better start in life? In places where people are divided into rich and poor, perched at the top and bottom of the ladders of opportunity, with no rungs between them (as in parts of Kensington); in places where everyone stands on much the same rungs of the ladder and an upward or downward step compels people to break with family, friends and neighbours (as in some of the Glasgow Council estates and the plusher Surrey suburbs); or in places where the steps to higher rungs in the labour market, the income distribution, the housing market and the education system are all within easier reach (in Camden perhaps, or in parts of Coventry and Reading)?

These questions are too complex to be answered conclusively: the springs of human aspiration and achievement run too deep and diverse to be described in simple generalisations. (Before we are tempted to vulgar environmental determinism we should recall the fountain of talent which has flowed from some of the one-class, one-industry valleys of South Wales.) But there is a growing volume of evidence to show that aspiration, attainment and mobility tend to be higher - liberty, that is, becomes a reality - in mixed and pluralistic societies where people are not segregated wholly amongst their own kind. (26)

The economic and social influences working upon us tend to have a mutually reinforcing character. In future the planners must ensure that vicious spirals grow virtuous. We should ask not merely whether the slums are being cleared or whether schoolchildren grow healthier - separate questions about different aspects of life, directed to different public services. We should be asking whether the location and distribution of housing ensure that the most deprived children attend schools where there are good teachers, *and* sufficient numbers of able and ambitious children to make high attainment a feasible and respectable aspiration; *and* whether the opportunities for work and leisure open to pupils from these schools are of a kind to encourage high attainment; *and* whether public transport and the location of housing and industry give everyone access to these opportunities; *and* whether family allowances, rate rebates, housing subsidies and other systems of income redistribution work in ways that extend the aspirations of the deprived, rather than restricting them; ... and much else besides. These demands will make the planners' task more comprehensive, and much more difficult.

4 Liberty will not have been effectively extended unless it provokes new demands and unlocks new talents for meeting them. For the extension of freedom, the promotion of innovation, and economic and social progress are all part of the same process.

Our habit of divorcing economic from social progress, and treating the latter as parasitic upon the former, has made us more concerned about production than about innovation, and more concerned about restraining inflation than about encouraging new and potentially creative demands. And that is very bad economics. Jane Jacobs, (27) although she repeatedly underrates the contribution of planners and the public services, shows clearly that economics and sociology are only different languages for discussing the same processes: the brassiere was invented and mass produced, not in countries where feminine crafts were most advanced, but where women had high status, readier access to credit, bigger incomes and greater self-confidence - on the eastern seaboard of the United States. We know from our own experience that fifteen years after teenagers secured (during the war) a bigger increase in incomes than anyone else, we experienced a boom in young people's music, consumer goods and tourism which was largely created by young people themselves, both as producers and as consumers. (Imagine the opportunities for innovation, growth and exports that a redistribution in favour of old people might one day create - in new forms of housing? heating systems? holidays? hearing aids ...?)

If equality, freedom and economic growth tend to go together, so do inequality, restraint and stagnation. But the British do not readily think in these socio-economic terms. When presented with a Report proposing reforms of the public schools, they embarked on an emotional orgy of dispute about class distinction, fagging, flogging ... never pausing amidst the welter of irrelevancies to note that a system which gave the old boys of six schools two-thirds of the seats in the cabinet and more than two-fifths of the directorships of our most prominent firms is a singularly inefficient way of choosing elites. Not surprisingly, they proved incapable of doing anything about the problem. Jeremy Bentham must have turned in his grave.

5 Eventually it should be possible to sustain the process by which policies for the equalisation of income, wealth and living standards extend freedom and promote innovation and development which ensure the continuing economic growth that makes further progress towards equality possible.

At the moment our wheels are firmly stuck in ruts that lead in the opposite direction: slow growth, repeatedly interrupted by economic set-backs, prohibits movement towards equality which would be inflationary in the short run. Hence we preserve a divided and deferential society, talent is wasted, innovation is difficult, and the economy stagnates.

More would have to be said to explain this philosophy properly, and far more must be learnt about the way our society works before we can decide how much faith to put in it. Even then, many will reject it - and reject it with greater conviction the sounder its assumptions prove to be. They do not want to turn the economy round. They fear that a society which grows too free, too equal or too rich will become coarsened, congested and quarrelsome. And they may be right. Freedom and growth bring unforeseeable changes, and every change is a kind of bereavement. Their point of view is a respectable one which deserves to be more frankly stated. It would provoke more productive argument about more important problems than this country's political debates customarily deal with.

NOTES

1 Second Report of the Public Schools Commission, 'Points of Disagreement', London, HMSO, 1970, vol. 1, p. 120.
2 See The Incidence of Taxes and Social Service Benefits in 1965 and 1966, 'Economic Trends', no. 172, February 1968, HMSO, which suggests that all forms of tax together take remarkably similar proportions of the income of rich and poor. Alan Peacock and Robin Shannon (The Welfare State and the Redistribution of Income, 'Westminster Bank Review', August 1968) argue that the evidence does not justify so simple a conclusion, but give no support to the conventional assumptions outlined above.
3 See Harold Lydall, 'The Structure of Earnings', Oxford University Press, 1968; and J. Frederic Dewhurst et al., 'Europe's Needs and Resources', London, Macmillan, 1961.
4 See W.G. Runciman, 'Relative Deprivation and Social Justice', London, Routledge & Kegan Paul, 1966.
5 S.M. Miller and Pamela Roby, 'The Future of Inequality', New York, Basic Books, 1970, p. vii.
6 'Equality', London, Allen & Unwin, 1931, p. 41.
7 'The Future of Socialism', London, Jonathan Cape, 1956, p. 190.
8 Thomas Balogh, 'Labour and Inflation', London, Fabian Tract No. 403, p. 61.
9 'Garden Cities of Tomorrow', London, Faber, 1965, pp. 146 and 150.

Chapter 8

10 Whose Welfare State? in 'Conviction', ed. Norman MacKenzie, London, MacGibbon & Kee, 1958, p. 68.
11 'The Future of Socialism', p. 205.
12 See C.B. Macpherson, 'The Political Theory of Possessive Individualism, Hobbes to Locke', Oxford University Press, 1962, chap. III.
13 'On Liberty', London, Dent, Everyman edition, p. 133.
14 Ibid., p. 68.
15 Ibid., p. 68.
16 'Utilitarianism', Everyman edition, p. 58; my italics. People's happiness, Mill says, must be 'supposed equal in degree (with the proper allowance made for kind)' - a qualification which led him to emasculate Bentham's original doctrine. Their equal claims to the means of happiness were likewise subject to limits, but 'those limits ought to be strictly construed'.
17 Bentham, Principles of the Civil Code, 'Works', 1843, vol. i, ch. xii; quoted in 'Equality', p. 133.
18 'Peter Bell the Third', Part the Third.
19 'Prometheus Unbound', Act II, lines 131 and 193.
20 Ralf Dahrendorf, 'Essays in the Theory of Society', London, Routledge & Kegan Paul, 1968, p. 214.
21 For a revealing and far more thorough treatment of the language of egalitarian debate, see Brian Barry, 'Political Argument', London, Routledge & Kegan Paul, 1965.
22 UN Economic Commission for Europe, 'Incomes in Postwar Europe: A Study of Policies, Growth and Distribution', Geneva, 1967, ch. 1, p. 1.
23 For a cross-national study of these questions see Torsten Husén, ed., 'International Study of Achievements in Mathematics', New York, Wiley, 1967. For a more detailed study of the workings of the British system see T. Christie and A. Griffin, The Examination Achievements of Highly Selective Schools, 'Educational Research', vol. 12, no. 3, June 1970.
24 But see Martin Rein (Social Class and the Health Service, 'New Society', 20 November 1969) who shows that the poor probably get more medical care than the rich under a nationwide, free health service. The unanswered question is whether this advantage matches their, presumably greater, medical needs.
25 Although the positive discrimination recommended in the Plowden Report ('Children and their Primary Schools', London, HMSO, 1967) for schools in the

most deprived areas would make a start in this direction, the Plowden Committee frankly recognised that it knew very little about the criteria and methods for such policies.
26 For a discussion of some of this evidence and an important new contribution to it, see B.T. Robson, 'Urban Analysis: A Study of City Structure', Cambridge University Press, 1969.
27 See 'The Economy of Cities', London, Jonathan Cape, 1970.

9   Who is my stranger?

R. M. Titmuss

1

In this chapter we return to the theme of 'the gift'. In an earlier one (Chapter 5), setting out a typology of donors, we drew attention to the similarities and dissimilarities between the blood gift in modern societies and forms and manifestations of giving and gift-exchange in primitive societies. The social and economic aspects of gift-exchange as a universal phenomenon offer material, as Lévi-Strauss has said, for 'inexhaustible sociological reflection'. No one has done more to provoke such reflection than Lévi-Strauss himself, especially in his book 'The Elementary Structures of Kinship'. (1)

Both Lévi-Strauss and Mauss, in analysing materials from an immense range of culturally diverse societies, are tempted from time to time to speculate about the relevance of the rules and functions of giving in such societies to present-day institutions in the West. Mauss was eventually led to see modern forms of social security, expressing 'solicitude or co-operation', as a renaissance of 'the theme of the gift'. Had he been born later he might well have explored comparatively the concept of socialized medical care as exemplified by Britain's National Health Service or the principles underlying systems of voluntary blood donorship. When he was in his seventies, blood transfusion services were in their infancy; today, they are practically universal and world demand for blood is estimated to be growing at a much faster rate than adult population growth, economic growth and other physical indicators. (2) What seemingly lags far behind this imperative demand from medical science in most countries - and especially in the United States and Japan - is the rate of 'social growth' in the form of adequate numbers of voluntary donors. This refusal to give without immediate reward could be interpreted - if translated into the context of the primitive societies studied by Mauss - as a 'refusal of friendship and intercourse'.

Lévi-Strauss had comparative pictures also in mind in deploying examples of gift transactions in the West.

In North American society, which often seems to seek the reintegration into modern society of the very general attitudes and procedures of primitive cultures, these occasions (festivals) assume quite exceptional proportions. The exchange of gifts at Christmas, for a month each year, practised by all social classes with a sort of sacred ardour, is nothing other than a gigantic *potlatch*, implicating millions of individuals, and at the end of which many family budgets are faced with lasting disequilibrium ... even in our own society the destruction of wealth is a way to gain prestige. (3)

These and other examples drawn from both complex and traditional societies indicate that the personal gift and counter-gift, in which givers and receivers are known to each other, and personally communicate with each other, is characterized by a great variety of sentiments and purposes. At one end of the spectrum, economic purposes may be dominant as in some forms of first-gifts which aim to achieve a material gain or to enhance prestige or to bring about material gain in the future. At the other end are those gifts whose purposes are predominantly social and moral in that as 'total social facts' they aim to serve friendly relationships, affection and harmony between known individuals and social groups.

Within all such gift transactions of a personal face-to-face nature lie embedded some elements of moral enforcement or bond. To give is to receive - to compel some return or create some obligation - either in the form of a similar or different material gift or in the overt expression of sentiment, pleasure or pain, manifested in physical acts of behaviour on the part of the recipient. No such gift is or can be utterly detached, disinterested or impersonal. Each carries messages and motives in its own language.

Both Lévi-Strauss and Mauss - and other anthropologists - have sought to show that exchange in primitive societies consists not so much in economic transactions as in reciprocal gifts, that these reciprocal gifts have a far more important function in these societies than in our own, and that this primitive form of exchange is not merely nor essentially of an economic nature but is what Mauss called 'a total social fact', that is, an event which has significance that is at once social and religious, magic and economic, utilitarian and sentimental, jural and moral. Dalton concluded from a survey of the literature that economic theory, developed to analyse the structures, processes and problems of market-organized industrialism, was not relevant to primitive economies. (4)

Tönnies in his classic study of European societies, 'Gemeinschaft und Gesellschaft' (strangely neglected by the French anthropologists) developed what he called the 'Fellowship Type' in Gemeinschaft-like relationships. Gift-exchanges in such community oriented societies were, he argued, essentially mutual depending on equality of knowledge or volition in performance. By contrast, Gesellschaft-like relationships (in which economic man was dominant) were governed by the principle, *Do, ut des* (I give, so that you will give). 'What I do for you, I do only as a means to effect your simultaneous, previous or later service for me. Actually and really I want and desire only this. To get something from you is my end; my service is the means thereto, which I naturally contribute unwillingly.' (5) Strong elements of compulsion, dominated this type of gift relationship which, according to Tönnies, often had as its purpose a desire for status, power or material gain.

But in our societies, argued Lévi-Strauss, the proportion of goods transferred according to the gift-exchange modalities of primitive societies is 'very small in comparison with those involved in commerce and merchandising. Reciprocal gifts are diverting survivals which engage the curiosity of the antiquarian ...'. (6) The examples he gives - whether they are regarded as 'survivals' or not - relate to physical objects all of which have utility; they are bought and sold in the market. They involve the use of money which could have been put to other purposes and which might have been more (or less) profitable to the giver. Other writers, like Schwartz and Veblen, discuss the psychology of the gift in the context of economic commodities being used as vehicles and instruments for realities of another order. Thus, such gifts presuppose some element of calculating 'economizing' behaviour. In so far as these forms of gift-exchange in modern societies are partly or mainly economic in form or intent then it could follow that

certain kinds of action or behaviour often regarded as
primarily social might be considered to be primarily
economic in intent. Like Blau, this would lead us to
apply the principles of marginal utility analysis from
economics to exchange in social life. (7)

Whatever the general validity of these theories concerning gift-exchange relationships of a Gesellschaft-like type they entirely neglect large areas of gift
actions and behaviour in both personal and impersonal
contexts which do not involve physical objects, which
are difficult or impossible to price and quantify in
economic terms, and which, while involving an act of
giving, carry no explicit right, expectation or moral
enforcement of a return gift. If it were possible to
apply to such actions the metaphysical concept of
utility it would be found that they are not processes,
relationships or things which generally people want to
acquire, possess or buy. They have no exchange value.

Yet, as we have argued in this study, social gifts
and actions carrying no explicit or implicit individual
right to a return gift or action are forms of 'creative
altruism' (in Sorokin's words). (8) They are creative
in the sense that the self is realized with the help of
anonymous others; they allow the biological need to
help to express itself. Manifestations of altruism in
this sense may of course be thought of as self-love.
But they may also be thought of as giving life, or
prolonging life or enriching life for anonymous others.
That they may, incidentally, create economic wealth by
sustaining life is subsidiary in conception, conduct
and objective.

We speak here, of course, of those areas of personal
behaviour and relationships which lie outside the reciprocal rights and obligations of family and kinship in
modern society. We are thus chiefly concerned - as
much of social policy is - with 'stranger' relationships, with processes, institutions and structures
which encourage or discourage the intensity and extensiveness of anonymous helpfulness in society; with
'ultra obligations' which derive from our own characters and are not contractual in nature. (9) In the
ultimate analysis it is these concerns and their
expression which distinguish social policy from economic
policy or, as Kenneth Boulding put it, '... social
policy is that which is centred in those institutions
that create integration and discourage alienation'. (10)

2

In an earlier chapter we pointed out that the gift of blood had certain attributes which distinguished it from many other forms of gift and in a series of propositions we described these attributes. Most if not all of them are not to be found in any total sense in the forms of gift-exchange analysed by Lévi-Strauss, Schwartz, Blau and others which, interpreted structurally, lead to the elaboration of marginal utility models. Such models or theories of market exchange are, we suggest, irrelevant to an understanding of the place of blood in modern systems of medical care.

As we have explained earlier, in reflecting on the nature of medical care and its associated social and psychological elements we were eventually forced, by a process of logical inevitability, to more concrete generalizations and to ask whether the blood transfusion services and the use and distribution of human blood should be treated as a market consumption good. From an affirmative answer much could flow; the implications could extend to affect our thinking over wide areas of social policy and what are conventionally called 'the social services'. Hospitals, nursing homes, clinical laboratories, schools, universities and even, perhaps, churches would no longer be protected by laws or common conventions of 'charitable' immunity; they would be exposed to the forces of economic calculation and to the laws of the marketplace.

Blood transfusion services were selected as material for a case study on a comparative basis to illumine the problems of social policy in general and medical care in particular. The reasons for this selection were explained in Chapter 1. But other areas of gift-relationships in modern society might have been chosen for detailed examination from a large and expanding social policy territory of stranger relationships and transactions of a non-economic character. Some indications of this territory, actual and potential, of a 'caring community' in Britain were given in the Seebohm Report: 'This new department (of social service) will, we believe, ... enable the greatest possible number of individuals to act reciprocally, giving and receiving service for the well-being of the whole community'. (11)

We could, for example, have taken for study the giving role of the patient as 'teaching material', and as research material for experimentation and the testing of new drugs and other diagnostic and therapeutic measures. Millions of people in Western societies every year are expected to give themselves, without price or a contractural reward, in these situations. Moreover, measured in terms of time and numbers, the demand is increasing. To qualify as a doctor in Britain, it is probable that the average medical student now needs access to or contact with in one form or another some 300 different patients. This contribution from patients to the training of a professional élite will be substantially higher when the recommendations of the Royal Commission are fully implemented. (12) They are no longer 'charity' patients and could not in the 1970s, whatever the future of the National Health Service, be treated as such. Should their contribution to medical education, therefore, be paid on market criteria?

At present, patients as strangers are asked or expected to behave as givers on the unspoken assumption that they may benefit; sometimes their consent is sought; sometimes they are simply informed; often nothing is said. (13) Their willingness to be 'taught on' and to give of themselves, physically and psychologically, is presumed. It is taken for granted in the name of research, the advancement of medical science, society's need for doctors, the better training and more rapid progression of doctors professionally and financially and, ultimately, for the good of all patients irrespective of race, religion, colour or territory.

Gift transactions of this type between strangers - at present unpriced in non-market situations - are by no means unilateral transfers. Patients may benefit immediately more from contact with medical students than with consultants. Doctors in teaching roles give more to patients than a strict definition of their duties may warrant. But the benefits of teaching, experimentation and research - often inextricably mixed up - mostly accrue in the long run. They are not immediately a 'return gift' to the individual patient. While there may be 'fall-out' benefits they are not at once obvious to the patient. Among medical students, doctors ascending career ladders, research workers and scientists, however, the connections are more obvious and more personal. As individuals they expect to benefit in the short run from these gift transactions. The benefits to patients mostly accrue in the long-run; they further the well-being of some future collectivity of patients. If old age pensioners with chronic bronchitis put to themselves the Hobbesian question - why should men do other than act to their own immediate advantage? - they might start charging for the gifts they make which are more likely to benefit future cohorts of chronic bronchitics.

All personal service professions in an increasingly professionalized world are becoming - like medicine - more dependent on other people to further their professional aspirations. Sociologists need co-operative field and control material; psychologists need laboratory volunteers; psychiatric students need the mentally ill; social workers-to-be need clients; various professional groups within and without the pharmaceutical industry need healthy volunteers as well as diseased patients for drug trials; student teachers need pupils, and so on.

Considered individually as examples of stranger relationships, more people are expected to contribute - to give - to serve the interests of other people. There is in all these transactions an unspoken assumption of some form of gift-reciprocity; that those who give as members of a society to strangers will themselves (or their families) eventually benefit as members of that society. More often than not, however, such donors are in captive situations; the transaction cannot, therefore, be considered to be spontaneously altruistic in its most attainable form. There is, nevertheless, a vague and general presumption of a return gift at some future date, but a gift that may not be deliberately sought or desired by the individual concerned - as with voluntary blood donors. Few people when well wish to be ill; few people desire operations, blood transfusions, inpatient treatment or social care from social workers. More and more instruments of social policy are in action requiring, as scientific knowledge advances *pari passu* with professionalization, these acts of 'voluntaryism' which carry with them no wish for return acts or return gifts.

This is but one brief illustration of a number of social policy areas in which gift transactions take place and which might have been developed at length as case studies in this book. Another unexplored area of a different type - though also containing elements of altruism and self-interest - relates to the institution of foster care. At present we know little about the attitudes and motivations of foster parents and about who gives and who receives in systems of child care outside the family. It would seem that foster care is in Britain an essentially working-class institution. (14) Why do not the middle classes participate to the same extent? Is this another area of unquantified redistribution because foster parents though receiving payment are not rewarded on market criteria? Or because - as Sir Denis Robertson once said - love is a 'scarce resource'? (15) In the interests of society as a whole this resource is needed if the children concerned (as well as society) are not to suffer harm immediately and in the future. In this area also we might have raised questions about foster parents and the gift of foster care of a similar nature to the questions asked about the characteristics and motives of blood donors.

Or, to take one other example, we might have explored the gift transactions of Regional Eye Banks under the National Health Service in the prevention and reduction of blindness. At one such bank, the South Eastern Regional Eye Bank, 448 eyes were donated in 1965 - a number that had been steadily rising. (16) Because the supply of donated eyes is much less in other countries without a National Health Service than it is in Britain, 73 of these 448 corneas were exported as free gifts to India, Jamaica, South Africa, Singapore, Turkey, Hong Kong and other countries. (17) Should human eyes, bequeathed by donors or given by relatives to unknown strangers, be treated as a consumption good and sold to the highest bidders? These are not just idle theoretical questions as experience in the United States and other countries has shown in recent years in the expanding area of organ transplantation. (18)

3

'Modern social welfare' wrote Wilensky and Lebeaux, 'has really to be thought of as help given to the stranger not to the person who by reason of personal bond commands it without asking. It assumes a degree of social distance between helped and helper'. (19) The degree will vary from the social distance separating the patient from medical students engaged in examining, feeling and questioning to that of blood donors who do not know and can never see the recipient of the gift.

The givers in these relationships - whether captive or altruistically voluntary - may themselves be harmed by the act of giving. Blood donors can be harmed - in rare cases mortally - by giving. Patients can be harmed, physically and psychologically, by giving themselves, willingly or unwillingly, knowingly or unknowingly, as teaching material. So can pupils, clients, foster parents and many other categories of people in a variety of 'giving' social policy situations. There are risks to the giver as well as to the receiver in these social gift transactions.

Welfare propositions in economic theory rest to a large extent on an often unexpressed ethical proposition - the 'Paretian optimum'. Any change is for the better as long as nobody is worse off and at least one person is better off, each in his own estimation. But in the whole area of social gift-relationships this proposition is inapplicable. Givers are in no position themselves to evaluate gains and losses to themselves or to others. Professional arbiters decide but they, in turn, can seldom estimate as individuals the gains and losses for either the givers or the recipients. Their interventions are transitory and episodic; they seldom know the ultimate outcome. Those economic theorists who in assuming God-like mantles apply the Paretian optimum to increasing areas of social transactions have been blinded by their own calculus. In their blinkered pursuit of economic arithmetic they and those who follow them endanger society's unmethodical knowledge of the living man.

While physicists have increasingly been yielding theoretical territory many economists have been claiming more. In a remarkable book 'The World View of Physics', first published in English in 1952 Von Weizsäcker had this to say:

> Yielding step by step to the pressure of new data, scientists have given up more and more completely the presupposition that classical mechanics or a theory modelled on it is valid for the whole of nature. Instead the attempt is made to develop an independent theory of the phenomena not apprehended by classical mechanics and, conversely, to understand classical mechanics as a 'limiting case' of the new theory, i.e. as the result of its application to a definite, restricted field of inquiry. (20)

Ethical considerations are, as we said earlier, also endangered when scientific, technological and economic considerations are uppermost. Concrete illustrations of this danger - particularly to captive donors - are increasingly being provided by those engaged in the world of medical science. (21) One example was given in earlier chapters of the use of plasmapheresis techniques by the pharmaceutical industry in the United States. Many others could be drawn - if this were a full-length survey - from what the 'British Medical Journal' described in 1963 as the 'alarming rate of increase in experiments on human beings'. (22) But two examples - relevant to this case study of human blood - must suffice. (23)

The first relates to a study of hepatitis infection undertaken at a University College of Physicians and Surgeons in the United States and reported in August 1969. (24) Earlier studies by other investigators had shown that a serum factor, hepatitis antigen, was specifically associated with viral hepatitis. The university investigators tested 2211 units of blood of which 16 were found to contain the antigen. These 16 units of blood were transfused into 16 different patients. A control group of patients received blood which did not contain the antigen. Of 12 surviving recipients of blood containing the antigen 9 (75 per cent) developed hepatitis. The incidence of hepatitis in recipients of antigen-negative blood was 5.8 per cent (4 of 69). 'Our observations', said the authors, 'indicate ... an impressive correlation between the presence of hepatitis antigen in donor blood and the development of hepatitis following transfusion'. The question raised by this investigation is whether in the light of the findings of earlier studies blood containing the hepatitis antigen should have been transfused to patients. It is assumed that these patients and/or their relatives were informed of the possible risks involved.

The second example concerns an experimental study, reported in 1967, which took place at Willowbrook State School, Staten Island, New York, an over-crowded institution containing some 6000 mentally retarded patients predominantly children. Those in the experiment were children aged 3 to 10 years of age 'whose parents gave written consent after being informed of the details, potential risks, and potential benefits of the investigation'. (25) No information was published about the actual methods of the consent procedure and how it was carried out.

The purpose of the experiment was an attempt to elucidate the origins of serum hepatitis and to evaluate the possibility that there are several immunologically distinct types of the disease. The institution had a history of endemic infections. This in part was said to be a justification for the experiment. Groups of these children were in a series of trials exposed to hepatitis.

Scientific lessons were, of course, learnt for the benefit of society from these studies of mentally retarded children who participated as givers. As the 'Journal of the American Medical Association' commented: 'these recent studies ... represented an important contribution to our knowledge of hepatitis that would have been impossible without the judicious use of human beings in carefully controlled experimental studies'. (26)

Judicious means justify the ends; a plea made more urgent by the increasing commercialization of blood in the United States and the increasing use of 'derelict' and Skid-Row populations as a source of blood. It is doubtful whether this experiment would have taken place had social policy considerations dominated the supply and distribution of blood rather than the economics of the market. (27)

In these expanding fields of human experimentation - as with plasmapheresis programs - virtually all the strangers who give, by inducement, for money or in captive situations, are poor people; the indigent, the deprived, the educationally handicapped, the socially inadequate (in and out of prisons and other institutions), and all those described by an American sociologist as 'inept' in advancing a hypothesis that modern economic systems 'utilize the inept more efficiently'. (28)

How some of the 'inept' in captive prison situations have been utilized for the presumed benefit of society in clinical trials undertaken for profit by an American drug corporation was described in Chapter 8. Among those who were utilized, some died and some were disabled. These are the human cost facts that can be and were counted but what cannot be assessed are the moral effects on all those who were involved, in one form or another, in this and similar experiments which 'utilize' the poor and the inept; physicians, prison staff, prisoners, technicians, administrators and officials of the pharmaceutical companies involved, and many others. What effects do such experiences have on their values and on their attitudes and behaviour towards the 'inept' in society? The ethical consequences - or disvalues - of market experiments of this kind extend far beyond the biological damage actually done to those who are utilized.

What is also a fact that could be counted - if anyone thought of counting - is that in the United States and certain other Western societies poor people and those classed as 'indigents' are the providers of most of the teaching and research material needed to sustain the fabric of medical systems. Many American teaching hospitals are facing a crisis in the 1970s as the relative proportions of indigents in the locality decline. The rapid growth of profit-making hospitals (referred to in Chapter 8) is likely to accentuate the shortage of 'clinical material' for teaching and research - with consequential effects on the American output of doctors. The corporations who operate these hospitals have decided not to treat 'indigent' or 'charity' patients and not to provide emergency, obstetrics or paediatric departments 'which, traditionally, are money-losers in hospitals'. (29)

With rising standards of living the availability and number of poor charity patients would also have presented problems in Britain but the advent of the National Health Service saved the situation as it brought in after 1948 millions of Health Service potential 'teaching cases'. Even so, some element of discrimination is still practised in favour of some private patients. They are not required or expected to the same extent to make stranger gifts for the eventual benefit of society at large - just as the rich of New York and Chicago write cheques for blood bills without thought of tomorrow or the social direction of their society.

4

We have continually in these discussions of gift relationships asked the question: who gives and why? In this chapter we have placed these same questions in a much broader social service context. An essential corollary is the further question: who in fact benefits from all these unpaid social transactions? Do the poor benefit proportionately as much or more in relation to their social and medical needs as the rich for the gifts they make in the interests of science, of medicine, of the medical and other professions and of society? What return gifts does society make?

In the preceding chapter we discussed certain social costs arising from the wastes, shortages, inefficiencies, unethical practices and hazards involved in the American commercial blood market. We concluded that despite the difficulties of measuring such costs in money terms a disproportionate part was borne by poor people, the sick and the handicapped.

In this chapter we have extended the discussion of costs and benefits to encompass a far wider area of social policy. An economic statistician, specializing in cost-benefit analysis, and looking at the scene with the aid of quantifying spectacles might see this whole area of social gift transactions as a great and growing redistributive process favouring - in some societies - the rich and the privileged; a process, moreover, stimulated by advances in science and technology, by the growth of professionalism and the personal service occupations, and by systems of buying and selling medical care and other social services through which gifts are received but are not returned in kind or money. (30)

Could our statistician then, pursuing further and on a comparative basis this statistical fantasy, bring together and merge, in an immense series of tables, all his social redistribution data with the conventional income and wealth data available for Britain, the United States and other countries? Is it not possible that the results would show for some economic and social systems large flows of total redistribution from the poor to the rich? In other words, would not the social gifts from the economically poor more than outweigh the combined effects of progressive taxation and the cash transfers of social welfare programs?

However many computers were provided for our statistician, and whatever advances were made on 'theories of public goods' developed by Samuelson (31) and others he would, in the end, have to confess to failure. The task would be beyond him because, in the first place, most of the hard facts about the beneficiaries of services in kind are missing. To take the case of blood transfusions again, no national data exist for any country in the world which show the distribution of blood recipients by sex, age, social class, income group and other characteristics. There are certain indications - particularly in the United States - of a positive relationship between the incidence of blood transfusions and the utilization by higher income groups of certain sectors of medical care services. (32) But none of the studies that have been made in the United States and Britain are comprehensive in scope and analysis.

The sample survey in 1967 of some 3800 blood donors, reported in Chapter 7, suggested that the families of higher income/social class groups received proportionately more blood than the families of lower income/ social class groups. This survey was, however, from the viewpoint of estimating the beneficiaries and benefits of blood transfusions on a limited scale. We have to conclude, therefore, that even in this relatively small area of social policy our statistician would not be able to answer on a national basis the question: who receives blood?

Nor could he even begin to answer some of the more metaphysical and distributive questions that have recurred again and again in this book. He would not, for example, be able to identify and evaluate all the 'externalities' or 'disvalues' in the total redistributive process. What implied money values would he place on the human lives saved and lost, on sickness induced and prevented, even if he had all the demographic data? What prices would he expect medical students, doctors and many other professional aspirants and groups to pay for the right to treat people as teaching, learning, research and scientific experimental material? What allowances would he make for the external costs of malpractice and counter-malpractice claims as more areas of stranger-relationships became subject to the laws of the marketplace? What profitability value would he accord to a spirit of altruism in society today and in the future, its absence or its presence as an element of free choice for individuals? How would he cost the consequences to a society in which people, by simply writing cheques for blood, say 'I need no longer suffer from or experience a sense of duty, of obligation, of responsibility for strangers'? How then would he quantify the costs of violence?

All this is not pure speculation. There is growing disquiet in the United States, Japan and other countries with expanding commercial blood programs that such programs are driving out the voluntary system. Insurance companies are said to be stifling the spirit of giving and thereby harming society by selling policies which provide for cash reimbursement of the cost of blood transfused. The pharmaceutical industry, in developing commercial plasmapheresis programs, is similarly under criticism for encouraging among the public at large the notion that dollars can substitute for blood. Even the President of the American Medical Association was led to say in 1968 '... money payments for blood can destroy the motivation of the family and friends to replace the blood and could result in the creation of many "semi-professional" donors who would contribute too frequently, to the detriment of their own health. It also would increase premiums and rates for this portion of insurance plans; would tend to commercialize what have been community-spirited voluntary contributions; and could affect the amount of blood available in time of national catastrophe'. (33)

Such externalities cannot be measured in statistical or monetary terms. As Edgeworth once said in another context: 'We cannot *count* the golden sands of life; we cannot *number* the "innumerable smiles" of seas of love'. (34)

It is here that we can discern some of the fundamental distinguishing marks of social policy which differentiate it from economic policy. Because it has continually to ask the question 'who is my stranger' it must inevitably be concerned with the unquantifiable and unmethodical aspects of man as well as with those aspects which can be identified and counted. Thus, in terms of policies, what unites it with ethical considerations is its focus on integrative systems: on processes, transactions and institutions which promote an individual's sense of identity, participation and community and allow him more freedom of choice for the expression of altruism and which, simultaneously, discourage a sense of individual alienation.

This book, centring on gift relationships, is an attempt at measurement in respect of one such institution. It has also advanced three inter-related theses. First, that gift-exchange of a non-quantifiable nature has more important functions in complex, large-scale societies than the writings of Lévi-Strauss and others would suggest. Second, the application of scientific and technological developments in such societies, in further accelerating the spread of complexity, has increased rather than diminished the scientific as well as the social need for gift relationships. Third, for these and many other reasons, modern societies now require more rather than less freedom of choice for the expression of altruism in the daily life of all social groups. While this requirement has been argued primarily on social, ethical and biological grounds it is also justified on scientific and economic criteria.

5

To end this chapter we move from abstract generalizations about gift relationships and unanswered questions about social redistribution to report concretely on some blood donor responses in England. We end, therefore, on an individual note by quoting what some donors had to say about their motives for giving when they took part in the questionnaire survey in 1967.

First, however, we have to repeat a few warnings scattered throughout this book and offer some general observations.

The assumption should not be drawn from the comparative material presented in this study that, in terms of moral values, there is anything particularly unique or meritorious about the British people in their commitment to and support of a voluntary blood donor program. In many other countries beside Britain and the United States there are countless numbers of voluntary community donors. If asked, there is no reason to doubt that many would respond by expressing similar sentiments of altruism and reciprocity. What we cannot write about (apart from a few countries) are their numbers, proportions, characteristics, representativeness, and so forth. But just because we have presented a mass of facts about voluntary donors in Britain and few facts about voluntary donors in many other countries there must not, we repeat, be thoughts about chosen people. In any event the blood donor, however he is classified by type (see Chapter 5), represents only a minority in a total eligible population.

Nor must it be concluded from what we have written that all is well with all British social institutions and distributive welfare systems; with, in short, the 'social condition of Britain'. As a corrective, perhaps for some who may err in interpretation, it needs to be said that the themes pursued in this book are linked to the issues of social justice raised in the author's 'Commitment to Welfare' and 'Income Distribution and Social Change'.

What is unique as an instrument of social policy among the countries we have surveyed is the National Health Service and the values that it embodies. Attitudes to and relationships with the National Blood Transfusion Service among the general public since 1948 can only be understood within the context of the Health Service. The most unsordid act of British social policy in the twentieth century has allowed and encouraged sentiments of altruism, reciprocity and social duty to express themselves; to be made explicit and identifiable in measurable patterns of behaviour by all social groups and classes. In part, this is attributable to the fact that, structurally and functionally, the Health Service is not socially divisive; its universal and free access basis has contributed much, we believe, to the social liberties of the subject in allowing people the choice to give or not to give blood for unseen strangers.

Of course, in probing the deeper human motives for giving and return-giving, for altruism and self-love, it would be facile to suggest that socialized medicine was wholly responsible. We have not said that at all. What we do suggest, however, is that the ways in which society organizes and structures its social institutions -

and particularly its health and welfare systems - can encourage or discourage the altruistic in man; such systems can foster integration or alienation; they can allow the 'theme of the gift' (to recall Mauss's words) - of generosity towards strangers - to spread among and between social groups and generations. This, we further suggest, is an aspect of freedom in the twentieth century which, compared with the emphasis on consumer choice in material acquisitiveness, is insufficiently recognized. It is indeed little understood how modern society, technical, professional, large-scale organized society, allows few opportunities for ordinary people to articulate giving in morally practical terms outside their own network of family and personal relationships.

We have from time to time in asking questions about gift relationships employed the words 'motives' and 'motivation'. Their use may have promised too much. We did, however, a long while ago - in Chapter 2 - draw attention to the association of blood, its possession, inheritance, loss and transfusion, with religious beliefs, theories and concepts of race, kinship, ancestor-worship and so forth and its many symbolical properties. The very thought of blood touches the deepest feelings in man about life and death. Consequently, we said, any attempt to study individual motives for giving or not giving blood would face some extremely demanding conceptual and analytical problems. In any event, we concluded, these could not even be formulated until we had the basic facts about the social and demographic characteristics of a sample of blood donors.

In Chapter 7 and Appendix 4 we presented an analysis of the facts derived from the pilot study in certain areas of England for some 3800 donors. We shall not attempt to repeat the findings here. As regards that part of the questionnaire which asked about reasons for giving blood, we expressed our hesitations about the value of such questions and the difficulties of interpreting the responses. Hence, the analysis of the results in Appendix 6 was undertaken in a relatively straightforward manner; no attempt is made to speculate widely and deeply, and no statistical tests of significance adorn the tables. The analysis is chiefly confined to a classification of the answers to question 5 under fourteen main heads. The generally uncomplicated way in which this question was answered does not justify a complicated motivational analysis.

These fourteen heads are set out in Table 38 along

with the proportions of donor replies judged to fall in one or other category. We now provide below some examples of individual replies to illustrate each category of answer to Question 5 ('Could you say why you *first* decided to become a blood donor?'). They were selected because they seemed to express more vividly different categories of replies than many stereotyped answers like 'Because I want to help to save lives in hospital'. A purely random selection would have been less interesting.

1 Altruism (26.4 per cent of answers)

The great majority of answers in this category expressed in general terms a desire to help:
'Knowing I mite be saving somebody life' (single woman, aged 40, power press operator, £10-15 a week, 10 donations).
'Anonymously, without financial reward to help others' (married man, aged 34, no children, insurance claims official, £20-30 a week, 23 donations).
'You cant get blood from supermarkets and chaine stores. People them selves must come forword, sick people cant get out of bed to ask you for a pint to save thier life so I came forword in hope to help somebody who needs blood' (married woman, aged 23, no children, machine operator, £15-20 a week [chief earner, electrician] 4 donations).
'No man is an island' (married man, aged 36, two children, foreman maintenance fitter, £30-50 a week, 21 donations).
'I thought it just a small way to help people - as a blind person other opportunities are limited' (married man, aged 49, no children, piano tuner, £30-50 a week, 26 donations).
'I felt it was a small contribution that I could make to the welfare of humanity' (married man, aged 45, four children, bank manager, £30-50 a week, 26 donations).
'A desire to help other people in need' (single man, aged 51, road labourer, £10-15 a week, 11 donations).
Some donors singled out for help the Health Service in its various manifestations:
'Just to help the Hospitals' (married woman, aged 61, two children, husband retired, £10-15 a week, 45 donations).
'At the age of 18 I decided that it was a good thing for anyone capable and healthy to donate blood for

the good of other people and the advancement of medical science' (married woman, aged 28, three children, husband carriage serviceman [railways], £10-15 a week, 12 donations).

'I get my surgical shoes thro' the N.H.S. This is some slight return and I want to help people' (married man, aged 53, one child, insurance agent, £15-20 a week, 20 donations).

A small proportion of donors specified those who should be helped:

'To help babies that are borne with bad blood' (married man, aged 23, one child, skilled boot polish worker, £15-20 a week, 12 donations).

2 Gratitude for good health (1.4 per cent of answers)

'Because I am fortunate in having good health myself and like to think my blood can help some-one else back to health, and I felt this was a wonderful service I wanted to be part of' (widow, aged 63, four children, widow's pension, less than £10 a week, 25 donations).

'Briefly because I have enjoyed good health all my life and in a small way it is a way of saying "Thank you" and a small donation to the less fortunate' (married man, aged 53, two children, retired police officer now welfare officer, £20-30 a week, 11 donations).

'To me it is a form of thanking God for my own good health' (married woman, aged 64, two children, clerk, £20-30 a week [husband also a clerk], 47 donations).

3 Reciprocity (9.8 per cent of answers)

In Chapter 7 we showed the proportions of donors who had themselves received transfusions. Many of them gave this as the reason in filling in the questionnaire:

'After being told that my own life had been saved by transfusions - childbirth. Determined to repay' (married woman, aged 46, five children, husband toolmaker, £20-30 a week, 6 donations).

'To try and repay in some small way some unknown person whose blood helped me recover from two operations and enable me to be with my family, thats why I bring them along also as they become old enough' (married woman, aged 44, three children, farmer's wife, more than £50 a week, 8 donations).

Over 40 per cent of those whose answers were classified under 'reciprocity' referred to transfusions received by relatives or friends:

'Some unknown person gave blood to save my wifes life' (married man, aged 43, two children, self-employed window cleaner, £15-20 a week, 56 donations).

'A young niece died from Luekemia after having several transfusions which prolonged her life a little. After discussing this with a friend who was already a donor, I went along with her to the next session' (married woman, aged 59, one child, husband sheet metal worker, £20-30 a week, 12 donations).

'My husband aged 41, collasped and died, without whom life is very lonely - so I thought my blood may help to save some-one the heart ache I've had' (transfusion received by husband before he died) (widow, aged 47, one child, school meals service cook, less than £10 a week, 16 donations).

Another substantial group of donors gave blood because they thought that in the future they or a member of their family might need it:

'Someone in my family may one day need blood, I would like to think that someone will be there then, so I give mine knowing that some unknown person will be eternally grateful' (married woman, aged 28, no children, industrial chemist [husband motor mechanic], £20-30 a week, 13 donations).

'I have a motor Bike and someday I may need blood to help me, so why shouldnt I give mine to help someone who may have had an accident' (married man, aged 50, two children, waterman textiles, £15-20 a week, 4 donations).

4 Replacement (0.8 per cent of answers)

These were donors who thought that someone in the family should give blood and who said that they were replacing a member who could not - or could no longer - donate:

'My mother was a donor for a number of years and when she died in 1958 I decided to carry on in her place' (married man, aged 49, five children, bricklayer, £20-30 a week, 16 donations).

'When my wife was refused as donor due to anaemia I stepped in' (married man, aged 63, one child, bus driver, £15-20 a week, 23 donations).

'My son was killed on the road, he was a Blood Donor and I knew they did their best to save him and because I know he would be pleased I am carrying on as long as I can to help someone I hope' (married woman, aged 63, four children, husband timber sawyer, £10-15 a week, 19 donations).

5 Awareness of need for blood (6.4 per cent of answers)

All donors in this category said that they gave blood because they had become aware of the need for it. The circumstances in which they recognized need varied considerably:

'Being in the construction side of building you see many people hurt and it makes you feel as though you have done a little bit to help' (married man, aged 25, no children, scaffolder, £30-50 a week, 3 donations).

'Owing to the nature of my work I feel the need to give to the unfortunate people who require blood after an accident. Having seen so much lost in the course of my work I thought my health could stand helping others' (married man, aged 49, three children, ambulance driver, £20-30 a week, 23 donations).

'A sister had to receive five pints after an illness and I realized how much benefit could be had by receiving blood from a donor' (married woman, aged 62, three children, husband company director, £30-50 a week, 17 donations).

'After seeing a bad accedent I thought it was the best way I could help' (single woman, aged 22, upholstress, father rubber tyre beader, £20-30 a week, 5 donations).

'In order to help maintain the supply of blood so urgently needed at all times' (married man, aged 59, three children, postman, £10-15 a week, 10 donations).

6 Duty (3.3 per cent of answers)

The distinction between 'Altruism' (Category 1) and 'Duty' was extremely difficult to draw. There were the donors who said quite simply that they *wanted* to help other people; there were donors who said or implied that as a matter of conscience, or duty or feelings of guilt they *ought* to help other people. The difference in these responses - if there really is or could be a difference - may well lie in the accidental choice of words by individual donors. But, as we said earlier, there is no justification for reading more into these responses about motives than appears on the surface of language. Hence, the classification into categories was undertaken on the basis of what people actually wrote on the questionnaire. Some examples of 'duty' answers are:

'Sense of duty to the community and nation as a whole' (married man, aged 31, three children, charge-hand fitter, £15-20 a week, 7 donations).

'My conscience - having served 5 years on active service in the war (1939-45) helping to destroy life, and during this period my wife was receiving blood to save her life, it occurred to me, after demobilization, that I could at least ease my conscience' (married man, aged 52, 1 child, clerical officer civil service, £20-30 a week, 58 donations).

'Feelings of guilt at receiving so much in life and giving so little' (single woman, aged 60, school teacher, £20-30 a week, 20 donations).

'Primarily to "conform" with teenage contemporaries - desire "to be of service" to others was a secondary reason' (married man, aged 37, two children, contracts engineer, £20-30 a week, 26 donations).

'During the war I was afraid I would be considered too old to help my country. Giving blood, as I started to do then, was just a balm to my pride. I was called up late for service, which restored my pride. Afterwards I just carried on donating. With other voluntary jobs I have undertaken, I have just felt the job was there, and I was available. Other jobs were in trade unions or political parties. I have never thought "Why should I do it? I'll leave it to someone else". I have thought "Why should not I do this?" I am not a do-gooder, at least, I don't feel like one nor think like one' (married man, aged 62, three children, compositor, £15-20 a week, 28 donations).

'I am a father of two, and feel that if I, or any of mine ever need blood, they have a moral right to it. It is an obligation of a father' (married man, aged 55, two children, motor mechanic, £15-20 a week, 33 donations).

'I have been a mental patient (PSYCOPATH) and I have always tried to help people. Also I tried to commit suicide by stabbing myself and a transfusion saved me' (single man, aged 19, labourer, £10-15 a week, 2 donations).

7 War effort (6.7 per cent of answers)

In comparison with the preceding category, most of the answers classified here were fairly straightforward. Naturally, they all came from donors over the age of 40:

'During war service in the WAAF I was made aware of the need to give blood to help injured servicemen and civilians and afterwards I realized that it was also necessary in peace time' (single woman, aged 45, bank clerk, £20-30 a week, 40 donations).

'Came unscathed through 1939-45 war; felt "owed" something' (married man, aged 43, three children, chief establishment assistant local government, £30-50 a week, 30 donations).

'1941. War. Blood needed. I had some. Why not?' (married man, aged 47, three children, sales representative, £20-30 a week, 10 donations).

'I first gave blood during the last war to try and help save people from the results of war to which I am very strongly opposed - prefer to preserve life as against destroying it' (married woman, aged 53, one child, part-time actress and housewife, £30-50 a week, [husband television producer], 20 donations).

8 The Defence Services since 1945 (5.0 per cent of answers)

This category, partly associated with the preceding one, comprises donors who said that they first gave blood as members of the Services. Some of the answers indicate that the respondents became donors at least partly because of certain benefits, e.g. 48-hour passes, being excused drill, etc. Other answers suggest that the act of donating was not entirely voluntary; that there were, as we discussed in our typology of donors, external pressures 'to volunteer'. However, the majority of donors placed in this category did not specify either benefits or pressures; the most usual wording employed took the form 'I answered an appeal for blood while in the Army.' Some illustrations of the responses of donors in this category who whatever the reasons given for the first donation had continued to donate are:

'Gave blood when in the services (seemed a good way to get out of an afternoons duties!). Later there was a general appeal for blood where I live' (married man, aged 37, two children, sales office manager, £30-50 a week, 9 donations).

'It was a good excuse for a good cup of tea and the afternoon off duty whilst serving in the Navy' (married man, aged 42, three children, maintenance engineer printing, £30-50 a week, 49 donations).
'Request for voluntary donors whilst serving in Forces' (married man, aged 41, no children, sales representative, £20-30 a week, 6 donations).
'Told to volunteer in RAF! Subsequently as a civilian happened to pass a blood donor session (not well advertised) and called in on spur of moment' (married man, aged 41, two children, local government clerk, £30-50 a week, 36 donations).

9 Rare blood group (1.1 per cent of answers)

The general idea expressed in this type of answer was that the discovery that they were in a rare blood group was instrumental in the donor deciding to give blood. Such answers further imply that because one's blood is rare or unique there is a particular responsibility to make it available to others who may need it. To learn also that one has in one's make-up some element of 'uniqueness' may contribute to feelings of self-respect as well as to acts of giving.

'My blood is fairly rare - this I did not discover until I had had my twins (4th pregnancy). I now have six children which is most unusual because of my group. Maybe my blood may help some other mother. I give blood in gratitude for my good fortune' (married woman, aged 42, six children, school teacher [husband also school teacher, £30-50 a week], 20 donations).
'Curiosity first. Then continued when I discovered I had a rare blood group. I like to think that a life may be saved by my blood' (married man, aged 53, two children, engineering toolmaker, £15-20 a week, 25 donations).
'My mother is of a rare blood group and I thought perhaps I would be. I was not, but felt my blood would still be needed' (married woman, aged 23, no children, hairdresser [husband advertising art director, £30-50 a week], 10 donations).

10 To obtain some benefit (1.8 per cent of answers)

These were fairly straightforward answers the great majority of which were concerned with benefits to the donor's physical health; nose bleeding, regular health checks, learning one's blood group, etc. A few donors, however, introduced more complex reasons:

'From being a boy I had suffered from constant nose bleeding and since I became a donor I have not had a single nose bleed' (married man, aged 43, two children, newsagent, £30-50 a week, 17 donations).
'I wanted to do something to convince myself I was 18 and I always wanted to be a blood donor - snob appeal' (married woman, aged 20, no children, donor attendant blood transfusion service [husband car fitter £15-20 a week] 6 donations).

11 Personal appeal (13.2 per cent of answers)

In this category were placed the answers of donors who said that they had been influenced to give blood by encouragement, requests and appeals on a personal basis:

'A workmate convinced me of the need for more donors' (married man, aged 35, one child, form grinder/miller [machine tools], £20-30 a week, 20 donations).
'A pretty young nurse walked round the factory I was working in' (married man, aged 41, three adopted children, development engineer [pressure diecasting non-ferrous], £30-50 a week, 17 donations).
'Coerced by my husband as I was rather apprehensive' (married woman, aged 35, two adopted children, husband teacher technical education, £30-50 a week, 16 donations).

12 General appeal (18.0 per cent of answers)

These were mainly short answers by donors who said that they had been influenced by a general appeal:

'I heard the appeal on the BBC' (married woman, aged 61, three children, husband old age pensioner, less than £10 a week, 16 donations).
'On seeing TV Advert I thought what great help to patients it could be, with so little effort by giving' (married man, aged 45, 1 child, builder's manager, £20-30 a week, 7 donations).
'I became a donor when the Unit came to the firm at which I worked, and ask for donors because of a shortage of blood' (married man, aged 42, six children, glass furnace operator, £15-20 a week, 19 donations).
'I read the notice the appeal for donors in the

Putney Hospital waiting room' (widower, aged 56, five children, manager [cleaning], £20-30 a week, 7 donations).

13 Miscellaneous (5 per cent of answers)

All types of answers occurring less than twenty times in the whole of the sample were put in this category. They varied greatly, ranging from the obviously frivolous to serious essays of a personal nature:

'To get a good cup of tea' (married man, aged 24, one child, store-keeper [lock and door closers], £15-20 a week, 4 donations).

'I went along to hold my husbands hand' (married woman, aged 39, two children, husband shop manager [grocery], £15-20 a week, 32 donations).

'No money to spare. Plenty of blood to spare' (married man, aged 35, two children, painter and decorator, £15-20 a week, 19 donations).

'After seeing fellow hitch hikers in Greece selling their blood for a few pounds a pint to raise some money for food. It made me realize what a good system the voluntary system is' (single man, aged 23, industrial chemist [abrasive wheel industry], £15-20 a week, 2 donations).

14 More than one type of answer (0.9 per cent of answers)

Some donors gave answers which included more than one of the categories we have employed in the analysis in Appenidx 6. Most of them seemed to recognize that the decision to give blood is often a complex process and that, consequently, they could not distinguish a single or predominant motive:

'I feel that with blood it would have to be used for the purposes it was given, no deductions for administrative purposes like so many Charity Organizations. Blood is something which could not come out of the rates. I have also now become a car driver and know that I use a dangerous weapon. And as a hypochondriac who has not visited a doctor for illness for some 7 years I felt that I would like to have some sort of blood test and felt sure, rightly or wrongly, that if I became a donor my blood would go through a test of some kind - at least I would know I had blood' (married man, aged 33, no children, company secretary, £30-50 a week, 2 donations).

'My group is rather rare. I drive every day, I see
blood on the road every week. One day it may be
mine. With that cheerful thought one may regard
donating as an investment' (single man, aged 25,
advertising copywriter, £20-30 a week, 4 donations).
'It is in my estimation, a good way to keep a half
yearly check on my own health. The thoughts of my
own children at some time needing a donor's blood'
(married man, aged 40, two children, foreman building maintenance, £20-30 a week, 4 donations).

This is what some of the donors had to say in their
own words about their reasons for giving. The vividness, individuality and diversity of these responses add
life and a sense of community to the statistical gener-
alities in Appendix 6. To speculate further about the
psychology of these relationships would require not only
depth interviews and a larger sample but, maybe, the
insights of a Freud, a Jung and a Lévi-Strauss.

All we can do is to call attention to the facts and
the donors' own statements. Over two-fifths of all
the answers in the whole sample fell into the categories
'Altruism', 'Reciprocity', 'Replacement' and 'Duty'.
Nearly a third represented voluntary responses to
personal and general appeals for blood. A further 6
per cent responded to an 'Awareness of Need'. These
seven categories accounted for nearly 80 per cent of
the answers suggesting a high sense of social responsibility towards the needs of other members of society.
Perhaps this is one of the outstanding impressions
which emerges from the survey.

NOTES

1 C. Lévi-Strauss, 'The Elementary Structures of Kinship', revised edition (ed. R. Needham), London,
   Eyre & Spottiswoode, 1969.
2 'Proc. Conf. American Association of Blood Banks',
   Los Angeles, 1966.
3 Lévi-Strauss, op. cit., p. 56.
4 G. Dalton, Economic Theory and Primitive Society,
   'American Anthropologist', vol. 63, February 1961.
5 F. Tönnies, 'Community and Association' ('Gemeinschaft und Gesellschaft'), translated and supplemented by C.P. Loomis, London, Routledge & Kegan
   Paul, 1955, pp. 20-1.
6 Lévi-Strauss, op. cit., p. 61.
7 P.M. Blaue, 'Exchange and Power in Social Life', New
   York, Wiley, 1964.

8 P.A. Sorokin, 'The Ways and Power of Love', Boston, Beacon Press, 1954.
9 For a philosophical discussion of 'ultra obligations' see G.R. Grice, 'The Grounds of Moral Judgement', Cambridge University Press, 1967.
10 K.E. Boulding, The Boundaries of Social Policy, 'Social Work', vol. 12, no. 1, January 1967, p. 7.
11 'Report of the Committee on Local Authority and Allied Personal Social Services', Cmnd 3703, 1968, p. 11.
12 'Report of the Royal Commission on Medical Education 1965-8', Cmnd 3569, London, HMSO, 1968.
13 For an explanation of the problems of defining 'true' or 'informed' consent see 'Medical Research Council, Annual Report 1962-3', Cmnd 2382, London, HMSO, 1964 and M.H. Pappworth, 'Human Guinea Pigs', London, Routledge & Kegan Paul, 1967.
14 See R. Parker, 'Decision in Child Care', London, Allen & Unwin, 1966, especially pp. 68-9, and R. Dinnage and M.L. Kellmer Pringle, 'Foster Home Care - Facts and Fallacies', London, Longmans, 1967.
15 D. Robertson, 'Economic Commentaries', 1956, p. 154.
16 Personal communication, Sir Benjamin Rycroft and P.V. Rycroft, December 1966 and see also G.E.W. Wolstenholme and M. O'Connor, ibid., pp. 43-50.
17 New eye donors in Britain were being registered at a rate of about 1000 a month in 1965 ('Report of the Central Health Services Council for 1965', HMSO, 1966).
18 For an informative discussion of the ethical and legal problems of organ transplantation see G.E.W. Wolstenholme and M. O'Connor, ibid.
19 H.L. Wilensky and C.N. Lebeaux, 'Industrial Society and Social Welfare', New York, Russell Sage, 1958, p. 141.
20 C.F. von Weizsäcker, 'The World View of Physics', London, Routledge & Kegan Paul, 1952, p. 69.
21 Western scientific medicine appears to be making increasing use of two 'captive volunteer' groups for research and experimental purposes, 1, primitive peoples in Africa and South America, 2, prisoners in the United States and South Africa. The main area of research interest in relation to the first group is coronary heart disease and its reported connection with diet (one of the major health preoccupations of Western man). Many studies involve the provision for a short period of comprehensive medical care. When the research facts have been collected medical care is withdrawn

(see, for example, A.G. Shaper and K.W. Jones, Serum-Cholestrol in Camel-Herding Nomads, 'Lancet', ii, 1305, 1962). As regards the use of prisoners, see references in this book to plasmapheresis; A.J. Davis, 'Trans-Action', December 1968 (describing extensive laboratory experiments in Philadelphia gaols) and Wolstenholme and O'Connor, op. cit.
22 'Brit. Med. J.', editorial Ethics of Human Experimentation, 6 July 1963, p. 1.
23 For more documentation and references to some 200 papers see Pappworth, op. cit., and letter to 'Brit. Med. J.', on the ethics of liver transplants, 7 June 1969, p. 631.
24 D.J. Gocke, H.B. Greenberg and N.B. Kavey, Hepatitis Antigen, 'Lancet', ii, 248, 1969.
25 S. Krugman, C.P. Giles and J. Hammond, Infectious Hepatitis, 'J.A.M.A.', vol. 200, no. 5, 1 May 1967, p. 365.
26 'J.A.M.A.', Editorial, vol. 200, no. 5, 1 May 1967, p. 407.
27 'In initial trials of any new agents, the investigator must be genuinely open-minded concerning the possibility that the drug is worth a trial and that it may be as good as, or perhaps better than, one or more of those already available. Strong convictions for or against its value in the treatment of a disease can render it unethical for him to use or withhold the agent under trial or to use a placebo; in this case he should not undertake the investigation' ('Principles for the Clinical Evaluation of Drugs, Report of a WHO Scientific Study Group', World Health Organization, Tech. Rep. Ser., 1968, no. 403, p. 6.
28 W.J. Goode, The Protection of the Inept, 'Amer. Soc. Review', vol. 32, no. 1, February 1967, pp. 5-19.
29 'Wall Street Journal', 13 October 1969.
30 In Britain, private patients who find the National Health Service uncongenial are not charged for blood received from the National Health Service.
31 See, for example, P.A. Samuelson, The Pure Theory of Public Expenditure, 'Review of Economics and Statistics', XXXVI, 1954, Diagrammatic Exposition of Theory of Public Expenditure, op. cit., XXXVII, 1955, and Aspects of Public Expenditure Theories, op. cit., XL, 1958.
32 Two of the main American sources of medical care utilization data are: 1, 'Vital and Health Statistics Data from the National Health Survey', National

Center for Health Statistics, Public Health Service, U.S. Department of Health, Education and Welfare, 1960-9 and 2, Commission on Professional and Hospital Activities, 'Medical Audit Program Reports', Ann Arbor, Michigan, 1963-9. Sources of data for England and Wales are the 'Report on Hospital Inpatient Inquiry' for 1961 and 1966 and 'Annual Report of the Ministry of Health', Department of Health and Social Security and General Register Office. See also J.N. Morris, 'Uses of Epidemiology' (2nd edn), Edinburgh and London, Livingstone, 1964.

33 M.O. Rouse, Blood Banking and Blood Use, 'Transfusions', vol. 8, no. 2, March-April 1968, p. 106.

34 F.Y. Edgeworth, 'Mathematical Physics', London, Kegan Paul, 1881, p. 8 (original italics).

10 The concept of community

John Benson

The term 'community' in the title cannot be said to mark off a clear topic for discussion. It is used in ordinary speech and in the semi-technical vocabulary of sociologists in a wide variety of applications and in different, and sometimes seriously ambiguous, senses. Its relations to and overlap with other terms in the same conceptual region, such as 'society', and 'association', are far from clear. To take 'community' and 'society'; sometimes 'society' is taken to refer to the most inclusive groupings, the most extensive collectivities felt to be marked by a significant degree of unity and integration, while 'community' is taken to refer to particular sub-divisions of such inclusive societies: regions, cities, national and racial groups, religious denominations, neighbourhoods, and so on. With this distinction we have a very wide sense for 'community', for it is obvious that these various groupings are marked off by quite diverse principles of classification, and one may question whether they have any significant features in common. At any rate it is clear that in this sense a community is a part of a wider social whole. But there are other uses of the two terms, not obviously illegitimate, in which this is not so. 'Community' may be used to refer to any group, large or small, whose members live together in such a way that they share, not this or that particular interest, but the basic conditions of a common life; (1) and 'society' to refer to the institutional organisation, political, legal, and economic, which may or may not be a feature of such groups. Again 'society' may be used as a generic term and 'community' as a specific term denoting societies characterised by particular kinds of relationship (e.g. 'face-to-face', or sympathetic as opposed to contractual) between the members.

An example of this use is the distinction between 'community' and 'association' derived from Tönnies' analysis of *Gemeinschaft* and *Gesellschaft*, supposedly fundamental types of social relationship providing a way of classifying actual social groupings.

There are then at least these three senses of 'community' which, even if not severally very clear, are pretty clearly different. Of course their areas of application overlap, but this is just where the danger lies, for though the word may apply in two or all of its senses to the same thing it does so by virtue of different criteria and says very different things depending on the criteria which are held to justify the application.

One further possible ambiguity should be mentioned, which is rather different from those considered so far, which consist in the currency of different *descriptive* senses of 'community'. 'Community' is often used with strong evaluative and emotive force, commonly signalled by the use of such intensifying adjectives as 'real' and 'genuine'. When people talk about 'real community' they are not referring to an objectively definable type of social structure so much as to a vaguely sensed quality of common life which is felt to be valuable and is assumed to depend for its existence on a specific type of social structure (such as the self-contained village). It may be unfair to label this an 'ambiguity' since many words have both descriptive and evaluative meaning without confusion being engendered. But it is important to keep separate the two kinds of meaning so that one may be clear about which descriptive features of a social grouping are relevant to the value-judgments that are made of it. This is particularly important when the descriptive content is itself variable, as we have seen is the case with 'community'.

It would be useful, though perhaps tedious, to elaborate these distinctions, so far only broadly indicated, and to examine in detail the concepts involved. But before this kind of clarification can get very far it seems to me necessary to discuss something more fundamental, namely the notion of 'the social' or 'the communal' as something essentially characteristic of, and peculiar to, the life of human beings. Is there anything to be said in general terms about what constitutes a 'common life'? It might be thought that the answer to this question is 'no'. To distinguish and classify various different groupings that are found to exist involves the analysis of different ways in

which individual human beings may be related to one
another and act *vis-à-vis* one another. These relationships and patterns of interaction are so various and
constitute such widely different kinds of group-life
that it may seem naïve essentialism to look for a common
factor, for some special bond which ties a man to his
fellows in whatever kind of social whole he may be a
member. It has been urged against the classical political philosophers that they went wrong in looking for
some such essential social bond and that this search
naturally led to such quasi-historical myths as the
social compact or to the dubious metaphysics of supra-individual wills and social 'organisms'. However, I
don't think that they did go wrong so obviously. What
they did - or some of them at any rate - was to give a
misleadingly concrete, in some cases quasi-historical,
expression to the attempt to specify *formal* conditions
for the existence of a human political community.
Part of what Rousseau was saying in 'The Social Contract', to mention one instance, was that a political
community in which it makes sense to distinguish between
legal and illegal actions by citizens or governments
must be a body of individuals each of whom recognises
as binding on himself rules which are for the common
good and not, at least directly, for his own good.
This is a formal condition in that it does not say anything about the content of the rules or about the
institutional machinery by which they are formulated.
Whatever criticisms may be made of this formulation it
is not hopelessly nebulous. The point of citing this
example is to show that the attempt to give a general
account of the most basic presuppositions of social
life does not necessarily lead to answers that are
vacuous or unilluminating.

What I mean to attempt then is to give in outline a
similarly formal account of what it is for a collection
of individuals to have a common life (at this level of
generality it makes little difference whether one
calls this 'social' or 'communal'). In this case the
account will be formal in the sense that it will not
say anything about the specific kinds of relationship
that can characterise human societies, though it will
be an attempt to answer the question what it is that
makes a relationship a human social relationship.

We are inclined to talk about animals having a
social or communal form of life when we find species
that are not only gregarious but whose collective
existence involves differentiation of function and
interdependence of individuals performing different

functions. As a definition this is too broad, for it would cover animals which come together to mate but are otherwise solitary. Two further conditions need to be added. First it seems necessary that to have a social life individuals must form groups that have some degree of continuity; a mating pair that breaks up immediately the mating is completed does not satisfy this condition. Second, the individuals must be dependent on others in some identifiable group in a reasonably high proportion of their activities and for some substantial portion of their life-span; this condition would exclude animals which, say, formed packs on infrequent occasions for hunting, but were otherwise solitary. Interdependence of individuals performing different functions, however, seems to be the most central feature, and the one which is so striking in the collective behaviour of certain species, such as the bee, and in them invites comparison with the social life of human beings. But this feature, even with the addition of the other necessary conditions mentioned, would not be enough to characterise the human form of social life. What more needs to be added? It seems obvious that what is necessary is that the distribution and performance of functions should be not merely *de facto* but should be governed by rules or norms.

To perform a function is to act in certain definite ways in specific types of situation, but to perform a function in a human society is to act in ways appropriate to certain types of situation *because of* the type of situation one is in, where the 'because' is the agent's and not merely the observer's. So, for example, a bus conductor who issues a ticket in response to a passenger's demand is not automatically responding to a stimulus but is acting for a reason, namely that he has been asked for a threepenny, or whatever it may be. If asked why he issued the ticket when the passenger asked for it he might well say: 'Well, that's what I'm paid for.' That is, acting on such requests, accepting them as reasons for acting in a certain way, is what the job consists in. There is of course the different question of why this man has this particular job, the answer to which would have to invoke a second level of rules, those governing the recruitment to roles in a society. I am concerned with the rules that operate within the role, which define the character of the role. In the case of the bus conductor this normative definition of the role is obvious enough, and may be explicitly set down in his terms of employment. There are obviously many roles of which this is not true, but which are defined by

rules that are not set down at all, for instance those
of a friend, or a son, or a host. To use the term
'role' in such a wide sense is in need of justification
and of some qualification. It depends perhaps on what
is no more than an analogy, if a strong one, between
such institutionalised roles as those of the bus conductor, the professor, and the income-tax inspector,
and the more private, commonly less formal, 'capacities'
in which a man may act in relation to other people.
The rules governing the former are no doubt more explicit and more precise; but the latter are just as much
governed by what is expected and what is recognised.
A son is expected to show his parents a particular
kind of respect, to help maintain them if necessary
and so on. A friend is expected, among other things,
to be willing to give and receive confidences and to
help in difficulties. There is a significant sense in
which talk of rules is appropriate here.

It can be illuminating to think of society as a network of roles, institutionalised and non-institution-
alised, of many different kinds, each regulated, indeed
constituted, by a set of rules. Each person's conception of his society consists in the knowledge that he
has of the network of roles, in his knowing what is
expected of him in the roles he occupies and what to
expect of others in theirs. S.F. Nadel, who brilliantly developed this approach to the description of
societies, puts this as follows:

> ... each actor in his role knows about all the other
> roles from which his own differs in some manner,
> and is guided by this knowledge in his own actions.
> We might say he carries a role map of his society
> in his head, indicating the way in which his role
> fits in amongst others. This map need only be a
> rough one, though one sufficiently accurate to show
> the boundaries between any actor's role and relevant
> others - similar, as it were adjacent, roles or
> perhaps opposed ones. So that a 'father' will act
> in full knowledge of how his position compares with
> that of an 'uncle' or 'teacher'; a 'doctor', of
> how his right to the confidences of his patients
> compares with that of a 'friend' or 'priest'; and
> so forth. (2)

It might be as well, before going further, to guard
against two misinterpretations to which this account
might be subject. The first is that to talk of society
as a network of roles might be thought to imply that
human action in a social context falls into a rigid,
stereotyped pattern. But no such inference need be

drawn. Few, if any, roles can be specified in terms of a set of rules which specify completely determinate actions for specific situations, the entire range of possible situations being explicitly and exhaustively set out in the rules. No one could give an exhaustive list of actions that ought to be performed by a friend in all the various situations that might arise in the course of a relationship. One must operate rather with a number of 'rules of thumb' that apply to situations of fairly common occurrence (such as being asked for a loan), and for the rest with much more general rules that call for interpretation to apply them to particular situations. But there must be some criteria by which it can be decided that an action is or is not a friendly one, and unless there were general agreement about these, no one could begin to know how to be friendly. One would not know how to be unfriendly either. For one thing which the recognition of roles summing up, however loosely, normal ways of behaving does, is to make intelligible certain kinds of departure from them. There is no real opposition between a description of a society in terms of roles and recognition of individual purposes. The framework of roles is the context in which individual purposes and actions become intelligible.

The second misinterpretation would be to suppose that the rules defining social roles are all moral rules. By and large, however, such rules do not prescribe what the occupant of a role must do on pain of being immoral. For instance, one of the things that may be expected of me as the friend of another is that I should lend him five pounds. He has more reason to expect me to lend him the money than someone else who is not his friend, and I have more reason to lend it to him than I would have to lend money to a stranger or casual acquaintance. It would be appropriate for me, as his friend, to lend him the money, but this is not to say that I am under an obligation. Here it may be objected that the 'appropriateness' in question has at least a moral flavour; I might be thought mean if I refuse the loan, and this would be a moral appraisal of the action. But it is easy to think of instances in which even this kind of moral significance is absent; if I drink his whisky or allow him to drink mine, both, in their ways, are acts of friendship.

Both of these misinterpretations derive from an oversimple notion of what a rule (or a 'norm' in the jargon) is, and the next task must be to indicate some of the kinds of rule that are relevant to the understanding of human action.

Accounts of the 'norms' which regulate behaviour in particular societies seem often to emphasise the kind of rule which *requires* a man to act in a certain way in a certain kind of situation. Professor Homans, for instance, writes: 'A norm, then, is an idea in the minds of the members of a group, an idea that can be put in the form of a statement specifying what the members or other men should do, ought to do, are expected to do, under given circumstances.' (3) 'We have defined norms as the expected behaviour of a number of men.... But some norms, though they may be held by all the members of a group, apply to only one of them: they define what a single member in a particular position is supposed to do. A father is expected to treat his children, a host, his guests, a foreman, his men, in certain special ways.' (4) The distinction made in the second of these quotations, between rules which apply to everyone and rules which may be held by everyone but apply only to certain classes of people, is an important one. But another distinction, particularly important as it applies to rules of the latter type, is ignored. This is the distinction between rules that require and rules that permit or license certain kinds of behaviour. A father must feed and clothe his children; he may send them to public school or encourage them to follow him in his trade: a host must give his guests food and drink, or at least houseroom and a chair, he may provide dancing girls or turn the conversation to the state of the weather or the parties. Rules of this second kind, defining modes of fatherly or hostlike behaviour, are quite as important in defining particular roles and relationships as rules of the first kind. Consider an example of Nadel's: 'the proverbial "salesman", who is not only the representative of an occupation understood in a strictly technical sense, but something like a "personality", being expected to be a "jolly good fellow", boisterous and perhaps overbearing on all occasions, to frequent particular entertainments and belong to particular associations, and the like.' (5) It would be strange to regard such activities as required of the salesman, in the way that it is required of him that he sell things.

It seems likely that Homans fails to recognise this distinction, between what we may term 'requirements' and 'permissions', because his definition of 'norm' is partly in terms of the notion of a sanction: 'A statement of the kind described is a norm only if any departure of real behaviour from the norm is followed by some punishment.' (6)   Plainly there cannot be sanctions for permissions.   'You may do so-and-so, and if you do not you will be punished' would be an absurd thing to say.   And so, if norms are introduced in the course of discussion of the regulation of behaviour or of conformity and deviance, it is inevitable that permissions should be ignored.

There is indeed something puzzling about rules of this kind; for not only does it make no sense to speak of their sanctions, but it seems also impossible to obey or disobey them, conform or fail to conform to them.   If there is a notice saying 'no smoking' I can obey the injunction by not smoking or disobey it by smoking.   But if I am in a compartment without such a notice (or suppose there is one saying 'you may smoke') am I disobeying a rule if I fail to smoke, or keeping a rule if I do smoke?   It would seem absurd to answer 'yes' to either part of this question.   In what sense then can permissions be said to be rules at all?   An illustration from chess may help here.   If the player with the white pieces opens $P-K_4$ there is a wide variety of ways in which he can continue, but there is a smaller if still very large range of recognised continuations, recorded in books on the game as 'openings'.   In the context of a game of chess each of the possible sequences of moves in this range can be thought of as a rule, and what gives sense to this is that each can be understood as related to the tactics and strategy of the game, for instance as an attempt to gain control of the centre, or as facilitating the development of one's pieces.   It does not make sense to speak of breaking such rules, and we should not normally speak of obeying them either, but it is quite natural to speak of *following* them.   It is perfectly possible to distinguish between moves which are in accordance with a rule and moves which, although permitted (i.e. not illegal), are not.   What counts as a permissive rule, and what counts as following one, depends on a context.

This can I think be quite readily seen to apply to actions in a social context.   The lover, or the host, knows that to occupy this role is to have at his disposal a range of actions, gestures, modes of expression, which are the recognised manifestations of the role and which are all related to the general point of the role - the gaining of affection, or making a guest feel comfortable.   It is rarely possible to indicate the context which gives sense to social permissions in so simple and clear-cut a way as was possible in the chess example. For this context can normally only be specified by reference to related rules defining other roles, and to ends which themselves are only possible given a certain kind of social context: to want to make a guest feel comfortable, for instance, is an end that is intelligible only in a society whose conventions create the special status of a guest.

The reference to actions, gestures, and expressions as recognised manifestations of a role suggests a further sense of rule. The actions which are characteristic of particular social roles can be thought of not only as rule-governed in the sense of being in accordance with requirements or permissions, but also as rule-governed in the way that a word is rule-governed. A linguistic rule, as such, is not a rule which requires or permits a speaker to use a certain expression in a specified situation, but a rule which determines both for the speaker and for his hearers what his utterances can be taken to convey. If I say, 'I'm very sorry to hear that you're better', intending to say, 'I'm very glad ...', my intention does not alter the fact that the words I spoke meant that I regretted your recovery. It is only because words have meanings determined in this way by rules that I can successfully use them to convey *my* meaning. The rule determining the meaning of the word 'dog' does not say that I must or may utter 'dog' when there is an animal of a certain sort in the vicinity; it determines that if I say 'there is a dog in the room' I am referring to an animal of a certain sort. This is why it is possible to tell a lie by making this statement, for it will convey the same information when I use it in the situation where there is a dog in the room and when I use it in the situation where there is not. Lying does not involve breaking language rules but making a special kind of use of them. It is true that if all speakers used the statement 'there is a dog in the room' as commonly when there was not as when there was, the rule determining the meaning of the word 'dog' would cease to exist. This shows that the existence of language-rules depends upon a certain consistency in the actual practice of speakers, but it does not mean that such rules tell speakers what they must or may say.

The point I have made about language applies to action as well. Here too there are rules that determine not what one ought to do or may do in a given situation, but what significance a given piece of behaviour will have, what it will count as. This is most obvious in the case of what everyone would recognise as 'conventional' behaviour. To go to a funeral wearing a gay tie and co-respondent shoes just does not count as behaviour expressing respect for the dead or for the feelings of the bereaved, whatever the wearer may claim to have meant by it. Such conventional behaviour may come to have meaning simply through becoming customary. Wearing black, or wearing a frock-coat, comes to signify observance of the formal dignity of an occasion simply by being regularly adopted for occasions that are formal and dignified. Someone who fails to conform is considered not only to have broken a rule, but to have made a gesture with a certain meaning, unless some special explanation is forthcoming.

Perhaps the importance of this kind of rule of meaning is less apparent in the understanding of actions which are not so plainly governed by explicit conventions. That rules of meaning have a wider application than this may be shown by consideration of a more complex example. In a paper called Two Villages in Orissa, F.G. Bailey describes two incidents which occurred in 1955 in the Kondmals, a subdivision of Orissa (India). Both were assaults by an untouchable on a man of clean caste, both led to hostility between the castes, but in one case to fiercer hostility than in the other. Bailey's problem is to understand why the incidents took place and why the subsequent conflicts took such different courses. I am concerned not with his approach to this problem but only with the way in which his account of the incidents makes clear that in order to understand the actions of the participants it is necessary to relate them to the systems of ideas of the society. To mention one case, an elderly *Pan* (an untouchable) met a youth of the warrior caste on a narrow path above a rice field; there was a scuffle and the youth fell into the muddy field. An understanding of this incident which assumed that the same features were significant as would be significant in a European context would no doubt fix on the respective ages of the two men and interpret the incident as an impudent youth being properly rebuked for not giving way to his senior. Though this seems a 'natural' way to look at it, it is mistaken. And that it is so brings out particularly well that in a European context what makes such an action what it is are the ideas we have about the respect due to old age. Such ideas exist in India, but the barrier of untouchability cuts across them in such a way that the action of the old man becomes an insult, and other associated ideas give it an even more complex significance:

Hindu ideas about pollution explain why the blows which were struck were not simple assaults, but were also attacks on a fundamental moral principle, governing the relationship between clean caste and untouchable. This ritual relationship is now seen as one part of a complex in which political and economic interests are also involved. [The *Pans* have no representation on the village council and only own such property as their masters choose to give them.] The blows now appear not only as an offence against all village morality, but also as an attack on the established political order of the village. Given that the rituals of untouchability symbolise also political inferiority, these assaults were tantamount to a revolution. (7)

What gives sense to an interpretation of this sort is that it is in terms of the way in which actions of this kind are understood by the participants. Reference to Hindu ideas about untouchability and to political and economic institutions helps to explain what happened because these things are incapsulated in the actions themselves. The distinction between rules of action (requirements and permissions) and rules of meaning is needed here, for the assaults are not in accordance with the 'norms' of society and yet are clearly significant. In any society there is common agreement about what actions mean, not merely common agreement about what should or should not be done in specified situations. Because of this it is possible to 'say' things with actions, and particularly to say unusual, unconventional, even defiant and revolutionary things, and be understood. It is because a description of society in terms of roles involves reference to rules of this kind that such a description does not imply that the behaviour of social beings is stereotyped and invariable, but rather lays bare a framework within which both conventional behaviour and innovation become intelligible.

I must now try to bring to a focus this rather long discussion of different types of rule. I suggested that an account can be given of society in terms of the roles that individuals occupy and the way in which these roles are related to one another. From this point of view society is thought of not as a collection of actual individuals interacting with one another in various complex ways, but as a system of roles that can be occupied by many individuals, and of which many can be occupied simultaneously by a single individual. The model does not deny that in one obvious sense it is precisely individual people who do constitute society. But it offers a way of speaking about the modes of behaviour through which individuals come to constitute a society, and which remain relatively constant while the agents themselves are replaced in the course of time. Nor is the model unduly artificial, for it is already implicit in the way in which people actually characterise their relationships with others.

When one proceeds to examine what is involved in the notion of playing a role and the way in which a man is related to others in his various roles one finds the fundamental place occupied by rules, since a role can only be defined in terms of the mutual expectations of the role-player and those towards whom his actions in the role are directed. 'Expectation' is here more than a psychological term, but is normative, and corresponding to the expectations of others are the rules that guide the agent in playing the role. An account of society in terms of roles therefore necessarily involves the notion of common agreement about rules. For a role is constituted by a set of rules and moreover a role exists not by virtue of its occupant's recognition of the rules only, but also by virtue of their recognition by others. A collection of individuals can be said to have a social existence, a common life, to the extent that there exists among them a consensus about the rules that define the various roles that individuals can occupy. This consensus should be understood in terms of the account I have given of the different kinds of role. It involves agreement not only about what actions are required or permitted in particular roles, but also about the significance of various kinds of action. A society is a collection of people who have the same ideas about what is involved in being a father, or a doctor or a friend, and so on through the indefinitely long list of recognised activities.

Such an account avoids both an individualistic analysis of society, according to which individuals take part in a co-operative enterprise in the pursuit of individual ends which are prior to the social relationships that they enter into, and the view of society as an organism, individuals having their being only as parts of a whole. On the sort of accounts that I have been giving there is no need to ascribe anything like purposes to social wholes that cannot be analysed in terms of individuals and the relationships between them, and yet the fact that we can ascribe actions, intentions, and purposes to individuals is owing to the existence of a common understanding of what constitutes various kinds of action.

In giving an account of what is essential the idea of a common life I have said nothing directly relevant to the question of how societies or communities may be individuated, i.e. what sorts of collection can usefully be regarded as social entities. It will follow from my account that some principles of individuation will be more important than others; neither geographical unity nor the existence of a single political system for instance would by itself be an important criterion in the absence of agreement on other rules concerned with family and group life and personal relationships. Similarly it is conceivable that two groups of people might have distinct territorial locations, distinct political and perhaps economic institutions, and yet have the same language, or languages with similar conceptual structures, the same family structure, the same ideas about love and friendship and so on, and so constitute a single society by virtue of this agreement. (However, it must be admitted that it is difficult to say in general to what extent such elements can be dissociated from one another; there are conceptual as well as causal links between them, which would need to be analysed in detail.) The notion of society being constituted by consensus also has implications for what can be regarded as an autonomous group. If one thinks of the tightly knit and self-contained group that the family can be one may be tempted to suppose that it constitutes an autonomous social unit. But however self-contained and inward-looking it may be, a family is part of a society that contains it not only in the sense that its members will have some relationships with people outside the family, and so will occupy other roles besides those of kinship, but also in the sense that the 'norms' which define kinship roles exist by virtue of a consensus that is wider than any single family. In this way even what may be thought of as personal, as distinct from social relationships, such as friendship, are dependent on such a consensus about the modes of behaviour appropriate to them.

This last point enables me to bring my account into relationship with the influential notion of community (*Gemeinschaft*) developed by Tönnies, which can all too easily lead to a kind of sociological sentimentalism. *Gemeinschaft* is characterised by a close bond of sympathy between the members, mutual trust, shared sentiments and beliefs, non-contractual co-operation in the carrying out of common tasks. *Gesellschaft* relationships by contrast are those into which people enter on the basis of 'I give, so that you will give', the prototype of which is barter or exchange; societies based on such relationships are impersonal and individualistic. The distinction is an important one, and Tönnies is alive to the fact that human society cannot be understood as an arrangement of convenience, based on contract, into which individuals enter as independent beings with certain interests which they seek to further by means of mutual services. To be able to enter into such relationships people must already have the institution of promising, or a common understanding of some gesture as an undertaking to perform, and this already constitutes a social relationship. Further, although Tönnies sees *Gemeinschaft* as originating in blood-relationships, he regards the community of mental life as 'the truly human and supreme form of community', and emphasises the way in which language is the necessary means by which a common understanding is brought about.

Even so, the sharp dichotomy between community as involving deep personal involvement and commitment, and an impersonal kind of association based on the rational (calculative) will, and the application of this dichotomy in classifying social groups, can be misleading. For the examples of *Gemeinschaft* societies are the family, the neighbourhood unit (agricultural village or city) and the fellowship of friends. These are the paradigm cases, and there is a twofold danger in presenting them as such. We may be persuaded to think of any large-scale society as a mechanical contrivance, hostile or at best indifferent to human values, and having nothing to do with genuine human relationships. And to the extent that we are persuaded of this we may lament as an irreparable loss, or try to create artificially, the small face-to-face community, in the belief that it is only in this kind of social environment that the sorts of norm can be developed that give significance and purpose to the projects of the individual. To accept these ideas is to beg too many questions. It is to beg important empirical questions about what kinds of social organisation are and are not compatible with the personal satisfaction of the individual and the development of satisfying personal relationships. But it is also to beg a different kind of question, for it is to suppose that the community which is creative of the rules defining social roles and relationships is identical with the particular group

which may be the setting of an individual's main
interests, activities and relationships. The purpose
of my contribution has been to indicate that these are
different senses of 'community', and more particularly
to develop the notion of a community as creative of
rules. This may be said to be an invisible community, but it is no less real for that.

NOTES

1 This definition of 'community' (though not the definition of 'society' immediately following) is given by R.M. MacIver and Charles H. Page, 'Society, an Introductory Analysis', London, Macmillan, 1950, p. 8.
2 S.F. Nadel, 'The Theory of Social Structure', London, Cohen & West, 1957, p. 58.
3 G.C. Homans, 'The Human Group', London, Routledge & Kegan Paul, 1951, p. 123.
4 Ibid., p. 124.
5 Nadel, op. cit., p. 27.
6 Homans, op. cit., p. 123.
7 F.G. Bailey, Two Villages in Orissa, in 'Closed Systems and Open Minds, the Limits of Naïveté in Social Anthropology', ed. Max Gluckman, Edinburgh and London, Oliver & Boyd, 1964, p. 64.

11 The function of social work in society
A preliminary exploration
Peter Leonard

1 INTRODUCTION

The purpose of this paper is to explore some questions concerning the philosophical and political basis of social work. This exploration will involve questions about the nature of knowledge as well as the nature of society and is based upon the conviction that unless social workers are prepared to examine some fundamental theoretical problems, the study of the activity of social work will continue to be reduced to issues of technological effectiveness. Such a reduction is characteristic of much of the work undertaken in the field of social policy study, where concentration is given to specific social problems, such as housing, education and employment, but little effort given to discovering the interaction between them as a whole, and their relationship to basic economic and political structure.

The reasons for the reluctance to come to grips with theoretical questions which raise as problematic assumptions which are usually taken for granted, are not difficult to discover. Principally, this reluctance arises from a distaste for theoretical discussion which results from the fact that social work is developing largely within a positivist, empiricist tradition. This tradition insufficiently emphasises that social facts have a dual nature, that they exist both in themselves and in the conceptualisations of those who observe them. Even psychoanalysis has striven to maintain its place within the empiricist tradition, and so it has sealed off, Habermas suggests, (1) fuller exploration of the problematic nature of 'facts'. A concern with the 'practical', the applied and the specific, which takes the 'common-sense' definitions of

social institutions as given, avoids the necessity of
facing the problem that definitions of social reality
are highly ideological.

As a first step in examining the function of social
work in society, we shall discuss some problems associated with the definition of social situations with
which social workers are concerned. This discussion,
in Section 2, will rest heavily on the work taking
place in the sociology of deviance, (2) and particularly
on the debate which is being conducted on the place of
phenomenology in the social sciences. (3) Having
looked at the problematic nature of social facts and
their implications, we shall, in Section 3 be able to
move to a consideration of the function of social work
in society from the point of view of different definitions of society and of the place of social work within
it. Here I shall draw especially on the work of sociological theorists (4) in examining alternative models
of society and of social work. Finally, in Section 4
we shall examine the implication of our theoretical
discussions for the practice of social work.

2 DEFINITIONS OF SOCIAL REALITY

A central problem for the social worker is how to
understand the meaning which the client gives to his
social situation. The social worker assigns some
meaning of his own to this situation, but how does he
take account of the client's meaning? The empiricist
tradition in social science suggests that if subjective
interpretation, *verstehen* is to be allowed, then it is
simply an intervening variable relating observable
stimulii to observable reactions. The problem, as
Hindess (5) suggests, is that 'if the actor acts in
terms of meanings, of his definition of the situation,
these meanings are never, as far as the social scientist is concerned, directly observable. Yet the
scientist must refer to these meanings in order to
account for the actions which he observes.'

In so far as the social worker attempts to base his
understanding on social science knowledge and approaches,
he faces a similar problem. A social relationship has
to be understood from a number of viewpoints. (6)
First, there is the understanding of the participants
themselves, who know the relationship from the *inside;*
then there is the understanding of others outside the
relationship to which it appears as an environmental
fact; finally there is the social worker himself who

tries to understand both the participants' subjective perception and the others' perception of the social relationship and then adds to it his own account. The point is that we are not here discussing observable facts, but second order constructs made by someone before the consciousness of a social relation arising exists. Schutz (7) argues that 'the constructs of the social sciences are ... constructs of constructs made by the actors on the social scene, whose behaviour the social scientist has to observe and to explain in accordance with the procedural rules of his science.' In attempting to understand social reality, social workers like social scientists are bound to get further and further away from direct experience as they give attention to a particular social action, try to control and use it, and typify and over-simplify the experience. Such a typification is essential to study and diagnosis, for the social worker's concept of the experience is sharpened, but it may also be false. In other words, the social worker does not have a true account of observed behaviour as though he had seen it in the head of the client; the social worker has a typification which may be clear but wrong. Equally, of course, in the client's interpretation of his own action there is the possibility of false consciousness, a point to which we shall return later.

Once we acknowledge the problematic nature of the social worker's (and others) interpretation of reality, we can no longer accept, without question, the given definitions of social situations and social problems which are presented by the major institutions of society. In constructing any kind of model of society, for example, what has to be taken into account is how the various elements in the model come to be defined and evaluated. Because of this subjective element, we can recognise that people may disagree as to the nature of the social world in general and the social relations in which they are involved in particular. Disagreement about the nature of the social world begins from the very concept 'society'. We may use the concept to refer to people, things and activities within a given geographical boundary and suggest that people's behaviour can be explained, in part, in terms of being members of a society organised in a particular way. However, it is possible to move from this point to a perception of society as something which *causes* behaviour, as if society were separate, mystical, and over and above people, things and activities. Thus, although men created society, definitions

of society have developed which suggest that society
created men. Such definitions of our social world
personify things, the arrangements of society, and reify
persons, reducing them to the status of things. The
personification of society and the reification of
persons, which summarises what Marx meant by alienation, prevents the individual in society, whether social
worker or client, from understanding the actual sources
of influence and power which affect his behaviour and
beliefs. The politician who talks of 'the national
interest', and the social worker who talks of 'being
responsible to society', are both suggesting definitions
of the social world which involve mystification.

In a critique of role theory in Western sociology,
Urbánek, the Czech sociologist, shows that reductionist
definitions of man may be accepted because men feel
powerless, are alienated from each other and themselves,
and therefore experience a false consciousness of their
social situation. Urbánek writes as follows:

> Reduction of man to an average, to a bearer of common
> social qualities, roles and masks, to an impersonal,
> outward, shared and forced character is ... the pro-
> duct of the evolution of that period of history....
> Thus man, although he is the unconscious author of
> his own life's drama, exists first of all as an
> actor of a role, where the conditions, relations,
> circumstances and institutions, though created by
> himself, are prescribed to him almost fatally and
> irrevocably. (8)

The problematic nature of definitions of social reality
are especially evident when one examines the definition
and treatment of 'social problems' by government and
other services. The established approach is based
upon a reified model of society in which it is assumed
that people are bound to the state by a common set of
values and that social problems and deviancy are an
aberration which has to be eliminated. It is assumed
that the population as a whole is healthy and integrated
and keep to the rules because they reflect a central
value system. Problems arise with individuals and
groups because they have been inadequately socialised
into society's norms, due, for example, to family
breakdown which prevents the individual from incorporat-
ing appropriate social values into his superego. Some
individuals are seen as lacking the opportunity to
benefit from what society offers and may then engage
in 'senseless', 'meaningless' and 'irrational'
behaviour.

Some members of society are seen as mentally disordered in some way, either as a result of environmental factors, or because of inherent, biological factors, or a combination of both. In either case, such people, the source of many social problems, are seen as not being responsible for their actions, for they are 'maladjusted', 'psychopathic', 'schizophrenic' or 'immature'.

We can see immediately that such an approach ignores the problematic nature of the definition of social problems and of the conflict of perceptions which may exist as between the problem individual and others. Nor is it clear that the problems which some individuals experience stem fundamentally from physical, mental and environmental factors over which they have little control. Also, many individuals internalise values which they perceive, albeit through false consciousness, as legitimate but who, through personality factors, are unable to respond to the demands made upon them. However, the liberal, humane, therapeutic approach of the established services fails to take account of the possibility of a conflict of values based upon radically different definitions of social reality. People with 'problems' are often seen as not understanding what has or is happening to them and of needing help to accept the definitions of their social situation which social workers, in particular, can provide. One of the major problems of this established, consensus approach to social problems is that it denies the meaning which those with problems, especially the deviants, place on their own actions. The 'real' causes have to be discovered and actions themselves are deprived of meaning. Theft, for example, is not seen as possibly expressing value conflict over the ownership of property; alternative norms are often seen as the absence of values due to personality failings. Ultimately, the deviant and other clients of the social services, are viewed as essentially lacking freedom of choice and, in the best empiricist tradition, as determined by physical, social and psychological factors, and hardly ever by their own intentions. Those who operate the services, including social workers, tend to see *themselves* as determined in their actions not only by internal and external forces, but by their intention based upon their definitions of social reality. In this way many clients of the social services are deprived of a moral status which social workers claim for themselves.

This discussion of definitions of the social world is not intended to suggest that a full phenomenological

approach to social work and social problems is the
answer to our difficulties. Schutz (9) argues that
the individual is free, that his acts proceed from
spontaneous activity, that these acts are determining,
not determined, and that we can only study conceptual
models, not real people.

An approach which gives much pre-eminence to subjective meanings ends up as a highly individualistic and
psychologically reductionist view of the world. Sociologists who have been heavily influenced by phenomenology, such as Becker (10) and Goffman, (11) emphasise
the importance of social interaction in small groups
in developing self-images and face a similar danger of
reductionism, where social phenomena are reduced to
views of the situation held by individual participants.
Rather than swallow phenomenology whole, social workers
should welcome the critique with which it confronts
the established social sciences and might, in part,
emulate the approach which Matza suggests is incumbent
on those who recognise the importance of the subjective
view:

> It delivers the analyst into the arms of the subject
> who renders the phenomenon, and commits him, though
> not without regrets and qualifications, to the
> subject's definition of the situation. This does
> not mean that the analyst always concurs with the
> subject's definition of the situation; rather that
> his aim is to comprehend and to illuminate the
> subject's view and to interpret the world as it
> appears to him. (12)

The social worker cannot, however, stop where Matza, a
sociologist, stops. He must view subjective meanings,
liable as they are to false consciousness, as one
determinant of behaviour alongside others and he must
take action to intervene in social situations. It is
the problem of social work intervention within a context of conflicting definitions that leads us to
examine alternative models of society and social work.

3 MODELS OF SOCIETY AND SOCIAL WORK

The preceding discussion has emphasised the importance
of recognising the range of definitions of social
reality which may exist, definitions which reflect the
social position and consciousness of the individual
and which may be an integral part of the ideology of a
social group. The definitions of social reality which
we are now going to examine are models of society and

the function of social work as perceived within the context of these models. A model, in the social sciences, is a general orientation to some social phenomenon usually by analogy from the natural sciences or technology (as, for example, in organic and mechanistic models) whose purpose it is to provide a framework within which theories can be tested. Thus, from the scientific stance, one does not ask of a model primarily whether it is true or false, but whether as a general orientation it fits the major features of the phenomenon and is a fruitful source of theory development.

However, models of society, as we have seen, define important social arrangements, are concerned with power and its legitimation and cannot, therefore, be seen simply as value-free scientific statements. It is important to recognise that the implicit models of society which lie behind statements about the nature of social problems and the role of social work in meeting them, are ideologically charged; they are value-laden definitions of social situations. How are we to choose between these definitions? Are personal authenticity and political commitment our only guide? Goldmann suggests that there is something more:

> Once the conscious or unconscious effect of value judgements on scientific theories is recognised, the problem of the criterion of truth is raised. Must a sociology of knowledge lead to relativism? Are all ideologies of equal value, at least, as far as the search for truth is concerned; and is the choice of one over another only a matter of individual preference?... Viewed in terms of their effect on scientific thought, different perspectives and ideologies do not exist on the same plane. Some value judgements permit a better understanding of reality than others. When it is a question of determining which of two conflicting sociologies has the greater scientific value, the first step is to ask which of them permits the understanding of the other as a social and human phenomenon, reveals its infrastructure, and clarifies, by means of an immanent critical principle, its inconsistencies and its limitations. (13)

Goldmann argues, and this paper is based upon a similar viewpoint, that on the criterion of its understanding of ideologies, the Marxist orientation provides a better definition of social reality than others.

We now turn to specifying some alternative models of

society and of social work having already made reference to one such model. This model has a long pedigree in conservative social theory (14) and is based upon an organic analogy in which society is conceived as a system of interacting parts which are cemented together by a common set of values. In this *consensus* model of society, social institutions are prior to individuals, the major purpose of society is to secure social order and this is achieved largely by the imprinting of values through the socialization process. Institutions and values are seen as essentially man-received rather than man-made. This reified model of society, in which common interests bind diverse social groups to a set of values which legitimate the authority of the central elites, is the basis of Western representative democratic theory. Such a model is also the basis, often unacknowledged, of an *integration* model of social work. Because, in the final analysis, the interests of the individual and society are the same, social work is able to function in the interests of all individuals and groups in society.

The focus of social work within this model is the resolution of conflict and tension, the mutual adjustment of the individual and his environment within certain limits, and the socialisation of deviant individuals and groups into the common value system. Social work with 'multi-problem' and 'inadequate' families, for example, focuses on rehabilitation and good child-rearing practices. Whilst within this model emphasis tends to be placed on defining problems in terms of the pathology of individuals and groups, there is place also for community development which lays stress upon self-help as a means of integrating values and encouraging citizenship. The approach to deviance of all kinds is liberal and compassionate, for deviants are not 'bad', but are to be pitied as unfortunate, disadvantaged or ill.

The integration model of social work is the model on which the established services are largely based. Social work is seen both as an agent of social control in the interests of society as a whole, and of social change within the limits demanded for the maintenance of social order and the major social institutions. The mainstream of social-work literature has reflected this integration model, though without reference to the model of society on which it is based.

The critique of the consensus model of society involves the outlining of an alternative model of society and enables us to add three further social-work models to our typology. We have already argued that the reified view of society is mystifying; it masks the fact that major social groups in society, especially those centrally involved in the means of production, have different interests and these are frequently expressed in different values. The consensus model in particular fails to take proper account of the differential distribution of power in society. The main features of a *conflict* model of society, which stands as the major alternative, are outlined by Rex (15) in the following way:

1. Instead of being organised around a consensus of values, social systems may be thought of as involving conflict situations at central points. Such conflict situations may lie anywhere between the extremes of peaceful bargaining in the market place and open violence.

2. The existence of such a situation tends to produce not a unitary but a plural society, in which there are two or more classes, each of which provides a relatively self-contained social system for its members. The activities of the members take on sociological meaning and must be explained by reference to the group's interests in the conflict situation. Relations between groups are defined at first solely in terms of the conflict situation.

3. In most cases the conflict situation will be marked by an unequal balance of power so that one of the classes emerges as the ruling class. Such a class will continually seek to gain recognition of the legitimacy of its position among the members of the subject class and the leaders of the subject class will seek to deny this claim and to organise activities which demonstrate that it is denied (e.g. passive resistance).

A significant point about this conflict model of society is that it provides a definition which includes an account of the ideological distortions which both the ruling class and the subject class may be involved in. The ruling class may propose a definition of society based upon a consensus model and thereby try to legitimate its dominant position by reference to common values and goals - the 'national interest'. The subject class may either resist such ideological distortion by proclaiming its conflicting interests, or by false consciousness come to accept the legitimacy of the ruling class. Marcuse (16) argues that the ideological hegemony of the ruling class has been established largely because the working class, especially in the United States, has been won over by relative affluence.

Two other points are worth noting about this model. Conflict may be institutionalised through the political parties and through trade unions and employers' associations; it then operates through arriving at a consensus as to the rules by which the conflict will be conducted. The conflict model may be applied to any social system and from the point of view of social work we may identify as a subject group or underclass those in society who form a large proportion of the clientele of the social services - the poor, the unemployed, the deprived and the deviant. This underclass may, of course, have little consciousness of its collective interests and may be particularly vulnerable to ideological distortion which suggests that their social situation is a 'natural' one, or due to their own inadequacy, or that radical alternatives may be 'worse' than the present injustice.

The conflict model of society presents the social worker with a dilemma. Once a reified view of society is abandoned social work can no longer be seen simply as balancing individual against society interests. As major social classes have different interests and are engaged in a struggle for power and legitimacy, so social work has to operate within this context especially as it directly affects the underclass clientele of the social services.

The conflict model, like all sociological models, is an abstraction which is bound to simplify and distort reality to some degree, and would need to be differentially applied to particular societies. In addition, it has been sketched here only in broadest outline. Nevertheless, the model suggests that there are three possible broad functions for social work in society, those of controller, adversary and mediator.

The *control model* of social work is appropriate when social work is clearly operating predominantly in the interests of the ruling class and its institutions. The ruling class, whether a majority or minority in society, uses social work primarily to contribute to the protection, expansion and legitimation of its power. The social services will be provided for the subject class and its casualties in order to improve the health and social functioning of the labour force and mitigate the extreme effects of structural inequality. Social work is especially important in legitimating the values of the ruling class by its emphasis upon the socialisation process. Social work aims, in other words, at re-education of the underclass clientele who are seen as irresponsible and immature. The subject class as a whole may be seen as aggressive and inadequate and needing more socialisation, as Eysenck (17) suggests in his discussion of working class psychopathy. The dividing line between deviant acts and political acts may be difficult to draw, as in Rhodesia and the Soviet Union. Above all, if social work is to operate in the interests of the ruling class then its social control functions will be to the fore.

The *adversary model* of social work may be applied to a situation where social workers are operating in the interests of the subject class or at least the underclass clientele of the social services, and in opposition to the ruling class. In the extreme case where a revolutionary war is in progress the subject class may, as in Angola and Mozambique, develop its own health and social services and provide some forms of social work. In the United States, Black communities may develop their own network of welfare services. In other situations, such as in Britain, where overt class struggle is less pronounced, the adversary model is difficult to apply to highly professionalised and institutionalised social work. Voluntary, fringe social service organisations working on behalf of deviant groups such as drug-takers may function as adversaries and so, at times, may other social workers, covertly, with individuals and community groups. Social workers trying to operate to this model have no commitment to the existing social order. Their primary tasks, with the individual and the family, may be seen as 'working the system' in the clients' interest, and combating false consciousness and ruling-class definitions of social situations by sharing a diagnosis with the client which sharpens his consciousness of his underprivileged position and urges his involvement, where appropriate, in social and political action. In working with community groups such as Claimants Unions, direct action, confrontation and subversion would be the most favoured approaches. Deviancy will be re-defined in terms of value-conflict and its political implications emphasised in the way that Taylor (18) suggests in the following passage:

> ... unless our conception of the criminal is that of someone fighting against the fundamental interests of a society we admire, we should surely seek to redirect his aggression, his anger, into political channels. Our therapy, our concern should surely be to raise consciousness of the possibilities for

external change and not to insist on the necessity for internal personality change. Here is a large group of predominantly working-class people who refuse to take quietly a society which steals from them products of their labour, which insists that they undergo periodic bouts of unemployment, that they live in inadequate houses, which ensures that their children will be processed through an educational system in such a way as to be only suitable to perform a similar depressed and alienated role in society. We hear a lot about the fatalism of the working-class, about lack of consciousness, but when we find a group of individuals who are taking a hand in determining their life chances we tend to treat them with no more than a rather condescending liberal humanitarianism.

Finally we come to the *mediation model* of social work.

In this model social work recognises a fundamental conflict of interests between ruling and subject class, and works towards institutionalising that conflict by mediating on behalf of the underclass clientele of the social services. Pressure group activity in the Fabian manner, such as Child Poverty Action Group, where the object is to achieve change by influencing the rulers, will be characteristic of this model. Considerable emphasis will be laid on the advocacy role of the social worker with individuals, groups and communities, especially with regard to 'welfare rights'. Social workers will favour both universal social services in order to gain positive discrimination in the interests of underprivileged groups. Social workers within this model will tend to have a conditional, though reluctant, commitment to the existing social order.

4 IMPLICATIONS FOR SOCIAL WORK PRACTICE

The purpose of the theoretical discussion in this paper has been to demonstrate that in order to clarify the functions of social work in society it is essential to explore the various definitions of social situations relevant to these functions which will be held by all the participants, including clients, social workers, administrators, and politicians.

The implication of this for social work is that the social worker's task is to place his own definition of social situations, with the value judgments that these imply, alongside definitions drawn out from clients and others in the social services. In attempting the very difficult task of revealing and understanding the client's subjective meanings, the social worker may draw not only upon the current work in the sociology of deviance which lays stress on identifying the client's intentions and the value orientation implicit in the intention, but also on recent developments in psychoanalysis. As Rycroft, (19) among others, has suggested, psychoanalysis may not be a causal theory at all, but a semantic one in which the client's psychic situation is explained through helping him to understand it and give it meaning. At the same time, however, we need to give more systematic attention to social workers' typification of social situations, and particularly the part which social workers play in the process of labelling deviants and other clients. One step in this direction is renewed emphasis on the fact that social workers' subjective meanings are important in their work and that they are to be understood not simply in terms of psychic processes, but also for the light they throw on ideological orientations.

The four models of social work which we have outlined have suggested that the functions of social work can be seen in terms of *integration, control, adversary* and *mediation* tasks. In reality, of course, the functions of social work are much more diverse and complex than a simple model allows. However, apart from elaborating and refining this preliminary work deriving from a Marxist sociological perspective, we can use the models to increase our understanding of the possibleddefinitions which the participants in social-work situations may develop.

In discussing these models with social workers, it becomes evident that some perceive themselves as controllers, adversaries *and* mediators, depending upon the particular situation in which they are placed. In part, this is due to the problems which these roles present to social workers. Given the established organisational and political context of most of social work, consistent adversary roles are very hard to maintain and often become no more than evening, off-duty activities. At the same time, it is important to recognise that work involving the meeting of physical and psychological needs of individuals and families can hardly be seen as inconsistent with ideological commitment to the adversary role of social work. Participation of clients in the social services, the aim of the mediator in social work, will be seen as ultimately unsatisfactory by those committed to the adversary role: client *ontrol* must be the eventual goal and participation may be simply a means diluting the conflict between the subject class and the ruling class.

Mediating roles, especially in severe conflict situations, such as those existing in Ulster, can also be difficult to perform, for as Goffman (20) puts it, the discrepant role of mediator is like 'a man desperately trying to play tennis with himself.'

If we use these social work models as a framework to examine the perceptions of the participants in social work as to its function, we can see how divergent they can be. It is not difficult to imagine a situation in which a social worker in a local authority is working closely with a client trying to obtain for him various financial benefits. The social worker sees his role as a mediating one, for though he is a tough, determined negotiator he is only working for that to which the client is strictly entitled and he believes that the existing organisational structures can be improved to provide better services. The chairman of the Social Services committee, however, sees the social worker as a trouble-maker and his perception is that the social worker is operating in the adversary role. The client has another perception; to him the social worker is a part of an indifferentiated 'them' and his well-meaning attempts are seen as ineffectual and not directed strongly to getting what the client wants - adequate housing. To him, then, the social worker is essentially a controller. Finally, the Director of Social Services, whilst he is also inclined to see this social worker in the adversary role, wishes that he would take the role of integrator working for a consensus which he believes is possible between all of those involved in the social services.

Clearly, this is simply a preliminary suggestion of the range of possible perceptions of a social work activity; substantial work needs to be done in order to explore this more adequately.

NOTES

1 J. Habermas, 'Knowledge and Human Interests', London, Heinemann, 1972.
2 See, for example, S. Cohen (ed.), 'Images of Deviance', Harmondsworth, Penguin, 1971; J. Young, 'The Drugtakers', London, Paladin, 1971; E.

Rubington and M. Winberg (eds), 'Deviance, the Interactionist Perspective', London, Macmillan, 1968.
3 See: A. Schutz, Concept and Theory Formation in the Social Sciences, in 'Sociological Theory and Philosophical Analysis', ed. D. Emmett and A. MacIntyre, London, Macmillan, 1970; B. Hindess, The 'Phenomenological' Sociology of Alfred Schutz, in 'Economy and Society', vol. 1, no. 1, 1972.
4 See: J. Rex, 'Key Problems of Sociological Theory', London, Routledge & Kegan Paul, 1968; A. Gouldner, 'The Coming Crisis of Western Sociology', London, Heinemann, 1971.
5 Hindess, op. cit., p. 16.
6 See: J. Rex, Sociological Theory and Deviancy Theory, paper presented at British Sociological Association Annual Conference, 1971.
7 Schutz in Emmett and MacIntyre, op. cit., p. 12.
8 E. Urbánek, Roles, Masks and Characters: A Contribution to Marx's Idea of the Social Role, in 'Marxism and Sociology', ed. P. Berger, New York, Appleton-Century-Crofts, 1969.
9 Schutz, op. cit.
10 H. Becker (ed.), 'The Other Side', London, Collier-Macmillan, 1964.
11 E. Goffman, 'The Presentation of Self in Everyday Life', New York, Doubleday Anchor, 1959.
12 D. Matza, 'Becoming Deviant', New Jersey, Prentice-Hall, 1969, pp. 24, 25.
13 L. Goldmann, 'The Human Sciences and Philosophy', London, Jonathan Cape, 1969, pp. 50-2.
14 See Gouldner, op. cit.
15 J. Rex, 'Key Problems of Sociological Theory', p. 129.
16 H. Marcuse, 'One-Dimensional Man', London, Routledge & Kegan Paul, 1964.
17 H.J. Eysenck, 'Sense and Nonsense in Psychology', Harmondsworth, Penguin, 1968.
18 L. Taylor, The Criminologist and the Criminal in 'Catalyst', no. 5, Summer 1970.
19 C. Rycroft (ed.), 'Psychoanalysis Observed', London, Constable, 1966.
20 Goffman, op. cit.

12 The art and science of helping

Alan Keith-Lucas

When I was first asked to talk to you about helping, my immediate thought was, 'What have I, a social worker and a teacher of social work students, to do with these people who are skilled in quite different things, things about which, to tell the truth, I know practically nothing at all?' But I really do have something, despite all that I do not know. For this matter of helping people is wider than any profession. What little I can add to it has already been taken up by groups of ministers, welfare workers, probation officers, guidance counsellors, Alcoholic Anonymous members, doctors studying character change and Deans of Students in our colleges. There does seem to be a common core, whether the help that one gives is in the form of money, advice, counselling or instruction, which is, of course, only common sense, since people are people whatever their problems and what all these professions are asking is basically the same thing. The teacher, the preacher, the social worker, the consultant, the agricultural expert, the marriage counsellor, the home demonstration agent are all saying to those they work with, 'Let me help you to change. Let me help you do something different. Let me help you begin to cope with whatever is making it hard for you to succeed'.

It is not surprising then that there should be the beginning, at least, of a little knowledge about how people can be helped. The surprising thing is rather that this beginning of knowledge should have been so little regarded - that we should have, in our universities and colleges, no curriculum in helping; that there should be so little common understanding of the problems and methods of helping, of even the basic principles that underlie this science and art. For, despite the intuitive helping that some people seem to be able to do without, it seems, being taught, the vast majority of people go about helping most casually, confident somehow that if one only knows one's subject and gives the right kind of advice one has done all that one could, and that if the person we're helping doesn't take that advice, or do what we want him to, it is his plain and obvious fault. He's either stupid, or idle, or obstinate, or weak, and he ought to be punished for it - either by not getting any help, or by being starved, or shamed, or made to do what's right by some process or other - the law, or our inherent authority, or the pressure of public opinion, or argument, or having us take over his thinking for him, or a thousand different ways of putting pressure on him. Fortunately we have dispensed with the whip, at least for adults, the branding-iron and the gallows as aids in the helping process, although all were used in the past. But one would have thought that our many failures should have shown us that something else was wrong, that we had not somehow got hold of some basic principles, that there was more to it than that.

What, then, have we failed to see? I would like to start with two statements that may seem extremely simple but lie, I think, at the heart of the matter. The first is that *all helping* - all real helping, that is, the sort that really induces change - *takes place within a relationship*. And a relationship is a two-way thing. It matters as much what I put into it as what the other fellow does. What may go wrong with helping may be as much my fault as the helper, as it may be on the part of the helped. The second is that *people rarely really want to be helped*.

This may sound like a strange statement, especially if one enlarges it, as I will, to include wanting to learn. It's true of course that many people profess an eager desire to learn. Others appear not only to ask for help but to demand it as if it were their right. But what these people profess to want, ask for, or even demand, is not real help or learning at all. It is help on their own terms - help that will not force them to change in any way. It is in fact a way of warding off any real offer of help, a way of going through the motions, of pretending to oneself, of placating the gods, even, rather than really getting help.

Perhaps we could understand this better if we looked a moment at what it takes really to ask for help. It takes:

1   a recognition that there is something wrong, and

that one cannot do anything about it by oneself,
without taking help, that is.
2 a willingness to confess this weakness to another,
to let him know what one really is.
3 a willingness to let him advise one, to have some
power over one's life, and
4 finally, a willingness to risk the unknown - to
give up one's present situation, however intoler-
able this may be, for some unknown that may look
better but may actually turn out worse.

I would add here, as an aside, and not to try to con-
vert anyone, but to make this process clearer and perhaps
to explain why I believe this to be something very
basic indeed, part of what men actually are and not a
psychologist's invention, that the Church, which is also
concerned with help, has long known this process. It
gives its elements different names - repentance, the
recognition that one is a sinner and needs God's help
to do any different; confession, submission and finally
faith - the evidence of things unseen. And anyone who
has had the experience of asking help from God may have
a little inkling of how difficult this entire process
really is. In addition, to ask help from a human
being is even harder than to ask help from God. One
has better reason to trust Him than one has to trust
another man.

Is it surprising, therefore, that people will do
almost anything to prevent themselves from being helped?
Is it surprising that many of them refuse to admit
their real need, that they demand help from us on their
own terms, that they find ways of neutralising our
help? My students do it to me, and I expect your
clients do it to you. One of the best ways, incidentally, of doing this is to agree with a great deal of
literalness with what the helping person wants - to
follow his advice blindly, and then be able to show
him that what he advised did not work. Some of you,
to be honest, will do this with what I have to say to
you today and it will work to show me up. Another way
is to go through all the motions yet somehow, somewhere,
to miss the really important point, the thing that
really matters - just as one of the best ways of not
getting help from God is to go to church, to sing all
the hymns, to be busy in 'church work' and never permit
the essential message to get across.

Those simple statements lead us to a number of
others, the first of which is the realisation that *what
prevents people changing is in fact, basically, fear* -
the fear of change, the inability to risk. It is this

which makes people refuse to do what in all common sense, what anyone else can see, ought or even has to be done. It is what makes people obstinate, hostile, weak or stupid or any other word we like to use to illustrate this paralysis. While there may be a few people who quite genuinely do not *know* what to do - and, of course, quite a lot of knowledge that can be helpful in deciding what to do - the basic problem is not generally lack of knowledge. It is fear of putting that knowledge to work. The person who is so often thought of as 'content with low standards' is often not that at all. He is by no means content. But he is afraid to act on his discontent, for fear that it will cost him what little contentment he has. Maybe his is a real fear; fear of failure, of unemployment, fear of not being able to compete, and in a depressed area like parts of West Virginia I would suspect that many of these fears are real. Sometimes the fear is unrealistic, and this is where helping can begin. For helping could in fact be described as a process of establishing the kind of relationship that can help exorcise fear.

It follows again, I think, that helping ought to be understood *as something that it is impossible for one man to give to another*. It's not a commodity, a thing. Even where material things are part of the help, such as in public assistance or surplus commodities, the help lies not in the thing but in the way that it is given. And this help cannot be given. *It can only be offered*. The kind of relationship can be set up that makes it possible for growth and change to take place, but you or I, or the greatest social scientist on earth, cannot ensure, cannot even predict that it will take place. We can only clear the way, make it possible for it to do so. And if it won't it won't.

This brings us then to another principle - that *help depends upon choice*. Now, this is a difficult word, because there are two kinds of choice in this world. There is the kind of choice that we exercise when we decided to wear a blue suit or a brown, or go for a walk or watch TV. And there's another kind of choice, that may or may not have anything to do with the choice of what we do in the purely material sense. This is the choice to do one of the three things when we are up against a problem that we can't manage by ourselves - the choice between accepting the problem and getting help for it, or fighting it blindly, or doing nothing at all, escaping from it, pretending even that it isn't there at all, hoping that it 'will go away'. This is the really essential choice that every

Chapter 12

man has, and which will determine what he does with his life. Sometimes, as doctors know, it is the thing that will, in fact, decide whether he lives or dies. The best word that I know for it - and again you must bear with me if I make reference to another framework of understanding to illustrate my point - is the word that the Church uses, 'commitment', to describe this kind of choice.

We don't know too much about it. But we do know a little, I think. One thing that we do not know is where it comes from. It isn't heredity. The power to make a positive choice turns up in the most unlikely people. It isn't environment, either. Good heredity, good environment may contribute to the ability to make a positive choice, but there is an unknown factor which upsets our most careful predictions. One thing we do know, however, is that it has little to do with choosing to do what one likes. It was this misunderstanding, this confusion about the meaning of choice, that led so many people to put their eggs in the basket of 'permissive' helping, of 'non-directive techniques', of giving the impression that all would be well if people didn't have to obey laws or even moral commands - a misunderstanding that has given my profession and many others the reputation of being soft hearted and soft in the head as well. It has, as a matter of fact, little to do with freedom in the ordinary sense of the word. It can, and must, be exercised by a prisoner in jail, a public welfare recipient on an inadequate grant, as well as by an executive at his desk.

We know also that it cannot be made by anyone else than oneself. A positive choice - which is, of course, what all of us want - cannot be made, it cannot even be too passionately wished by the person offering help. It doesn't come from being exhorted, or persuaded (except in the special religious sense of the word), or shamed, or encouraged, or praised. It has nothing to do with reason. One can't argue anyone into it. One doesn't do it because someone else wants one to do it. All that someone else can do is to make it more possible that the choice we dare to make is the forward-looking one, the one that will really solve our problem instead of fighting it or ignoring it.

We know something else, too. This is a paradox, a problem, for it goes against our instinctive way of wanting to help people. But the truth is that the *positive choice* - the choice to accept the problem and do something about it, *is possible only if a person is free to do exactly the opposite, to deny it, to fight against it.*

Intellectually this may not be too hard to see. Man cannot choose to be good unless he can also choose to be bad. To take another religious example, if God had compelled man to be good he would not be good at all. Again, man cannot choose to live fully unless he can also choose (or accept) death. He would never dare get up in the morning. Nothing is gained without risk and to say 'Yes' sincerely always means that I could have said 'No'. We recognise this when we speak slightingly of the 'yes-man' - for of all people the yes-man can never really say 'yes'.

But this truth is terribly hard to recognise in practice. We so much want the man we are helping to make the *right* decision, to choose independence and not dependence, to take our excellent advice, to learn what we have to teach him. Even to recognise the possibility that he may choose the wrong seems like treason to us. Perhaps we work for an agency whose whole purpose is to improve our client's lot. How can we freely tell a man that he is free not to improve.

And yet he cannot choose to get well unless he can choose to be ill. He cannot be pushed or forced or even gently manipulated (one of the strongest forces I know of) into choosing to improve - not if we want a real decision. This is the mistake that so many of us make time and time again - churches, courts, protective agencies, teachers and consultants. I would not like to have to confess to you how many students I have failed because I could not let them fail - but, clear as I am on the matter, I am tempted every time.

Perhaps I can make the point clearer by exploring a little further what is meant here by the opposite, or negative choice. By this I do not mean merely a failure to choose the good (or the supposed good). That is what happens when we try to *make* someone into something that he has not chosen to be, and he fails to live up to expectations. It is utterly defeating. But there is always a negative choice - even a kind of failure - that in itself is a choice and that has something of triumph about it. It is the choice, the determination, not to do what is expected of one, not to have anything to do with this kind of help. It is the decision to 'go it alone' or 'to take the consequences'. And being free to make this choice does not and cannot ever mean being spared these consequences. It is this, that man, if he is to be helped, must always be free to do - even to 'curse God and die'. And we, and even our cherished values, are not, of course, God. What we think of as the wrong choice may for another person be right. Even if it cannot be, the choice must still be there. The risk must be taken. And the person who makes the wrong choice is much closer to help than he who makes no choice at all.

Another way of looking at this is to liken the human predicament to a trolley. This trolley has an engine that tends to move it in the direction that it both needs and wants to go - the very same direction that we, too, would want it to go. Some trolleys do not move. They overcome minor obstacles, and sometimes, big ones, too. But some are held by a spring, pushing in the other direction - a spring of fear, of anger, of shame, of hopelessness and despair.

Now our natural reaction on coming across this trolley is to give it a push. Perhaps we do move it a little. But if it really has a spring this movement is at the cost of a tightening of its coils. If we relax our pressure, or perhaps turn away to try to push another trolley awhile, the spring will recoil. The trolley is then less far on even than when we started. And in any case our pushing will become harder hour by hour.

The sensible thing, of course, is to get at the spring and uncoil it. This is why it is usually true that *people need a great deal more help with their negative feelings than with their positive*. They need to look at their negative feelings, to examine them, to discover their weaknesses. Their positive feelings usually get a lot of support. They are acceptable and everyone can weigh in with reassurance, hope, or praise. It's their negative feelings with which they must struggle - their fears, their doubts, their hates, their despair. And this cannot be done, some psychologists and some preachers to the contrary, by pretending that the negative feelings are not there. They are. The man who exhorted us to 'accentuate the positive and eliminate the negative' may have discovered a rule of social intercourse, but he never had to help people in real trouble - which is why the extroverted, Pollyanish kind of helper who always wants to keep things pleasant is sometimes more harmful than helpful.

It follows therefore, fourthly, that *the helping relationship must be one in which negative feelings can be expressed without fear of blame, anger, sorrow or loss of face*. This means in turn that it cannot be a relationship of superior and inferior, saint and sinner, wise and foolish, judge and judged, or even their modern equivalent, adjusted and unadjusted. These things may objectively be true, or society may have

given one pair the responsibility to act as if they were
true, as in the case of a judge or a teacher. But as
helped and helper struggle together to understand, to
come to a point where the helped person makes his essential choice, they must struggle as equals either of
whom could have felt and thought like the other. This
is what we mean when we use the rather glib phrases
such as 'respect for human dignity' and 'accepting
people as they are'; that both helper and helped are,
for all their difference, fallible and imperfect
creatures who, if not capable of the particular weaknesses in question, are capable of many others. One
of the greatest helpers of delinquent children I ever
knew, when I asked once how he was so able to have children share with him their real hopes and fears, said,
'Because I could be a criminal too'.

A number of other conditions that make possible the
commitment to change more or less follow from these:

First, *the relationship must be centred entirely on
the interests of the person served*. It cannot be
centred in the helper's need to be liked or to control
or even to satisfy his own conscience. It cannot
immediately be centred on any other good, such as the
good of society, the honour of one's department or
school, public morality, justice or fair play, although
once real help is given these generally will be added
to it. This is a frequent mistake - to try to kill
two birds with one stone, and miss them both. The
helped person's need is antecedent. It must come
first.

Even more so, of course, helping cannot be centred
on goals of the helper's own - his desire to succeed,
or to be thanked, or to control another's life, or
satisfy his own conscience. These are the things,
often subtle, that prevent us helping another, and it
takes sometimes a great deal of self-discipline and
personal insight to be sure that they do not get in the
way. They crop up in the most unexpected places. I
know myself that the kind of people that I find hardest
to help are those whom I dislike the most, against whom
I have to fight, and those whom I like the most, the
people whom I want to like me, whom I can't bear to see
suffer, whom I want to protect.

Second, *helping must deal with real things*, however
unpleasant they may be. A doctor who refused to consider cancer of the anus because he was afraid of cancer
or he preferred to ignore the bathroom would be no
doctor at all. So help with social problems must deal
with what is really there - with real sorrow, real hate,

real sin, and real despair. It cannot deal with false reassurances, with polite evasions, with 'pie in the sky'. And it must deal with them here and now. It cannot, as in a case I read lately, assure a woman that she ought to be able to get support from an absent husband and do nothing about the fact that her gas and heat were to be turned off that afternoon.

Then again, *it must be based on trust; on the belief that man can be helped, however wayward he may seem.* I say this in contradiction to what seems to me the trend in the social sciences today, which progressively appears to see man as sicker and sicker and needing more and more control and advice from his stronger fellows. But this kind of trust is necessary if one is to stand by the whole process of helping. Often this is very difficult. Man's first choices in the process of finding himself again are often apparently negative and are in any case quite unpredictable.

And finally, and proceeding from this, the helping person needs not only courage - and plenty of that; any idea that helping people is a sissy undertaking is entirely wide of the mark - not only knowledge, not only self-understanding, but an entirely different virtue, which Christians call humility - and perhaps there isn't another word. I don't mean by this short-changing oneself, or being hypocritically modest. But I do mean facing the real facts. I do mean being clear with oneself that one doesn't know what is right for another person. One is extremely lucky if one knows this for oneself. I do mean understanding that however much one can feel and think with and for another, it is his problem and not yours. You don't have to face what he is facing. You may think that you have, or are, but you don't know. One of the most dangerous kinds of helpers, or teachers, is the one who has solved a problem and has forgotten what it cost him to do it. He expects everyone else to be able to solve it as he did. He gets impatient when the other finds it harder than he remembers that it was for him. And I do mean knowing that you will never know; that the more you think you know, the less you can really claim to know, the more you will find that there are factors not dreamed of in your philosophy, the less certain you will be that you really have the answer. For man is not a mechanical being who will someday be known in all of his depth and breadth and height. He is a living soul.

So far, perhaps, you will have the feeling that most of what I have said is negative. Perhaps all I have done is to tell you how not to help. I hope that it does not feel like that - but this is a difficult subject, and one that needs a lot of self-discipline, of knowing not what to do. I am going to end my talk, however, by suggesting three principles that do, I believe, lie in a very positive way the very core of help.

These three principles are a Trinity. By that I mean they are triune. No one is effective without the other. They cannot be separated. I won't conceal from you also something that you don't have to believe - that they are actually reflections of another Trinity of which we have heard - far-off, faint reflections, but nevertheless the three ways in which God comes to us. But that is not how I learned them, and you don't need to make the connection, for they are very real and practical things in themselves that exist wherever man is helped. They have technical names - Reality, Empathy and Support - but I like to try to bring them to life by putting them into the natural language that we use when we are talking to people.

Let us look at them in such terms. So expressed they come out this way:

(Reality) 'This is it'.
(Empathy) 'I know that it must hurt, or that it is difficult'.
(Support) 'I am here to help you if you want me and can use me'.

The first principle - reality - we discussed a few minutes ago. Let me see, however, if I can give it a little more depth. It means all that we said then - not pretending that a problem doesn't exist, not taking it away from a person, not disarming him about it, so that he has no way of dealing with it. It means not giving false reassurance. But it also means respecting a person enough to share the truth with him. It means not being over-protective. As you may know, my principal work is with children in institutions, and I have seen far more children - yes, children, not adults - hurt because people wanted to protect them from life, or the truth, or the consequences of their actions than I have from facing them with these things.

Reality also means not being indirect. For some reason or other consultants, teachers, and social workers, more than anyone else have gained the reputation of being rather wily birds who 'work round things', who tread like Agag, who don't come out with the obvious truth but are 'tactful' or 'considerate'. These words

can be good ones, of course, but all too often they
describe the person who gently manipulates another,
who tries to get him subtly to do what the helping
person wants and thinks that he thought it up himself.
And all too often what this means is that the helping
person doesn't want to face the truth himself. It is
not a bad adage to say that the fear of the unknown is
much worse than fear of the known - that the truth,
told with love, will set you free. I could give you
many examples from my work; I am sure that you can
find them in yours.

Empathy is the second requirement. 'I know that
this must hurt'. It is not too common a gift. All
too easily it, or she, becomes confused with her much
less difficult sister, Sympathy, and sometimes even
with her puffed-up stepsister, Pity. Let's see if we
can distinguish the three - for sympathy can be destructive, and pity is nearly always so.

Empathy is an act of compassionate understanding.
It says, 'I can understand how you feel, and feel it
with you in a limited way, but I don't feel that way
myself'. It maintains an essential difference between
the helper and the helped, and it is indeed this difference, set in the framework of the likeness, that
provides the means of help. Empathy feels *with* a
person. Sympathy feels *like* him. To take a rather
flippant example, suppose a man tells you that he cannot
stand his wife. The empathic person says, and means,
'I can understand how hard this makes your daily life.
I cannot judge, for I am not you, but with this feeling
you have for her what do you feel that you can do?'
Sympathy, on the other hand, would say, 'Oh, I know
how you feel, exactly. I can't stand my own wife
either'. This, of course, leads nowhere. And pity
would say, 'Oh you poor, poor fellow, to have to live
with a wife like that. I'm glad that mine is a wonderful girl. Why don't you come and eat with us sometimes
and see what married life can be like'.

One of the problems one frequently finds in trying
to help people to help is that when one describes a
person who is in trouble, perhaps has behaved badly,
has at least negative feelings, is angry, bitter, caught
up in lust or any other ill man is heir to, the helping
person fears that if he tries to understand he will
increase the other's weakness. He will be condoning
wrong. You hear it said over and over again, 'Sympathy
would make it worse. It doesn't do to sympathise with
such people. You can have too much sympathy, you
know'. The very term 'bleeding heart' applied to

those who try to help is a reflection of this fear. And if it's sympathy we're talking about, the objectors are right. One can have too much sympathy for another. Sympathy does condone. It does encourage the weakness. It is, on the whole, a weakness.

But empathy comes from strength, not weakness. It is strong because, though it never judges, though it strives to understand, it never condones. It maintains its difference. It is what my friend meant when he said, 'I could be a criminal, too', and everyone knew that he wasn't.

Empathy, too, is not a passive virtue. It doesn't mean just listening to someone's troubles, and empathising with them, helpful as this may sometimes be. It is a positive act of the imagination, and properly used breaks through even hidden defences. I think perhaps we can see this best if we go back to our trolley diagram. We said, rather blithely, that the sensible thing to do is to uncoil the spring. But what - and this so often happens - if the spring is enclosed in a tight casing of shame, of refusal to face the truth? What if the person can't tell us about it and so help us to get it uncoiled? Then the one key may be that act that we are trying to describe - imaginative empathy, trying to know what the casing must look like from the inside. Even the statement, 'It must be hard not to be able to talk about it' may be the thing that starts the talk.

Empathy is the part of our Trinity that deals, of course, with negative feelings, that encourages their expression, that works with them in the here and now. Support is its further dimension.

Support is both tangible and intangible - material and in feeling. We know that because we use the word in both ways in our common speech. We may support someone through money, or gifts, count him as a dependant on our income tax, or we may also give him what we call 'moral support', which is, unfortunately, not deductible. But let's not ignore the importance of material support. One of the worst misunderstandings about helping that I know, since it is so subtle, is the down-grading of material means of support in favour of counselling or advice. It is tremendously important that material support be sound - that, for instance, a relief budget is enough to live on and not something to starve on, or struggle desperately along on, or something on which one cannot count, so hedged around is it with uncertainty. It is important that the means of doing things are there. There is a type of helper who considers practical helping somehow below his dignity and there are programmes which exist, I think, sometimes, only to conceal the fact that people don't have enough to eat. There is even a theory around that if people have something to count on then they will never grow, or change - but the reverse is actually true. Only as people have something to rely on do they become free to change.

For every person who is dependent because help is too easy to get there are two or three who become dependent because they have never been freed from the necessity of clinging to everything they can get. There used to be a description of certain men as being of 'independent means' - and the men really were independent. They were really free to make something of their lives.

But moral support is also important. The key to it is in the word 'here'. 'I am here to help you if you want me and can use me'. The last is important, too. One cannot force help on another. But so is the first - I am here. Whatever you do, I will not desert you. I may not be able to help you through this agency, of course, but I will respect your decision, will still be concerned about you.

None of these three is easy to give. We'd all like to avoid reality. We do find it very difficult to let people talk out their real feelings, particularly when these feelings are hostile (and of course particularly when the hostility is directed towards us). We all feel like quitting on someone who won't, as we say, help himself. This is why, I think, helping is both a science and an art. It is a science - there are principles, even, though I don't like the word, 'techniques', but it takes a human being, a highly disciplined human being who is at the same time natural and full of feeling, to put this science to work - and this is what true professionals are - not people who simply know how, but people who have made this know-how part of their very being itself.

As I said when I started, I know nothing of your particular line or work. What I have said may not be relevant, but I doubt it. You deal with people. You are one of the many new helping professions that have come into being in this century, more or less. If I have spoken a foreign language, I hope that there are among you enough good translators that it may be of some use to you.

NOTE

This talk was given in 1964 to a conference of agricultural field agents and home demonstration workers in West Virginia, USA.

13 Knowing by living through

Dorothy Walsh

Many philosophers, of recent years, have emphasized the asymmetry of self-ascription and other-person-ascription of certain psychological characteristics. How is this view concerning asymmetry to be understood? Is it to be understood as constituting a challenge to the doctrine of philosophical behaviorism, in that cases of self-ascription provide an exception to the application of behavioristic methodology, or can the view be interpreted as constituting a challenge in a more ambitious sense?

It is the purpose of this paper to argue for the following claims. 1 What is chiefly characteristic of self-knowledge in certain cases is not privacy of knowledge or certainty of knowledge but manner of knowing. 2 This manner of knowing is capable of extension to our knowledge of others, even though it is less reliable in such cases. 3 Therefore what we need to recognize is not an exception to the application of behavioristic methodology but, rather, the possibility of an alternative, noncompetitive, method for the understanding of persons. This may be called humanistic knowledge as contrasted with scientific knowledge. Humanistic knowledge is knowledge as realization, that is, the realization of the qualitative character of some actual or possible lived experience.

1

Let us first of all consider the doctrine of philosophical behaviorism. The essential claim is that statements about mental events or conditions can be interpreted as statements about overt behavior, or as statements about dispositional tendencies to behave in certain ways.

However much philosophical behaviorism may have been motivated by the desire to avoid dualism in favor of an emphasis upon mind-body unity, yet the manner in which this unity is understood - the emphasis on behavior - is, I believe, testimony to the continuing influence of the earlier doctrine of logical positivism. Logical positivism, we may remember, was characterized by a special regard for science. It does not take much reflection to see that the program of behavioristic interpretation is admirably adapted to bring knowledge of persons within the sphere of scientific inquiry. The task of philosophy is to clear away the misconceptions or verbal confusions that might seem to present impediments to such inquiry.

Now, as to this, I think it should be said that the behavioristic program of interpretation is a *possible* program, and, moreover, the appropriate program for scientific inquiry. Scientific psychology must be behavioristic. If a person in pain reports that he is in pain, a scientist may attend to that report, he may regard the report as a suggestive clue, or as partial evidence for something, but he cannot rest on it. This is not because the scientist is a highly skeptical fellow given to entertaining doubts about whether a person in pain is in a position to know that he is in pain, or given to doubts about the veracity of speakers. It is because the only way he can use the pain report is to treat it as he would treat nonverbal pain behavior such as grimaces or cries. Let us remember that a necessary requirement for a scientific statement is its membership in a connected scientific discourse. Within the domain of a scientific discourse there must be paths of transition from any one part to any other part, and unless pain report is treated as pain behavior it cannot be related to nervous system behavior.

The psychologist, as scientist, need recognize no exceptions to the application of his scientific methodology. The question, therefore, is not whether a behavioristic interpretation of mental statements is a possible interpretation. It is. And the question is not whether persons can be objects of scientific inquiry. They can. The question is whether those who endorse philosophical behaviorism are justified in the belief that this program of interpretation is not simply a program but *the* program.

A proper respect for the enterprise of science is compatible with the recognition of the importance, in our personal and social life, of non-scientific modes of knowledge. If you are ambitious to achieve a more adequate understanding of stars or of volcanoes you cannot do better than acquaint yourself with the most up-to-date scientific account, but if you are ambitious to achieve a more adequate understanding of persons, it is not the case that science has the same claim to your attention. This is because we *are* persons.

2

Let us now turn to the consideration of the claim concerning the asymmetry of self-ascription and other-ascription of certain psychological characteristics. It should be obvious that the use of the word 'psychological' here implies or suggests nothing whatever about the science of psychology. It is important to keep this in mind because the example most commonly cited to bring out the claim concerning asymmetry is the example of pain. Every psychologist will say that pain is a sensation, and, from the point of view of scientific psychology, he is perfectly correct. Whether or not something is to be classified as a sensation is not at all a matter of how it is experienced; it is a matter of whether we can specific a sense organ such as free nerve endings. Thus, from the point of view of scientific psychology, apprehension of color and apprehension of pain are both cases of sensory response. However, if we turn to the consideration of *how things are experienced* - the phenomenology of experience - the situation is different. Pain is experienced as phenomenally subjective; it is 'in me.' Color is experienced as phenomenally objective; it is 'out there.' This is why, if we trust simply to the direct deliverance of experience, putting aside any beliefs we may entertain as a consequence of scientific inquiry, it seems perfectly plausible to say: 'There may be unseen colors but there cannot be unfelt pains.' Now the uprush of anger and the euphoria of elation are experienced as phenomenally subjective, and this is why if we find it natural to say: 'When I am in pain I know I am in pain,' we shall also find it natural to say: 'When I am angry (or elated) I know I am angry (or elated).'

I do not wish to deny that, for certain purposes, it may be useful to recognize that pain is a sensation, anger is an emotion, and elation is a mood. Even from the point of view of the phenomenology of experience the difference between anger and elation can be relevant in that anger is experienced as directed towards something. We cannot be aware of anger without being aware of something else. We cannot be 'just angry' as we can be 'just elated' or 'just in pain.'

Now the claim concerning asymmetry of self-ascription and other-ascription of certain characteristics is usually presented as the claim that self-ascription has a certainty that we cannot assume in the case of other-ascription, in short, I cannot be mistaken about 'I am in pain' though I may be mistaken about 'He is in pain.' But what, exactly, does this mean? Why can I speak so authoritatively about my own pain? Some philosophers wish to say that self-knowledge in such a case, is non-inferential and noncriterial. Accordingly, they hold that the question: 'How do you know you are in pain?' is a senseless question. The only answer that can be given is: 'I just do.' But the question: 'How do you know?' need not be interpreted as a question that asks for evidence; it can be interpreted as a question that asks about manner of knowing. So interpreted, the question has an answer and the answer, I suggest, is: 'I know that I am in pain by living through the pain experience.'

There is a difference between experiencing in the sense of living through, and experiencing in the sense of simply being aware of. We can be aware of a color, but we would not normally speak of living through the experience of apprehending a color. Accordingly, lived experience is something more than just experience. No doubt, anything experienced is experienced by someone, but lived experience is personal experience. If I know that I am in pain by living through the pain experience, I know more than that I am in pain, I know more than the pain, I know what it is like for me to suffer this pain. My pain, my anger, my elation, my memory of my childhood, my religious conversion, and so on, are mine. Our sense of personal identity is closely bound up with the sense of ownership, the sense of 'myness.'

Because of the individuality of persons and the uniqueness of their life histories, there is a sense in which my lived through experience cannot be identical with yours. Nevertheless, there can be similarity. When someone says: 'I know what your experience must be like. I too have undergone, lived through, that kind of experience,' he is claiming that there is a kind of understanding common to those who have lived through a certain kind of experience and not shared by those who have not. Consider the common remark: 'You don't really know what it is, unless and until you've experienced it.' The claim is that no amount of informational 'knowledge about,' no matter how reliable, can be a substitute for understanding by undergoing, by participation, by living through. The former can be described as knowledge from without, the latter as knowledge from within. It is not a question of which is better. They serve different purposes; they afford different kinds of understanding.

3

Since I wish to claim that the kind of knowing from within, knowing by living through, which we have of our own experience, is capable of extension to the experience of others, it will be necessary to draw attention to our human capacity for self-transcendence. We can transcend ourselves and see ourselves as 'other,' and we can transcend ourselves and enter into the situation of another. Let us consider these in turn.

Some philosophers wish to say that statements such as, 'I am in pain' or, 'I am angry,' are not based on observation. It is understandable that they should wish to say this, for there would be something odd about the request: 'Look and see whether you happen to be in pain, whether you happen to be angry.' Also, when I am angry (or in pain) I know this without undertaking some particular act of looking or peering or scrutinizing. But though it is proper to say: 'I don't have to observe myself to know I am angry,' we should *not* say: 'I never observe myself being angry.' If we say this latter, we say something that is not in accordance with experience. Consider the following recital of events.

'Before I had my interview with him I realized that I might get angry, and I was fully aware of how unfortunate this would be. Accordingly, I resolved not to get angry. But, alas, as the interview progressed, I was aware that I was getting angry. I kept telling myself not to get angry, but I was unable to prevent this happening. With helpless frustration I watched myself getting angrier and angrier.'

It is to be noted here that the frustration is a response to the state-of-affairs of me-being-angry, and this means that we must distinguish between the phenomenal self (the angry self) and the spectator self who witnesses the activity of the phenomenal self. I-and-myself talk is a product of I-and-myself experience, and there are many cases of such experience. Consider the following: 'I observed with satisfaction that I was enduring the pain with composure.' There is the suffering self which, as suffering, is not in a state of satisfaction, but there is also the self who can experience satisfaction with reference to the way the suffering self is enduring its suffering. The spectator self can respond in a variety of different ways to the behavior of the observed phenomenal self. 'I surprised myself, I didn't think I had it in me to make that witty remark.' 'I was revolted to hear myself pompously uttering those platitudinous comments.' 'I was appalled to witness this uprush of vindictive hatred in myself.' 'I was relieved to observe that I didn't hesitate to forgo the unfair advantage.' 'I saw myself awkward and embarrassed in the situation and felt a certain compassion for that poor unhappy self.'

Now, to be sure, the use of 'observe,' 'see,' 'witness' in these contexts is not exactly the same as their use in other contexts. All I wish to claim is that the use is intelligible *in* context. If remarks such as those cited above pass as intelligible in ordinary discourse, the fact that they do is evidence of something about us as self-conscious beings. As self-conscious beings we have a capacity to transcend ourselves and see ourselves as 'other.' If we recognize this, we should also recognize that we have a capacity to transcend ourselves and enter into the situation of another.

When we hear the imperative: 'Put yourself in his place, see the situation as he sees it, realize how he must feel!' we understand what we are being asked to do. This is the request for an act of imaginative projection, imaginative identification. It will not be considered that we have made any attempt at imaginative identification if we simply reply: 'Well, I recognize that he feels disappointed, threatened, humiliated....' Knowing that such and such is the case is not the same thing as 'realizing what it is like.' The only way to realize what it is like is to live vicariously through the experience of the other person.

To the question: Can we always be sure of doing this successfully? the answer must be no. 'I thought I understood just what his experience must have been, but his subsequent behavior was so discordant with this as to make me believe that I was mistaken.' How did I come to misimagine? There might be several answers to this. For example, I did not have sufficient background information about the person and his situation to provide an adequate basis for the act of imaginative projection. Or, again, I did not, on this occasion, detach myself from myself sufficiently. I imagined myself in the situation instead of imagining myself *as him* in the situation. However, if it be acknowledged, as I believe it should be, that there is a kind of understanding to be achieved by this means, an understanding for which mere informational report is no substitute, we shall be justified in seeking this understanding despite the fact that success in its achievement is not guaranteed.

It is one thing to observe human behavior and accept what we observe as data for inference; it is another thing to 'read' the behavior as expressive. If we recognize this difference we will understand why we can most readily enter into the experience of fictional characters and dramatis personae. Artistic talent can present experience as expressively articulate and, by exercising control over our imagination, render it perspicacious. But though, with the not inconsiderable assistance of Shakespeare and some talented actor, we can more readily enter into the experience of Lear than into the experience of many actual persons, our response to literary and dramatic art would not be intelligible except on the basis of the assumption of our human capacity for imaginative projection and vicarious experience.

4

My claim is that knowing by living through, whether this living through be actual or vicarious, is a distinctive mode of knowing. The only thing that can be known in this way is what can be lived through, and the only thing that *we* can live through is some actual or possible human experience. The kind of knowledge this mode of knowing affords is knowledge as realization.

There are contexts in which for the word 'realize' we can substitute 'recognize' without distortion of meaning. For example, 'I realize that he is certain to be disappointed,' 'I realize that it would be judicious to postpone decision.' But there are other contexts in which this substitution is not regarded as adequate. If someone claims to realize the situation of a victim of persecution or irrational prejudice, we can intelligibly question whether, in fact, he does. It makes sense to say: 'He *recognizes* that the situation of the victim is unfortunate, but he does not enter into the situation, there is a failure in imaginative understanding and he does not *realize* it.'

Recognizing that such and such is so with reference to some kind of human experience is not the same thing as realizing what this experience might be like as lived experience. Confession of failure to understand, in the sense of realize, is perfectly compatible with absence of doubt concerning matter-of-fact. For example, 'I do not doubt that certain persons enjoy situations of physical danger, and even seek them out, but I don't understand it.' What the speaker does not understand is the lure, the fascination, of danger. Again, 'I do not doubt that certain persons believe in a life after death, believe in the immortality of souls, and that they believe this with complete conviction, but I don't understand it.' What the speaker does not understand is what it would be like to live in the light of this conviction. If we distinguish, as we should, between the tenability of a belief and the experience of entertaining the belief, or the experience generated by that entertainment, we will recognize that anything that would effect a transition from nonunderstanding to understanding can properly be said to extend the range of our humanistic knowledge.

When someone says: 'I know what it's like. I've lived through it. I've experienced it,' we commonly accept that he does know, even when he cannot convey this knowledge. Knowing beyond saying is acceptable in such a case, not because saying is impossible, but because the only kind of saying that would be relevant is a saying that requires some degree of literary talent. Mere fluency in the language is adequate for informational report, but talent is necessary for the imaginative evocation of vicarious experience.

The notion of knowing by living through, and the belief that there is a kind of understanding to be achieved by this means, will not, I think, strike the ordinary person as in any way odd. We have all heard the remark: 'Oh, if only you could experience it, or something like it, you would understand!' Even the philosopher, when not in the grip of epistemological anxiety about whether he *may* use a cognitive term without having credentials of verification in his pocket, will relapse into these assumptions. The solicitous father, who must deal with the fear of the child, will assume that he must enter into his experience and understand it as lived experience. He will struggle to achieve this imaginative understanding regardless of whether such understanding has received acknowledgment in his officially endorsed epistemological theory.

What we need to assume, and do assume, in our personal dealings with persons, ought perhaps to receive recognition in philosophy.

14   On not being judgmental

Ian T. Ramsey

THE PROBLEM

What I hope to do in this lecture is to come to grips with an issue in the field of Pastoral Care that constantly arises when clergy, ministers, counsellors and social workers come together. It is an issue which I think needs a very great deal of clarification and it can be easily and seriously misunderstood. The issue is this: The attitude of the minister towards human problems is often condemned as 'judgmental' and then contrasted to its loss with the attitude of 'acceptance' adopted by the well-trained caseworkers, the sensitive doctor and so on. The point is made for instance in the recent British Council of Churches Report 'Pastoral Care and Training of Ministers'. We read, page 36:

> The aim of the doctor is usually to reduce guilt on the grounds that it is a rather useless feeling and to palliate anxiety with tranquillisers. Traditionally the minister has made use of guilt to move his flock to penitence. There may even have been times in the past when this has come perilously close to spiritual blackmail. There are issues here which neither doctors or ministers, have squarely faced and surely they should face them together.

But the paragraph grants: 'Here however, doctor, caseworker and minister may well find themselves on occasion in opposite camps and the issues are by no means easy to resolve'.

It is this tension and opposition which I shall seek to analyse and clarify as far as I can. Incidentally, doctor as well as minister can be deceived by appearances:

Chapter 14

The factors which are undermining health may not be obvious on the surface. Human beings who bear their sufferings with fortitude often have little idea how far they are the unconscious architects of their own misfortunes. It is fatally easy for even the experienced family doctor to collude with a patient's lack of insight. In a series of studies, Dr Michael Balint and his associates have shown that the doctor can unwittingly attract to himself a series of patients who are, by their own choice of this particular doctor, insulated from the risk of getting well.

Or again, still introducing the issue with which we are going to be concerned, this time as it arises in the field of Marriage Guidance, we read in the same BBC report, page 36:

> The saintly spouse, husband or wife, may well be driving the partner to the verge of breakdown and the children into ill-health yet this spouse may be the one who stands well with the congregation. The minister in dealing with a member of his Church may not be as clear sighted in the matter as he might be. He may even resent the suggestion that religious belief may be used at this point as a means not of facing but of evading real issues.

The report comments: 'All this is not to suggest that the minister is intrinsically more likely than anyone else to make this kind of mistake but merely that up to the present he has often been singularly ill-prepared to realise his mistakes'. Another way of expressing the issues before us in this lecture is to say that I shall try to clarify what precisely is the mistake which the minister may be making and which he may be 'singularly ill-prepared to realise'.

Still continuing to get the problem rather more into focus let us consider an example of an adolescent girl which is discussed on pages 37-38 of the Report. The girl, who had been sent for a behaviour problem to an approved school, was illegitimate and had since childhood lived with her grandmother who was now a widow. The quote from the Report:

> The minister was contacted by the Social Case Worker to see if he could include the girl in parish youth activities. On hearing that she was returning to her grandmother he objected as he thought the old lady was not a good influence on the girl. He took what the social worker considered to be a judgmental attitude to the grandmother. [Later the Report, commenting on the minister's attitude, remarked:] The Minister thinks in terms of 'defending' - as we

may say 'protecting' - the girl; the social worker regards this as treating the girl as immature and thus preventing maturity from being achieved. There are times when the minister as a result of his training will look on life from a judgmental point of view springing perhaps from his own defensiveness, [though in fairness it adds that] on the other hand the minister may have felt in this case that there were too many risks involved in the social worker's concurrence with the girl's wishes. [The Report then continues] There is no easy answer to this dilemma, both sides of the matter need to be taken into account. The ideal way with such a matter is to begin as far as possible with a full awareness of one's presuppositions and the safe way to continue is by constant vigilance without too much interference. There may be much to learn here about the openness of faith and the capacity of faith to take risks.

Again I may say that this lecture is concerned precisely with the background presuppositions of this kind of learning, with what in fact is involved in 'the openness of faith and the capacity of faith to take risks'.

Yet again, in discussing the example of a boy's behaviour and his relationship with his very 'proper' mother after the death of his delinquent father who had been strongly addicted to alcohol, the Report comments:

At this point the minister might have been tempted to speak to the child to warn him, to exhort him to behave, or to remind him that his mother had enough worries without his adding to them. By doing this he would adopt the role of disciplinarian, and might even earn merit with his congregation but this would not touch the real problem. The solution lay here in the minister's ability to get the woman to face her feelings about her (dead) husband. [Later the Report adds] The minister by trying to articulate her real feelings could begin the necessary Grief work to release tension and avert the breakdown which would otherwise probably take place. Perhaps a word like 'well you really must have loved him a lot at one time' or some such sentiment may be enough to get the natural processes working. The mistake not to make [the Report continues] would be to commend her for being brave in the face of death. This is not a case for the minister to support the defences of the woman but gently to encourage grief to work its way out and support her while this is happening. Only by placing her true feelings could this woman find real resources for living and be reconciled to the boy.

In those remarks about this particular case is implied something of the contrast between the 'judgmental' and the 'acceptance' approach. Another line on the distinction is given in some remarks by Miss Jean Heywood in her book 'Casework and Pastoral Care'. She asks, page 72:

> ... are there differences between the way the Priest and the Social Worker look at behaviour [and her answer is] I think there are. To the Caseworker sin is irrelevant in the context of his work. He knows and recognises that certain things are morally wrong, irresponsible and evil but he looks at acts of behaviour this way - Why did this person feel he must do this, what did it mean to him, what lies behind it all? The casework method is designed to find this way out. Sometimes, as in the case of the suddenly bereaved child who steals something of value to symbolise replacing the treasured mother he has lost, the act is seen as an appeal to compassion, a cry for help; sometimes it is an act of hate against a cruel world. The worker cannot change the behaviour except by giving to the child a repairing experience of love either through himself, or through providing some closer relationship.

The implication all through is that this is very different indeed from the approach of the Priest or the Minister to such a person.

There then is the issue with which I shall be concerned in this lecture and the kind of context in which it arises and I now propose first to look at what is involved in calling an attitude 'judgmental', and then to follow this by a similar examination of the attitude of 'acceptance' with which 'judgmental' is often contrasted. Thereafter I shall attempt a critical evaluation of the two terms. It seems to me that when the word 'judgmental' has been used to express the kind of criticism to which I have referred, we can discover at least seven different contexts for it, and I will try to segregate them as well as I can.

CONTEXTS FOR 'JUDGMENTAL'

1 First, to be judgmental is, in one sense of the word, to make a particular kind of judgment of someone's behaviour namely to condemn that behaviour as sinful or guilty. For it is claimed that to judge someone's behaviour as, for example, 'sinful' is either as Miss Heywood said, irrelevant or, especially when set in a

condemnatory context, sets up the very conditions which hinders a caring ministry from being effectively exercised. Miss Heywood tells us that even the Christian caseworker is 'wary about arousing too much guilt because he knows its paralysing effect and the serious depression which may follow it'. There then is my first sense of judgmental.

2 Broadening that first sense, being 'judgmental' can next mean imposing some dogmatic interpretation on a situation. For instance we may refuse to accept a divorced person's need for re-marriage on the grounds that since a metaphysical *vinculum* or bond had been created at his Wedding Service, that first marriage had not been broken nor could it ever be broken despite the fact that now at any rate there seems to be no evidence whatever for it. This would be a case of imposing a dogmatic interpretation on a situation which from the point of view of every empirical fact seems plainly to run counter to it. Or a text from scripture might be used in isolation to provide a judgment of a universal kind. Though I know that this particular text is open to many misunderstandings, it is good enough for an example and it might be used by people who have never known what the scriptures said or didn't say: 'Better to marry than to burn'.

3 More generally still to be judgmental may be to work with prior notions. Notice the way in which the first three senses become more and more generalised as we pass from 1 to 3. To be judgmental in this third sense then is to work with prior notions and so to make far too speedy and superficial reactions to the complexities of the human situation whose complexities, thanks to developments in the Behavioural Sciences, we are coming increasingly to recognise. In this way people who are judgmental would have greater concern for their conceptual frame than for those to whom they were supposed to be ministering. The judgmental would attempt to impose stereotypes on empirical fact and a number of these stereotypes come readily to mind. I have mentioned one or two already tonight. The dutiful daughter, the saintly spouse, the good for nothing brother, the lazy scoundrel, the merry widow, are some of them.

4 Judgmental is sometimes a way of characterising a disciplinarian, who has strict rules of how people ought to behave and sees human behaviour at its best as conformity to such rules and considers that any violation is to be condemned outright.

5 The judgmental need not to register an altogether

condemnatory attitude. We have seen already that it can be used of those who seek to protect a person. You remember the minister in relation to the child he thought ought not to go to the grandmother. Closely related to judgmental as used by those who in a particular way 'protect', is judgmental used of those who seek to manipulate a person in any particular way.

6 Another example of being judgmental is that of someone constantly uttering warnings and exhortations forbidding this and urging that - in this way bringing harsh and sometimes unfair pressure, authoritarian and insensitive pressure, to bear on people.

7 Something quite different - a judgmental attitude has sometimes been associated with the pronouncing of absolution. For someone might seek forgiveness in this way, and absolution be pronounced, in a situation whose complexities demanded a much more searching and a much more prolonged exercise. Penitential exercises, it would be said in this connection, are altogether too easy and too superficial for the complexities of human behaviour and it might be added that ironically enough, these prescriptions of traditional piety may only conceal what is in fact needing forgiveness, a situation which needs to be faced frankly and analysed very carefully.

Those are the seven senses in which so far as I can gather from the literature, the word judgmental can be used and has been used by way of criticism. What characteristic features do we now find looking back on these seven senses? What features do we find a judgmental attitude to display which can account for the caseworker's suspicion of it? I think we can group our answer broadly under two headings.

First the caseworker is suspicious of it because of the shallow and superficial understanding of human nature which it often implies. It represents the desire, so it would be said, to get by without any of the knowledge which can be given by techniques or other ways of knowing human nature. Second, the caseworker is suspicious of the judgmental attitude because it uses methods or concepts which, whether because of implied hostility or otherwise, inhibit response and oppress the spirit of man by being embodied in some authoritarian judgment. The judgmental attitude often names or condemns a situation, or both, rather than reacts creatively to it. There then are the seven senses of judgmental, and the caseworker's reasons for being suspicious, if you like, of them all.

FEATURES OF 'ACCEPTANCE'

Now contrasting with that judgmental attitude is the attitude of acceptance. What do we make of this? I think there are three features distinctive of this attitude of acceptance.

First of all it describes an attitude, relatively passive, which helps someone in need to articulate freely feelings which have been hitherto repressed or unacknowledged or undiscriminated and whose repression is proving a danger to health and well-being. The evidence for such a claim is that when these feelings have been articulated freely there is an obvious growth in health and well-being. Second, the attitude of acceptance is meant to build up and to develop, as far as knowledge and skills can go, all the empirical particularity of a certain situation. It is meant to create empathy and sympathy between those who accept and those who are accepted. Third, it is avowedly non-authoritarian in character, so much so that some have criticised it, I do not say necessarily unfairly, but have criticised it for being an altogether casual attitude - so open-minded as to be empty-minded.

But the claim would be that the caseworker and counsellor working with this approach is never off-putting, wins the confidence of the client and provides a climate and an atmosphere in which men and women can be helped to grow freely to maturity. Now it might seem that the case is absolutely clear-cut, that there is every need in a caring ministry, whether of priest or caseworker, not to be judgmental but always to develop an attitude of acceptance. What more could there be to say? I fear, however, that we have not completed the story. Let us now see how the edges of that clear-cut judgment begin to be rather blurred. There are some five points for us to consider.

BLURRED EDGES

First, in rightly criticising many judgments expressed in terms of sin and guilt as being either irrelevant or unhelpful we must not go so far as to exclude from our assessment all moral or theological interpretations of human behaviour. Recalling as an illustration the case of the 'suddenly bereaved child who steals something of value to symbolise replacing the treasured mother he has lost', there are at least three points to make. (i) In regard with this case, first of all the act of stealing as such is wrong. That I hold, we take for granted. (ii) But second, and following very quickly on that first reflection, no-one knowing, by the skills and techniques and knowledge now available to us by the Behavioural Sciences, no-one knowing the whole situation in this way would, I think, ever condemn the child or want to speak of sin or guilt in relation to the full circumstances. Here we may recall an obvious distinction of which, it seems to me, in this whole field we make use far too rarely. This is the distinction between right and wrong, good and evil on the one side and praise and blame on the other. There may be many actions, good and right for which people could and should be blamed; and there are many actions wrong and evil for which people could and should be praised. I think this is a logical possibility that the kind of hard and fast distinction between the judgmental and acceptance attitudes often fails to make. In judging an action wrong or a situation evil, we do not necessarily blame anyone, still less the person or persons who seem to be directly involved. This distinction which G.E. Moore discussed at length in his book on 'Ethics' (Home University Library pp. 187-95) is sometimes entirely lost sight of in the field of social work and yet it is clearly important to make a distinction between right and wrong, good and evil on the one side and praise and blame on the other. There is no reversible entailment between the one set of concepts and another. We have got to be very careful indeed how we move from the one set to the other and no doubt many of the condemnations of the judgmental have resulted from a confusion in this conceptual area. (iii) Third when on some particular occasion a moral judgment is made it must be genuinely moral which ensures in particular that it will not be authoritarian. How do we ensure this? The answer is: when and because the judgment discloses an ideal in relation to which a moral judgment is made. A moral judgment has lost its point and importance, and does not deserve to be called a moral judgment, unless it succeeds in mediating an ideal, a moral obligation which people acknowledge spontaneously and to which they respond freely.

Incidentally it would seem as if Miss Jean Heywood cannot in any way be surprised at this, cannot at all escape moral categories in her discussion of and assessment of social work cases. For instance she remarks, page 73, 'No casework, no caseworker ever knows the struggle which goes on in a person's mind as he wrestles with "want" or "thought", how easy it was to come down on the right side or how difficult'. I should have thought the implication of this comment was that, while no caseworker would ever know the moral struggle in all its intensity, this was certainly a feature of the situation which anyone concerned with a reliable assessment of it ought to do his best to know and certainly to acknowledge. Again the only way to change the child's behaviour Miss Heywood would say is to give him 'a repairing experience of love' on which obviously Miss Heywood would set extremely high value and make of that repairing experience of love is the moral level at which she would assess it. My point is, you see, that the distinction between judgmental and acceptance attitudes begins to be blurred. We see that the caseworker cannot avoid making moral judgments, or embracing some kind of moral ideal as the very presuppositions of his or her work, can't avoid engaging people in moral exercises. Yet at the same time we must rightly doubt whether the way to display these presuppositions or to initiate these moral exercises is by means of terms like 'sin' or 'guilt', not least when these are set within an authoritarian context. For then they fail to mediate the redeeming love which is the Gospel, a love in response to which men find freedom and life and the confidence of ultimate triumph. I think that one of our greatest needs in theology, as it bears on casework examples, is so to style terms like 'sin' and 'guilt' that they make evidently clear the Gospel the good news which they should be articulating. So often when I hear sin and guilt discussed in theological contexts they appear to be part of the worst possible news that has ever at any time come to man from anywhere, and they certainly do not initiate appropriate or beneficial moral exercise.

Second, having said all that in relation to the term 'judgmental' let us now note that the term 'acceptance' is not without its ambiguities. Very often in casework it is said that whether with ourselves or other people we must accept the evil that is in us and them. Now here, it seems to me, are two very important points. Acceptance by itself cannot possibly be a term strong enough to bear all the weight which the caseworker puts on it. Acceptance by itself is not a term strong enough to avoid being misleading, for it can be far too passive in its overtones. It can register far too little involvement and concern. For instance day by day, year in year out I accept the fact that Newcastle

is north of London and south of Edinburgh but there is
never an occasion I get warmed up about it. I even
accept the fact that we have a two-tier postal structure
and I am not much fussed about that either, and we can
all recall the lady who said she was perfectly prepared
to accept the universe and who prompted the remark
'ma'am, you had better'. Now it is to meet this difficulty that 'acceptance' is far too weak a term to use,
that it is ambiguous in its context, that very often
you will find in the literature that another word is
added to it. We have to get people to accept and to
'face' a particular situation. The word 'face' is
often added. So far so good and indeed much better.
But now comes my main point. When we accept and face
the evil around us what is quite clear is that the
alternatives are not denunciation and toleration. What
is quite clear is that we have not to choose between
denunciation on the one hand which oppresses and imperils
the spirit of man, and toleration on the other if that
is supposed to be, as it often is, a just-couldn't-care-
less attitude. For Christians at least there is a
third possibility, redemption and loving concern, the
conviction that by the love of God shown forth in
Christ, and reflected at least in true Christians,
there is no evil which cannot in measure be already re-
deemed and have its part in a creative development.
So here there arises a context for 'acceptance' and
'facing' which allows (unless we think that 'denunciation' and 'toleration' are exhaustive alternatives) for
having the third possibility which at once introduces a
theological interpretation even into and associated
with the attitude of acceptance and facing.

    Third, as we try to bring together the judgmental
and acceptance attitudes in a critical evaluation, let
us remember that appearances especially in human nature
are indeed often deceptive. But judgments are made
on situations even by caseworkers. Naturally as a
matter of pastoral expediency and professional discretion it is recognised that they will not always call
to be, nor should they be, publicised beyond ourselves.
But that does not mean that they are not made. The
important point here in an area where appearances can
be very deceptive and misleading and where judgments
are particularly intricate and hazardous would seem to
be this: always keep these judgments which, it seems
to me, that caseworkers as much as priests inevitably
make, always keep these judgments tentative and ready
for reform. Never let them be dogmatic. Let them
be open and at risk. But this is a feature of course

which many people would argue has not enough belonged to theology and needs to belong to theology, and that while it has belonged to theology in its most devout and creative eras, for instance in New Testament times, that is by no means to say that it always has belonged to theology, or does largely belong to theology today.

My fourth point concerns this matter of absolution. Now undoubtedly absolution can describe an activity which is as empirically naive as it is ritually stereotyped and theologically suspect. Undoubtedly it can, it may, tempt a priest to play the God role and in this way to pretend to an infallibility, an omnipotence and a divine status which since they are given to no finite person are inevitably and necessarily parodied and contorted. That needs to be said. But another interpretation altogether can be given to the act of absolution. In relation to sin and wrong-doing, it can in principle occur as an expression of the Gospel, just as indeed in relation to a community the Church occurs as an expression of the Gospel, and as in relation to written words the Bible occurs as an expression of the Gospel, and just as in relation to food, the Lord's Supper, the Holy Communion, occurs as an expression of the Gospel. What I am saying is that in relation to sin and wrong-doing absolution may occur as one of many legitimate expressions of the Gospel, the Gospel of God's redeeming love. In this sense absolution can be a feature of the reconciled community which in this way shares through its spokesmen in the unsearchable riches of Christ. This I believe to be the true interpretation of verses 19-23 of the twentieth chapter of St John's Gospel viz. that absolution is a characteristic feature of the forgiven, reconciled community, reminding its members of the redeeming love of God in which they constantly live. What I am saying is that absolution may in its rite and ceremony and when justified always will in its rite mediate this redeeming reconciling love in a disclosure. Absolution in this theological context can surely do nothing but good for it mediates God's redeeming love, in such a way that men freely and spontaneously accept it, as they respond to genuine inspiration. Absolution in this way creates and mediates that atmosphere which is the context of the Gospel and it is an atmosphere which we see also mediated in the word of God and the sacraments, and indeed by all Christian doctrine when they reliably express the Christian Gospel.

Which leads me, fifth, back to our talk about guilt. The BCC Report to which I referred earlier and from which I quoted some relevant remarks on guilt, comments in relation to the dilemma over guilt.

> The premature removal of guilt and anxiety may be detrimental to spiritual and mental health while the perpetuation of either feeling may be equally detrimental [and it continues] presumably the answer lies in solely treating guilt as to increase responsibility [but it concludes] the path which religious belief should play has yet to be adequately worked out [and here comes the quotation I made at the start] Doctor, caseworker and minister may well find themselves on occasion in opposite camps. The issues are by no means easy to resolve.

Well, may I make an attempt to resolve them and in this way to take a little further points which I have made already? There surely can be no objection to judgments of guilt or sin where, first of all, these are reliably made by people themselves (and notice that I inserted the word 'reliably'); and/or second, when they arise not as superficial or conventional or authoritarian interpretations of certain behaviour but as a response to the incoherence and the discord which has been disclosed when certain behaviour is set in the context of an inspiring ideal which we freely and spontaneously affirm. We can surely not object to judgments of guilt when they arise not in some authoritarian or dogmatic context but as a response to our discerning discord between certain behaviour and an inspiring ideal which we freely and spontaneously affirm. For to make such judgments would surely be an accepting and a facing. But the very accepting and facing of the situation on the one hand, and of the ideal on the other, would surely involve making a judgment which itself reveals the hope and possibility of redemption and initiates a growth to maturity indeed. Ironically enough it would seem to be judgments of sin and guilt which when properly articulated and reliably exercised that must lie at the heart of any growth to maturity. We all know that terrible agonising cry: 'They don't care enough to say that I am guilty'.

THE MEETING OF JUDGMENT AND ACCEPTANCE

Now all this may seem startling. Does it mean, you might say, an entire volteface? Is there then no defence whatever for the caseworker's 'acceptance', nothing to be said for 'not being judgmental'? No, to make my own central point quite briefly, criticism of the judgmental attitude is at its heart a criticism of an authoritarian theology, and of practices that show a shallow and superficial understanding of human nature and men's needs. Yet it often rests also on an inadequate understanding of the character of genuine moral judgments. In short, it is a devastating criticism somewhat weakened, however, by being expressed in terms of a shallow understanding of moral judgments. In other words, the point is this. For men and women to grow to maturity they need to respond spontaneously and freely to something which wins them over, to something which inspires them. Now in that sense to grow to maturity demands a response to something taken as authoritative but not, never, authoritarian. Neither caseworker nor priest can ever hope to succeed in their concern for maturity unless somewhere along the line they can effect some authoritative disclosure in responding to which men and women can find their freedom and life and fulfilment. The good caseworker and the good priest will both seek to create the conditions for such a disclosure to occur. Meanwhile what we have come to see and what I have implied is that much traditional theology and many traditional Christian practices so often fail to evoke such a disclosure, whereas ironically enough many of the natural techniques and skills and understandings of the social workers do. Now there, it seems to me, is the real tension between being judgmental and not being judgmental. Here, so to say, is the rub, the devastating contrast between an ineffective, harsh theology, a polished cistern which contains no water, no living water and the knowledge and skills of the Behavioural Sciences which seem to minister so obviously and creatively to the spirit of man. To overcome this tension we need to restyle our theology and our Christian practices from the one side and from the other side we must look for the fulfilment of natural concepts and practices in a Christian framework whose dominant theme is redeeming love. That it seems to me is the task which the judgmental controversy sets us.

A true theology that mediates the Gospel will never be, and can never logically be, authoritarian for it will always have the power and authority of God which in Whitehead's phrase is, 'the worship he inspires', or to give that remark a Christian context we may say that a true theology will have the power and authority of a love which never lets us go. Again moral judgments are worth nothing whatever, indeed they aren't even moral judgments, unless they mediate a moral ideal which freely inspires and spontaneously wins our acceptance. It is perfectly true that no good can ever come from a judgmental attitude which is hostile, repressive of the spirit of man, which imposes *a priori* dogmatic interpretation, which despises or ignores the wealth of our knowledge about human personalities, about their needs and hopes and fears, the kind of knowledge that the psychological and behavioural sciences can give us. (Incidentally, in case I have misled anybody when I said 'Behavioural Sciences', I hope that all the way through the reader will translate this as 'Psychological and Behavioural Sciences' for I always had both of them in mind.) But once theology has learned that it is primarily the purveyor of a vision, and that its authority is that of an inspiring ideal, and that moral judgments are worth nothing unless they arrive as a response to a disclosure of obligation around all the relevant empirical facts, then a judgmental attitude, so called, loses everything of its harsh, oppressive, inhibited, ignorant character. Furthermore, the attitude of acceptance receives in its turn the fuller setting and explication it must have if it is to be responsible and creative and point to freedom and maturity and fulfilment. The truly judgmental and the truly accepting attitudes come to the same point from quite opposite directions, the one coming from a theological and a moral direction, the other from a natural and behavioural direction. They meet together when they are both genuine at the point of all those who stand in need of adequate help.

But when we realise that the image of the Church is often judgmental in the bad sense, and its officers in that some sense are supposed to be judgmental too; we also realise what an appallingly difficult task lies ahead of us, those of us in the Church as Christians or in the Church as its officers. Not only must we ensure that the overall image is changed, but that the character of the Church's caring ministry makes certain that it will be. Until that happens there will not only be a lie instead of the Gospel in our right hand, but we shall have failed to minister God's Grace to the needs and hopes of humanity, and the cry of judgmental will be heard and rightly heard in our clinics and in our streets, not to say at our casework discussions. Not only will it be heard, but the condemnation it expresses albeit in a misleading way, will be amply deserved.

Bibliography

This bibliography includes all those sources referred to in the Editors' Introduction and others which may be useful in the study of particular topics raised by the essays collected. The topics to which the items listed are relevant are indicated by their titles, with the possible exception of Benn and Peters (1959), Feinberg (1973) and Peters (1966), which have directly relevant chapters, but are also good general introductions to moral and social philosophy. Other references can be found within the essays or their notes.

ARISTOTLE, 'The Nicomachean Ethics', trans. by Sir David Ross, Oxford University Press, 1925.
ARROW, K.J. (1972), Gifts and Exchanges, 'Philosophy and Public Affairs', vol. 1, no. 4.
ATTFIELD, R. (1974), On Being Human, 'Inquiry', vol. 17.
BEALES, H.L. (1945), 'The Making of Social Policy', Hobhouse Memorial Lecture, no. 15.
BENN, S.I. and PETERS, R.S. (1959), 'Social Principles and the Democratic State', London, George Allen & Unwin.
BROOKE, R. (1972), Social Administration and Human Rights in P. Townsend and N. Bosanquet (eds), 'Labour and Inequality', London, Fabian Society.
CAMPBELL, T.D. (1976), Discretionary 'Rights' in Timms and Watson (1976).
DOWNIE, R.S. (1971), 'Roles and Values', London, Methuen.
FEINBERG, J. (1973), 'Social Philosophy', Englewood Cliffs, Prentice-Hall.
HALL, P. (1952), 'The Social Services of Modern England', London, Routledge & Kegan Paul.
HARE, R.M. (1952), 'The Language of Morals', Oxford University Press.
HARRIS, E. (1968), Respect for Persons in R.T. DeGeorge (ed.), 'Ethics and Society', London, Macmillan.

HENDERSON, C.R. (1902), 'Introduction to the Study of the Dependent, Defective, and Delinquent Classes, and of their Social Treatment'.
HNIK, F.R. (1938), 'The Philanthropic Motive in Christianity'.
JONES, O.R. (1971), ed., 'The Private Language Argument', London, Macmillan.
KEITH-LUCAS, A. (1953), The Political Theory Implicit in Social Casework, 'American Political Science Review', vol. 4.
MACLAGAN, W.G. (1960), Respect for Persons as a Moral Principle - I, 'Philosophy', vol. 35, July, and, Respect for Persons as a Moral Principle - II, 'Philosophy', vol. 35, October.
MARSH, D. (1970), 'The Welfare State', London, Longmans.
NAGEL, T. (1975), 'The Possibility of Altruism', Oxford University Press.
PETERS, R. (1958), 'The Concept of Motivation', London, Routledge & Kegan Paul.
PETERS, R. (1966), 'Ethics and Education', London, George Allen & Unwin.
PINKER, R. (1970), Stigma and Social Welfare, 'Social Work', vol. 27, no. 4.
PINKER, R. (1971), 'Social Theory and Social Policy', London, Heinemann.
PINKER, R. (1974), Social Policy and Social Justice, 'Journal of Social Policy', vol. 3, no. 1.
PLANT, R. (1970), 'Social and Moral Theory in Casework', London, Routledge & Kegan Paul.
PLANT, R. (1974), 'Community and Ideology', London, Routledge & Kegan Paul.
RAPHAEL, D. (1967), 'Political Theory and the Rights of Man', London, Macmillan.
RAPHAEL, D. (1970), 'Problems of Political Philosophy', London, Macmillan.
RESCHER, N. (1972), 'Welfare', University of Pittsburgh Press.
ROBSON, W. and CRICK, B. (1970), 'The Future of the Social Services', Harmondsworth, Penguin.
SINGER, P. (1973), Altruism and Commerce: A defense of Titmuss against Arrow, 'Philosophy and Public Affairs', vol. 2, no. 3.
SLACK, K. (1966), 'Social Administration and the Citizen', London, Michael Joseph.
STALLEY, R.F. (1976), Non-Judgmental Attitudes in Timms and Watson (1976).
STRAWSON, P.F. (1959), 'Individuals', London, Methuen.
STRAWSON, P.F. (1962), Freedom and Resentment, British Academy Lecture reprinted in P.F. Strawson (ed.),

'Studies in the Philosophy of Thought and Action', Oxford University Press, 1968.
STRAWSON, P.F. (1971), Categories, in O.P. Wood and G. Pitcher (eds), 'Ryle', London, Macmillan.
TELFER, E. (1970), Friendship, 'Proceedings of the Aristotelian Society', 1970-71.
TIMMS, N. and WATSON, D. (1976) (eds), 'Philosophy in Social Work', London, Routledge & Kegan Paul.
TITMUSS, R.M. (1968), 'Commitment to Welfare', London, George Allen & Unwin.
TITMUSS, R.M. (1970), 'The Gift Relationship', London, George Allen & Unwin.
TITMUSS, R.M. (1971), Welfare 'Rights', law and discretion, 'Political Quarterly', vol. 42.
WATSON, D. (1976), Social Services in a Nutshell, in Timms and Watson (1976).
WILENSKY, H.L. and LEBEAUX, C.N. (1958), Conceptions of Social Welfare, ch. 6 of their 'Industrial Society and Social Welfare', London, Macmillan and New York, Free Press.
WINCH, P. (1958), 'The Idea of a Social Science', London, Routledge & Kegan Paul.
WINCH, P. (1964), Understanding a Primitive Society, 'American Philosophical Quarterly', vol. 1.

Routledge Social Science Series

Routledge & Kegan Paul   London and Boston
68–74 Carter Lane   London EC4V 5EL
9 Park Street   Boston   Mass 02108

Contents

International Library of Sociology 3
General Sociology 3
Foreign Classics of Sociology 4
Social Structure 4
Sociology and Politics 5
Foreign Affairs 5
Criminology 5
Social Psychology 6
Sociology of the Family 6
Social Services 7
Sociology of Education 8
Sociology of Culture 8
Sociology of Religion 9
Sociology of Art and Literature 9
Sociology of Knowledge 9
Urban Sociology 10
Rural Sociology 10
Sociology of Industry and Distribution 11
Documentary 11
Anthropology 11
Sociology and Philosophy 12
International Library of Anthropology 12
International Library of Social Policy 13
International Library of Welfare and Philosophy 13
Primary Socialization, Language and Education 13
Reports of the Institute of Community Studies 14
Reports of the Institute for Social Studies in Medical Care 14
Medicine, Illness and Society 15
Monographs in Social Theory 15
Routledge Social Science Journals 15

Authors wishing to submit manuscripts for any series in this catalogue should send them to the Social Science Editor, Routledge & Kegan Paul Ltd, 68–74 Carter Lane, London EC4V 5EL

●*Books so marked are available in paperback*
All books are in Metric Demy 8vo format (216 × 138mm approx.)

International Library of Sociology

General Editor John Rex

GENERAL SOCIOLOGY

Barnsley, J. H. The Social Reality of Ethics. *464 pp.*
Belshaw, Cyril. The Conditions of Social Performance. *An Exploratory Theory. 144 pp.*
Brown, Robert. Explanation in Social Science. *208 pp.*
● Rules and Laws in Sociology. *192 pp.*
Bruford, W. H. Chekhov and His Russia. *A Sociological Study. 244 pp.*
Cain, Maureen E. Society and the Policeman's Role. *326 pp.*
●**Fletcher, Colin.** Beneath the Surface. *An Account of Three Styles of Sociological Research. 221 pp.*
Gibson, Quentin. The Logic of Social Enquiry. *240 pp.*
Glucksmann, M. Structuralist Analysis in Contemporary Social Thought. *212 pp.*
Gurvitch, Georges. Sociology of Law. *Preface by Roscoe Pound. 264 pp.*
Hodge, H. A. Wilhelm Dilthey. *An Introduction. 184 pp.*
Homans, George C. Sentiments and Activities. *336 pp.*
Johnson, Harry M. Sociology: *a Systematic Introduction. Foreword by Robert K. Merton. 710 pp.*
●**Keat, Russell,** and **Urry, John.** Social Theory as Science. *278 pp.*
Mannheim, Karl. Essays on Sociology and Social Psychology. *Edited by Paul Keckskemeti. With Editorial Note by Adolph Lowe. 344 pp.*
Systematic Sociology: *An Introduction to the Study of Society. Edited by J. S. Erös and Professor W. A. C. Stewart. 220 pp.*
Martindale, Don. The Nature and Types of Sociological Theory. *292 pp.*
●**Maus, Heinz.** A Short History of Sociology. *234 pp.*
Mey, Harald. Field-Theory. *A Study of its Application in the Social Sciences. 352 pp.*
Myrdal, Gunnar. Value in Social Theory: *A Collection of Essays on Methodology. Edited by Paul Streeten. 332 pp.*
Ogburn, William F., and **Nimkoff, Meyer F.** A Handbook of Sociology. *Preface by Karl Mannheim. 656 pp. 46 figures. 35 tables.*
Parsons, Talcott, and **Smelser, Neil J.** Economy and Society: *A Study in the Integration of Economic and Social Theory. 362 pp.*
Podgórecki, Adam. Practical Social Sciences. *About 200 pp.*
●**Rex, John.** Key Problems of Sociological Theory. *220 pp.*
Discovering Sociology. *278 pp.*
Sociology and the Demystification of the Modern World. *282 pp.*
●**Rex, John** (Ed.) Approaches to Sociology. *Contributions by Peter Abell, Frank Bechhofer, Basil Bernstein, Ronald Fletcher, David Frisby, Miriam Glucksmann, Peter Lassman, Herminio Martins, John Rex, Roland Robertson, John Westergaard and Jock Young. 302 pp.*
Rigby, A. Alternative Realities. *352 pp.*

INTERNATIONAL LIBRARY OF SOCIOLOGY

Roche, M. Phenomenology, Language and the Social Sciences. *374 pp.*
Sahay, A. Sociological Analysis. *220 pp.*
Strasser, Hermann. The Normative Structure of Sociology. *Conservative and Emancipatory Themes in Social Thought. About 340 pp.*
Urry, John. Reference Groups and the Theory of Revolution. *244 pp.*
Weinberg, E. Development of Sociology in the Soviet Union. *173 pp.*

FOREIGN CLASSICS OF SOCIOLOGY

●Durkheim, Emile. Suicide. *A Study in Sociology.* Edited and with an Introduction by George Simpson. *404 pp.*
Professional Ethics and Civic Morals. Translated by Cornelia Brookfield. *288 pp.*
●Gerth, H. H., and Mills, C. Wright. From Max Weber: *Essays in Sociology. 502 pp.*
●Tönnies, Ferdinand. Community and Association. (*Gemeinschaft und Gesellschaft.*) Translated and Supplemented by Charles P. Loomis. Foreword by Pitirim A. Sorokin. *334 pp.*

SOCIAL STRUCTURE

Andreski, Stanislav. Military Organization and Society. *Foreword by Professor A. R. Radcliffe-Brown. 226 pp. 1 folder.*
Coontz, Sydney H. Population Theories and the Economic Interpretation. *202 pp.*
Coser, Lewis. The Functions of Social Conflict. *204 pp.*
Dickie-Clark, H. F. Marginal Situation: *A Sociological Study of a Coloured Group. 240 pp. 11 tables.*
Glaser, Barney, and Strauss, Anselm L. Status Passage. *A Formal Theory. 208 pp.*
Glass, D. V. (Ed.) Social Mobility in Britain. *Contributions by J. Berent, T. Bottomore, R. C. Chambers, J. Floud, D. V. Glass, J. R. Hall, H. T. Himmelweit, R. K. Kelsall, F. M. Martin, C. A. Moser, R. Mukherjee, and W. Ziegel. 420 pp.*
Jones, Garth N. Planned Organizational Change: *An Exploratory Study Using an Empirical Approach. 268 pp.*
Kelsall, R. K. Higher Civil Servants in Britain: *From 1870 to the Present Day. 268 pp. 31 tables.*
König, René. The Community. *232 pp. Illustrated.*
●Lawton, Denis. Social Class, Language and Education. *192 pp.*
McLeish, John. The Theory of Social Change: *Four Views Considered. 128 pp.*
Marsh, David C. The Changing Social Structure of England and Wales, 1871-1961. *288 pp.*
●Mouzelis, Nicos. Organization and Bureaucracy. *An Analysis of Modern Theories. 240 pp.*
Mulkay, M. J. Functionalism, Exchange and Theoretical Strategy. *272 pp.*
Ossowski, Stanislaw. Class Structure in the Social Consciousness. *210 pp.*
●Podgórecki, Adam. Law and Society. *302 pp.*

SOCIOLOGY AND POLITICS

Acton, T. A. Gypsy Politics and Social Change. *316 pp.*
Clegg, Stuart. Power, Rule and Domination. *A Critical and Empirical Understanding of Power in Sociological Theory and Organisational Life. About 300 pp.*
Hechter, Michael. Internal Colonialism. *The Celtic Fringe in British National Development, 1536–1966. 361 pp.*
Hertz, Frederick. Nationality in History and Politics: *A Psychology and Sociology of National Sentiment and Nationalism. 432 pp.*
Kornhauser, William. The Politics of Mass Society. *272 pp. 20 tables.*
●**Kroes, R.** Soldiers and Students. *A Study of Right- and Left-wing Students. 174 pp.*
Laidler, Harry W. History of Socialism. *Social-Economic Movements: An Historical and Comparative Survey of Socialism, Communism, Co-operation, Utopianism; and other Systems of Reform and Reconstruction. 992 pp.*
Lasswell, H. D. Analysis of Political Behaviour. *324 pp.*
Mannheim, Karl. Freedom, Power and Democratic Planning. *Edited by Hans Gerth and Ernest K. Bramstedt. 424 pp.*
Mansur, Fatma. Process of Independence. *Foreword by A. H. Hanson. 208 pp.*
Martin, David A. Pacifism: *an Historical and Sociological Study. 262 pp.*
Myrdal, Gunnar. The Political Element in the Development of Economic Theory. *Translated from the German by Paul Streeten. 282 pp.*
Wootton, Graham. Workers, Unions and the State. *188 pp.*

FOREIGN AFFAIRS: THEIR SOCIAL, POLITICAL AND ECONOMIC FOUNDATIONS

Mayer, J. P. Political Thought in France from the Revolution to the Fifth Republic. *164 pp.*

CRIMINOLOGY

Ancel, Marc. Social Defence: *A Modern Approach to Criminal Problems. Foreword by Leon Radzinowicz. 240 pp.*
Cain, Maureen E. Society and the Policeman's Role. *326 pp.*
Cloward, Richard A., and **Ohlin, Lloyd E.** Delinquency and Opportunity: *A Theory of Delinquent Gangs. 248 pp.*
Downes, David M. The Delinquent Solution. *A Study in Subcultural Theory. 296 pp.*
Dunlop, A. B., and **McCabe, S.** Young Men in Detention Centres. *192 pp.*
Friedlander, Kate. The Psycho-Analytical Approach to Juvenile Delinquency: *Theory, Case Studies, Treatment. 320 pp.*
Glueck, Sheldon, and **Eleanor.** Family Environment and Delinquency. *With the statistical assistance of Rose W. Kneznek. 340 pp.*
Lopez-Rey, Manuel. Crime. *An Analytical Appraisal. 288 pp.*
Mannheim, Hermann. Comparative Criminology: *a Text Book. Two volumes. 442 pp. and 380 pp.*

Morris, Terence. The Criminal Area: *A Study in Social Ecology.* Foreword by Hermann Mannheim. *232 pp. 25 tables. 4 maps.*
Rock, Paul. Making People Pay. *338 pp.*
●Taylor, Ian, Walton, Paul, and Young, Jock. The New Criminology. *For a Social Theory of Deviance. 325 pp.*
●Taylor, Ian, Walton, Paul, and Young, Jock (Eds). Critical Criminology. *268 pp.*

SOCIAL PSYCHOLOGY

Bagley, Christopher. The Social Psychology of the Epileptic Child. *320 pp.*
Barbu, Zevedei. Problems of Historical Psychology. *248 pp.*
Blackburn, Julian. Psychology and the Social Pattern. *184 pp.*
●Brittan, Arthur. Meanings and Situations. *224 pp.*
Carroll, J. Break-Out from the Crystal Palace. *200 pp.*
●Fleming, C. M. Adolescence: Its Social Psychology. *With an Introduction to recent findings from the fields of Anthropology, Physiology, Medicine, Psychometrics and Sociometry. 288 pp.*
● The Social Psychology of Education: *An Introduction and Guide to Its Study. 136 pp.*
●Homans, George C. The Human Group. Foreword by Bernard DeVoto. *Introduction by Robert K. Merton. 526 pp.*
● Social Behaviour: *its Elementary Forms. 416 pp.*
●Klein, Josephine. The Study of Groups. *226 pp. 31 figures. 5 tables.*
Linton, Ralph. The Cultural Background of Personality. *132 pp.*
●Mayo, Elton. The Social Problems of an Industrial Civilization. *With an appendix on the Political Problem. 180 pp.*
Ottaway, A. K. C. Learning Through Group Experience. *176 pp.*
Plummer, Ken. Sexual Stigma. *An Interactionist Account. 254 pp.*
Ridder, J. C. de. The Personality of the Urban African in South Africa. *A Thermatic Apperception Test Study. 196 pp. 12 plates.*
●Rose, Arnold M. (Ed.) Human Behaviour and Social Processes: *an Interactionist Approach. Contributions by Arnold M. Rose, Ralph H. Turner, Anselm Strauss, Everett C. Hughes, E. Franklin Frazier, Howard S. Becker, et al. 696 pp.*
Smelser, Neil J. Theory of Collective Behaviour. *448 pp.*
Stephenson, Geoffrey M. The Development of Conscience. *128 pp.*
Young, Kimball. Handbook of Social Psychology. *658 pp. 16 figures. 10 tables.*

SOCIOLOGY OF THE FAMILY

Banks, J. A. Prosperity and Parenthood: *A Study of Family Planning among The Victorian Middle Classes. 262 pp.*
Bell, Colin R. Middle Class Families: *Social and Geographical Mobility. 224 pp.*
Burton, Lindy. Vulnerable Children. *272 pp.*
Gavron, Hannah. The Captive Wife: *Conflicts of Household Mothers. 190 pp.*

George, Victor, and **Wilding, Paul.** Motherless Families. *248 pp.*
Klein, Josephine. Samples from English Cultures.
  1. Three Preliminary Studies and Aspects of Adult Life in England. *447 pp.*
  2. Child-Rearing Practices and Index. *247 pp.*
Klein, Viola. Britain's Married Women Workers. *180 pp.*
  The Feminine Character. *History of an Ideology. 244 pp.*
McWhinnie, Alexina M. Adopted Children. *How They Grow Up. 304 pp.*
● **Morgan, D. H. J.** Social Theory and the Family. *About 320 pp.*
● **Myrdal, Alva,** and **Klein, Viola.** Women's Two Roles: *Home and Work. 238 pp. 27 tables.*
Parsons, Talcott, and **Bales, Robert F.** Family: Socialization and Interaction Process. *In collaboration with James Olds, Morris Zelditch and Philip E. Slater. 456 pp. 50 figures and tables.*

SOCIAL SERVICES

Bastide, Roger. The Sociology of Mental Disorder. *Translated from the French by Jean McNeil. 260 pp.*
Carlebach, Julius. Caring For Children in Trouble. *266 pp.*
George, Victor. Foster Care. *Theory and Practice. 234 pp.*
  Social Security: *Beveridge and After. 258 pp.*
George, V., and **Wilding, P.** Motherless Families. *248 pp.*
● **Goetschius, George W.** Working with Community Groups. *256 pp.*
Goetschius, George W., and **Tash, Joan.** Working with Unattached Youth. *416 pp.*
Hall, M. P., and **Howes, I. V.** The Church in Social Work. *A Study of Moral Welfare Work undertaken by the Church of England. 320 pp.*
Heywood, Jean S. Children in Care: *the Development of the Service for the Deprived Child. 264 pp.*
Hoenig, J., and **Hamilton, Marian W.** The De-Segregation of the Mentally Ill. *284 pp.*
Jones, Kathleen. Mental Health and Social Policy, 1845-1959. *264 pp.*
King, Roy D., Raynes, Norma V., and **Tizard, Jack.** Patterns of Residential Care. *356 pp.*
Leigh, John. Young People and Leisure. *256 pp.*
● **Mays, John.** (Ed.) Penelope Hall's Social Services of England and Wales. *About 324 pp.*
Morris, Mary. Voluntary Work and the Welfare State. *300 pp.*
Morris, Pauline. Put Away: *A Sociological Study of Institutions for the Mentally Retarded. 364 pp.*
Nokes, P. L. The Professional Task in Welfare Practice. *152 pp.*
Timms, Noel. Psychiatric Social Work in Great Britain (1939-1962). *280 pp.*
● Social Casework: *Principles and Practice. 256 pp.*
Young, A. F. Social Services in British Industry. *272 pp.*
Young, A. F., and **Ashton, E. T.** British Social Work in the Nineteenth Century. *288 pp.*

SOCIOLOGY OF EDUCATION

Banks, Olive. Parity and Prestige in English Secondary Education: a Study in Educational Sociology. *272 pp.*
Bentwich, Joseph. Education in Israel. *224 pp. 8 pp. plates.*
●Blyth, W. A. L. English Primary Education. *A Sociological Description.*
  1. Schools. *232 pp.*
  2. Background. *168 pp.*
Collier, K. G. The Social Purposes of Education: *Personal and Social Values in Education. 268 pp.*
Dale, R. R., and Griffith, S. Down Stream: *Failure in the Grammar School. 108 pp.*
Dore, R. P. Education in Tokugawa Japan. *356 pp. 9 pp. plates.*
Evans, K. M. Sociometry and Education. *158 pp.*
●Ford, Julienne. Social Class and the Comprehensive School. *192 pp.*
Foster, P. J. Education and Social Change in Ghana. *336 pp. 3 maps.*
Fraser, W. R. Education and Society in Modern France. *150 pp.*
Grace, Gerald R. Role Conflict and the Teacher. *150 pp.*
Hans, Nicholas. New Trends in Education in the Eighteenth Century. *278 pp. 19 tables.*
● Comparative Education: *A Study of Educational Factors and Traditions. 360 pp.*
●Hargreaves, David. Interpersonal Relations and Education. *432 pp.*
● Social Relations in a Secondary School. *240 pp.*
Holmes, Brian. Problems in Education. *A Comparative Approach. 336 pp.*
King, Ronald. Values and Involvement in a Grammar School. *164 pp.*
  School Organization and Pupil Involvement. *A Study of Secondary Schools.*
●Mannheim, Karl, and Stewart, W. A. C. An Introduction to the Sociology of Education. *206 pp.*
Morris, Raymond N. The Sixth Form and College Entrance. *231 pp.*
●Musgrove, F. Youth and the Social Order. *176 pp.*
●Ottaway, A. K. C. Education and Society: An Introduction to the Sociology of Education. *With an Introduction by W. O. Lester Smith. 212 pp.*
Peers, Robert. Adult Education: *A Comparative Study. 398 pp.*
Pritchard, D. G. Education and the Handicapped: *1760 to 1960. 258 pp.*
Richardson, Helen. Adolescent Girls in Approved Schools. *308 pp.*
Stratta, Erica. The Education of Borstal Boys. *A Study of their Educational Experiences prior to, and during, Borstal Training. 256 pp.*
Taylor, P. H., Reid, W. A., and Holley, B. J. The English Sixth Form. *A Case Study in Curriculum Research. 200 pp.*

SOCIOLOGY OF CULTURE

Eppel, E. M., and M. Adolescents and Morality: *A Study of some Moral Values and Dilemmas of Working Adolescents in the Context of a changing Climate of Opinion. Foreword by W. J. H. Sprott. 268 pp. 39 tables.*

●**Fromm, Erich.** The Fear of Freedom. *286 pp.*
● The Sane Society. *400 pp.*
Mannheim, Karl. Essays on the Sociology of Culture. *Edited by Ernst Mannheim in co-operation with Paul Kecskemeti. Editorial Note by Adolph Lowe. 280 pp.*
Weber, Alfred. Farewell to European History: *or The Conquest of Nihilism. Translated from the German by R. F. C. Hull. 224 pp.*

SOCIOLOGY OF RELIGION

Argyle, Michael and **Beit-Hallahmi, Benjamin.** The Social Psychology of Religion. *About 256 pp.*
Nelson, G. K. Spiritualism and Society. *313 pp.*
Stark, Werner. The Sociology of Religion. *A Study of Christendom.*
 Volume I. *Established Religion. 248 pp.*
 Volume II. *Sectarian Religion. 368 pp.*
 Volume III. *The Universal Church. 464 pp.*
 Volume IV. *Types of Religious Man. 352 pp.*
 Volume V. *Types of Religious Culture. 464 pp.*
Turner, B. S. Weber and Islam. *216 pp.*
Watt, W. Montgomery. Islam and the Integration of Society. *320 pp.*

SOCIOLOGY OF ART AND LITERATURE

Jarvie, Ian C. Towards a Sociology of the Cinema. *A Comparative Essay on the Structure and Functioning of a Major Entertainment Industry. 405 pp.*
Rust, Frances S. Dance in Society. *An Analysis of the Relationships between the Social Dance and Society in England from the Middle Ages to the Present Day. 256 pp. 8 pp. of plates.*
Schücking, L. L. The Sociology of Literary Taste. *112 pp.*
Wolff, Janet. Hermeneutic Philosophy and the Sociology of Art. *150 pp.*

SOCIOLOGY OF KNOWLEDGE

Diesing, P. Patterns of Discovery in the Social Sciences. *262 pp.*
●**Douglas, J. D.** (Ed.) Understanding Everyday Life. *370 pp.*
●**Hamilton, P.** Knowledge and Social Structure. *174 pp.*
Jarvie, I. C. Concepts and Society. *232 pp.*
Mannheim, Karl. Essays on the Sociology of Knowledge. *Edited by Paul Kecskemeti. Editorial Note by Adolph Lowe. 353 pp.*
Remmling, Gunter W. The Sociology of Karl Mannheim. *With a Bibliographical Guide to the Sociology of Knowledge, Ideological Analysis, and Social Planning. 255 pp.*

Remmling, Gunter W. (Ed.) Towards the Sociology of Knowledge. *Origin and Development of a Sociological Thought Style. 463 pp.*
Stark, Werner. The Sociology of Knowledge: *An Essay in Aid of a Deeper Understanding of the History of Ideas. 384 pp.*

URBAN SOCIOLOGY

Ashworth, William. The Genesis of Modern British Town Planning: *A Study in Economic and Social History of the Nineteenth and Twentieth Centuries. 288 pp.*
Cullingworth, J. B. Housing Needs and Planning Policy: *A Restatement of the Problems of Housing Need and 'Overspill' in England and Wales. 232 pp. 44 tables. 8 maps.*
Dickinson, Robert E. City and Region: *A Geographical Interpretation 608 pp. 125 figures.*
 The West European City: *A Geographical Interpretation. 600 pp. 129 maps. 29 plates.*
● The City Region in Western Europe. *320 pp. Maps.*
Humphreys, Alexander J. New Dubliners: *Urbanization and the Irish Family. Foreword by George C. Homans. 304 pp.*
Jackson, Brian. Working Class Community: *Some General Notions raised by a Series of Studies in Northern England. 192 pp.*
Jennings, Hilda. Societies in the Making: *a Study of Development and Redevelopment within a County Borough. Foreword by D. A. Clark. 286 pp.*
●**Mann, P. H.** An Approach to Urban Sociology. *240 pp.*
Morris, R. N., and **Mogey, J.** The Sociology of Housing. *Studies at Berinsfield. 232 pp. 4 pp. plates.*
Rosser, C., and **Harris, C.** The Family and Social Change. *A Study of Family and Kinship in a South Wales Town. 352 pp. 8 maps.*
●**Stacey, Margaret, Batsone, Eric, Bell, Colin,** and **Thurcott, Anne.** Power, Persistence and Change. *A Second Study of Banbury. 196 pp.*

RURAL SOCIOLOGY

Chambers, R. J. H. Settlement Schemes in Tropical Africa: *A Selective Study. 268 pp.*
Haswell, M. R. The Economics of Development in Village India. *120 pp.*
Littlejohn, James. Westrigg: *the Sociology of a Cheviot Parish. 172 pp. 5 figures.*
Mayer, Adrian C. Peasants in the Pacific. *A Study of Fiji Indian Rural Society. 248 pp. 20 plates.*
Williams, W. M. The Sociology of an English Village: *Gosforth. 272 pp. 12 figures. 13 tables.*

SOCIOLOGY OF INDUSTRY AND DISTRIBUTION

Anderson, Nels. Work and Leisure. *280 pp.*
●**Blau, Peter M.,** and **Scott, W. Richard.** Formal Organizations: *a Comparative approach. Introduction and Additional Bibliography by J. H. Smith. 326 pp.*
Dunkerley, David. The Foreman. *Aspects of Task and Structure. 192 pp.*
Eldridge, J. E. T. Industrial Disputes. *Essays in the Sociology of Industrial Relations. 288 pp.*
Hetzler, Stanley. Applied Measures for Promoting Technological Growth. *352 pp.*
  Technological Growth and Social Change. *Achieving Modernization. 269 pp.*
Hollowell, Peter G. The Lorry Driver. *272 pp.*
Jefferys, Margot, *with the assistance of Winifred Moss.* Mobility in the Labour Market: *Employment Changes in Battersea and Dagenham. Preface by Barbara Wootton. 186 pp. 51 tables.*
Millerson, Geoffrey. The Qualifying Associations: *a Study in Professionalization. 320 pp.*
●**Oxaal, I., Barnett, T.,** and **Booth, D.** (Eds). Beyond the Sociology of Development. *Economy and Society in Latin America and Africa. 295 pp.*
Smelser, Neil J. Social Change in the Industrial Revolution: *An Application of Theory to the Lancashire Cotton Industry, 1770–1840. 468 pp. 12 figures. 14 tables.*
Williams, Gertrude. Recruitment to Skilled Trades. *240 pp.*
Young, A. F. Industrial Injuries Insurance: *an Examination of British Policy. 192 pp.*

DOCUMENTARY

Schlesinger, Rudolf (Ed.) Changing Attitudes in Soviet Russia.
  2. The Nationalities Problem and Soviet Administration. *Selected Readings on the Development of Soviet Nationalities Policies. Introduced by the editor. Translated by W. W. Gottlieb. 324 pp.*

ANTHROPOLOGY

Ammar, Hamed. Growing up in an Egyptian Village: *Silwa, Province of Aswan. 336 pp.*
Brandel-Syrier, Mia. Reeftown Elite. *A Study of Social Mobility in a Modern African Community on the Reef. 376 pp.*
Crook, David, and **Isabel.** Revolution in a Chinese Village: *Ten Mile Inn. 230 pp. 8 plates. 1 map.*
Dickie-Clark, H. F. The Marginal Situation. *A Sociological Study of a Coloured Group. 236 pp.*
Dube, S. C. Indian Village. *Foreword by Morris Edward Opler. 276 pp. 4 plates.*

India's Changing Villages: *Human Factors in Community Development.* *260 pp. 8 plates. 1 map.*
Firth, Raymond. Malay Fishermen. *Their Peasant Economy. 420 pp. 17 pp. plates.*
Firth, R., Hubert, J., and **Forge, A.** Families and their Relatives. *Kinship in a Middle-Class Sector of London: An Anthropological Study. 456 pp.*
Gulliver, P. H. Social Control in an African Society: a Study of the Arusha, Agricultural Masai of Northern Tanganyika. *320 pp. 8 plates. 10 figures.*
Family Herds. *288 pp.*
Ishwaran, K. Shivapur. *A South Indian Village. 216 pp.*
Tradition and Economy in Village India: *An Interactionist Approach. Foreword by Conrad Arensburg. 176 pp.*
Jarvie, Ian C. The Revolution in Anthropology. *268 pp.*
Little, Kenneth L. Mende of Sierra Leone. *308 pp. and folder.*
Negroes in Britain. *With a New Introduction and Contemporary Study by Leonard Bloom. 320 pp.*
Lowie, Robert H. Social Organization. *494 pp.*
Peasants in the Pacific. *A Study of Fiji Indian Rural Society. 248 pp.*
Smith, Raymond T. The Negro Family in British Guiana: *Family Structure and Social Status in the Villages. With a Foreword by Meyer Fortes. 314 pp. 8 plates. 1 figure. 4 maps.*

SOCIOLOGY AND PHILOSOPHY

Barnsley, John H. The Social Reality of Ethics. *A Comparative Analysis of Moral Codes. 448 pp.*
Diesing, Paul. Patterns of Discovery in the Social Sciences. *362 pp.*
●**Douglas, Jack D.** (Ed.) Understanding Everyday Life. *Toward the Reconstruction of Sociological Knowledge. Contributions by Alan F. Blum. Aaron W. Cicourel, Norman K. Denzin, Jack D. Douglas, John Heeren, Peter McHugh, Peter K. Manning, Melvin Power, Matthew Speier, Roy Turner, D. Lawrence Wieder, Thomas P. Wilson and Don H. Zimmerman. 370 pp.*
Jarvie, Ian C. Concepts and Society. *216 pp.*
●**Pelz, Werner.** The Scope of Understanding in Sociology. *Towards a more radical reorientation in the social humanistic sciences. 283 pp.*
Roche, Maurice. Phenomenology, Language and the Social Sciences. *371 pp.*
Sahay, Arun. Sociological Analysis. *212 pp.*
Sklair, Leslie. The Sociology of Progress. *320 pp.*

International Library of Anthropology
General Editor   Adam Kuper

Brown, Paula. The Chimbu. *A Study of Change in the New Guinea Highlands. 151 pp.*

Hamnett, Ian. Chieftainship and Legitimacy. *An Anthropological Study of Executive Law in Lesotho. 163 pp.*
Hanson, F. Allan. Meaning in Culture. *127 pp.*
Lloyd, P. C. Power and Independence. *Urban Africans' Perception of Social Inequality. 264 pp.*
Pettigrew, Joyce. Robber Noblemen. *A Study of the Political System of the Sikh Jats. 284 pp.*
Street, Brian V. The Savage in Literature. *Representations of 'Primitive' Society in English Fiction, 1858–1920. 207 pp.*
Van Den Berghe, Pierre L. Power and Privilege at an African University. *278 pp.*

International Library of Social Policy
General Editor Kathleen Jones

Bayley, M. Mental Handicap and Community Care. *426 pp.*
Butler, J. R. Family Doctors and Public Policy. *208 pp.*
Davies, Martin. Prisoners of Society. *Attitudes and Aftercare. 204 pp.*
Holman, Robert. Trading in Children. *A Study of Private Fostering. 355 pp.*
Jones, Kathleen. History of the Mental Health Service. *428 pp.*
 Opening the Door. *A Study of New Policies for the Mentally Handicapped. 260 pp.*
Thomas, J. E. The English Prison Officer since 1850: *A Study in Conflict. 258 pp.*
Walton, R. G. Women in Social Work. *303 pp.*
Woodward, J. To Do the Sick No Harm. *A Study of the British Voluntary Hospital System to 1875. 221 pp.*

International Library of Welfare and Philosophy
General Editors Noel Timms and David Watson

● **Plant, Raymond.** Community and Ideology. *104 pp.*

Primary Socialization, Language and Education
General Editor Basil Bernstein

Bernstein, Basil. Class, Codes and Control. *3 volumes.*
 1. *Theoretical Studies Towards a Sociology of Language. 254 pp.*
 2. *Applied Studies Towards a Sociology of Language. 377 pp.*
 3. *Towards a Theory of Educational Transmission. 167 pp.*
Brandis, W., and **Bernstein, B.** Selection and Control. *176 pp.*
Brandis, Walter, and **Henderson, Dorothy.** Social Class, Language and Communication. *288 pp.*

Cook-Gumperz, Jenny. Social Control and Socialization. *A Study of Class Differences in the Language of Maternal Control.* 290 pp.
● **Gahagan, D. M.,** and **G. A.** Talk Reform. *Exploration in Language for Infant School Children.* 160 pp.
Robinson, W. P., and **Rackstraw, Susan D. A.** A Question of Answers. 2 volumes. 192 pp. and 180 pp.
Turner, Geoffrey J., and **Mohan, Bernard A.** A Linguistic Description and Computer Programme for Children's Speech. 208 pp.

Reports of the Institute of Community Studies

Cartwright, Ann. Human Relations and Hospital Care. *272 pp.*
● Parents and Family Planning Services. *306 pp.*
Patients and their Doctors. *A Study of General Practice.* 304 pp.
Dench, Geoff. Maltese in London. *A Case-study in the Erosion of Ethnic Consciousness.* 302 pp.
●**Jackson, Brian.** Streaming: *an Education System in Miniature.* 168 pp.
Jackson, Brian, and **Marsden, Dennis.** Education and the Working Class: *Some General Themes raised by a Study of 88 Working-class Children in a Northern Industrial City.* 268 pp. 2 folders.
Marris, Peter. The Experience of Higher Education. *232 pp. 27 tables.*
Loss and Change. *192 pp.*
Marris, Peter, and **Rein, Martin.** Dilemmas of Social Reform. *Poverty and Community Action in the United States.* 256 pp.
Marris, Peter, and **Somerset, Anthony.** African Businessmen. *A Study of Entrepreneurship and Development in Kenya.* 256 pp.
Mills, Richard. Young Outsiders: *a Study in Alternative Communities.* 216 pp.
Runciman, W. G. Relative Deprivation and Social Justice. *A Study of Attitudes to Social Inequality in Twentieth-Century England.* 352 pp.
Willmott, Peter. Adolescent Boys in East London. *230 pp.*
Willmott, Peter, and **Young, Michael.** Family and Class in a London Suburb. *202 pp. 47 tables.*
Young, Michael. Innovation and Research in Education. *192 pp.*
●**Young, Michael,** and **McGeeney, Patrick.** Learning Begins at Home. *A Study of a Junior School and its Parents.* 128 pp.
Young, Michael, and **Willmott, Peter.** Family and Kinship in East London. *Foreword by Richard M. Titmuss. 252 pp. 39 tables.*
The Symmetrical Family. *410 pp.*

Reports of the Institute for Social Studies in Medical Care

Cartwright, Ann, Hockey, Lisbeth, and **Anderson, John L.** Life Before Death. *310 pp.*
Dunnell, Karen, and **Cartwright, Ann.** Medicine Takers, Prescribers and Hoarders. *190 pp.*

Medicine, Illness and Society

General Editor W. M. Williams

Robinson, David. The Process of Becoming Ill. *142 pp.*
Stacey, Margaret, *et al.* Hospitals, Children and Their Families. *The Report of a Pilot Study. 202 pp.*
Stimson, G. V., and **Webb, B.** Going to See the Doctor. *The Consultation Process in General Practice. 155 pp.*

Monographs in Social Theory

General Editor Arthur Brittan

● **Barnes, B.** Scientific Knowledge and Sociological Theory. *192 pp.*
Bauman, Zygmunt. Culture as Praxis. *204 pp.*
● **Dixon, Keith.** Sociological Theory. *Pretence and Possibility. 142 pp.*
Meltzer, B. N., Petras, J. W., and **Reynolds, L. T.** Symbolic Interactionism. *Genesis, Varieties and Criticisms. 144 pp.*
● **Smith, Anthony D.** The Concept of Social Change. *A Critique of the Functionalist Theory of Social Change. 208 pp.*

Routledge Social Science Journals

The British Journal of Sociology. *Managing Editor – Angus Stewart; Associate Editor – Michael Hill. Vol. 1, No. 1 – March 1950 and Quarterly. Roy. 8vo. All back issues available. An international journal publishing original papers in the field of sociology and related areas.*
Community Work. *Edited by David Jones and Marjorie Mayo. 1973. Published annually.*
Economy and Society. *Vol. 1, No. 1. February 1972 and Quarterly. Metric Roy. 8vo. A journal for all social scientists covering sociology, philosophy, anthropology, economics and history. Back numbers available.*
Religion. Journal of Religion and Religions. *Chairman of Editorial Board, Ninian Smart. Vol. 1, No. 1, Spring 1971. A journal with an interdisciplinary approach to the study of the phenomena of religion.*
Year Book of Social Policy in Britain, The. *Edited by Kathleen Jones. 1971. Published annually.*

361.001 T14   98142

TALKING ABOUT WELFARE

College Misericordia Library
Dallas, Pennsylvania 18612